My Boy Elvis

My Boy Elvis

The Colonel Tom Parker Story

By

Sean O'Neal

Barricade Books, New York

Published by Barricade Books, Inc.
150 Fifth Avenue
New York, NY 10011

Printed in the United States of America.

Book design and page layout by CompuDesign

Library of Congress Cataloging-in-Publication Data

O'Neal, Sean.
    My boy Elvis : The Colonel Tom Parker story / by Sean O'Neal.
        p.   cm.
    ISBN 1-56980-127-4
    1. Parker, Tom. 1909–   . 2. Impresarios—United States—
Biography.   I. Title.
ML429.P33054   1998
782.42166'092—dc21
    [B]   98-3056
                                                                        CIP
                                                                         MN

For Tracy, Lauren, Sean Jr., Mom, and Dad

Contents

★ ★ ★ ★

Introduction

$$\bigstar \qquad \star \qquad \bigstar \qquad \star$$

It was the middle of the afternoon, August 16, 1977, in Portland, Maine. Colonel Thomas A. Parker was resting in his suite at the Sheraton Hotel. The next day he would be traveling to Utica, New York, and Elvis Presley would be arriving in Portland to give the first of two scheduled performances at the Cumberland Civic Center.

Elvis had been on what seemed like a giant, never-ending concert tour since his return to the stage in 1969. In total, between 1969 and August 1977, he had performed 1,094 times. The Colonel was determined to continue this frantic pace indefinitely. As long as the crowds would pay to see Elvis, the Colonel would supply him.

The Colonel served as Elvis's advance man as part of his duties as personal manager. Parker always preceded Elvis by a day or two when he was on a concert tour. He would make certain that the city was whipped into an appropriate fever to ensure a sell out for "My Boy's" concert. Empty seats meant money lost. Now that he was confident that both Portland shows were sold out, the Colonel was planning his strategy for the next city.

When the phone rang that afternoon, the Colonel probably assumed that it was another reporter wanting an interview or a free ticket to Elvis's concert. The caller would be disappointed if he was looking for a freebie. The Colonel never gave free tickets to Elvis's shows. As was his custom, the Colonel answered the phone with a "ya!"

Joe Esposito, the foreman of Elvis's group of hired companions known as the Memphis Mafia, was on the other end of the line calling from Memphis. Esposito said, "I don't want you to hear it from a radio bulletin, Colonel." "Hear what, for Christ's sake?" the Colonel asked. "Elvis is dead. We found him in his bathroom about an hour ago slumped on the floor. We tried to revive him, but we couldn't," Esposito answered.

The Colonel took a single deep breath and said, "Oh dear God." It was the only expression of grief that he made. After the single exclamation, he sat in silence. For one of the few times in his life, the Colonel was speechless. However, his time as a mute only lasted a few seconds. "Nothing has changed," he said aloud to himself. "This doesn't change a thing."

He was wrong. The minute Elvis stopped breathing, a time bomb was set in motion. When the clock stopped ticking, the Colonel's purpose in life disappeared in an instant. He was left only with memories of the past. Memories of a life that began sixty-eight years earlier in a small town half a world away from Portland, Maine. Back in a time when Colonel Tom Parker did not yet exist except in the mind of a Dutch boy named Andreas Cornelis van Kuijk, in Breda, Holland.

Chapter 1

Holland

★ ★ ★ ★

$\mathcal{A}$ndreas Cornelis van Kuijk was born in Breda, Holland, on June 26, 1909. He was Adam and Maria van Kuijk's fifth child. Andreas, named after his grandfather van Kuijk, was called Dries by his family.

Adam and Maria van Kuijk came from opposite backgrounds. Adam's was a military family. He was accustomed to a life of discipline. His stern no-nonsense personality reflected this. Maria, on the other hand, had come from a happy-go-lucky gypsyish family. She was constantly surrounded with action. The marketplace in which she spent most of her time had a festive carnival-like atmosphere.

Adam was born in Raamsdonk, Holland, in 1866. In 1887, he was drafted into the Dutch army and assigned to an artillery division in Breda, some twelve miles from his hometown. One of his duties was to care for the horses that pulled the artillery guns. Adam enjoyed army life and reenlisted when his initial tour of duty ended.

On leaving the service in 1899, he found a job tending horses for a freight company in Breda. Adam was allowed to live in an apartment over the stables. It was in that apartment that he bedded his girlfriend, Maria Ponsie.

Maria Ponsie was born on September 2, 1876. She had seven older brothers and sisters. Maria's parents were Johannes and Marie Ponsie. The Ponsies earned their living as traveling salesmen. They sold a variety of flea-market quality items, from toys to pots and pans. They traveled throughout Holland by boat, peddling their wares.

In December 1899, Maria became pregnant by Adam. On May 10, 1900, Adam and Maria were married. Four months later, their son Joseph was born. Following Joseph were Adriana (born in 1902), Marie (1904), Nel (1907), Andreas Cornelis (1909), Engelina (1910), Ad (1913), Johanna (1916), and Jan (1918).

According to Dries's brother Joseph, despite his family's modest circumstances, Maria never worked. She had a maid clean her house. Her daughters assumed the responsibility of caring for their brothers and sisters. Adam was constantly taking side jobs to support the family. Dries's older sister, Adriana, was his surrogate mother as an infant and toddler. Caring for Dries was a challenge. Among other things, he had peculiar sleeping habits. He often slept with his eyes open. He also had a habit of sleepwalking as a child (a habit he shared with Elvis Presley). Doors had to be kept locked to keep him from walking out into the street.

As a child no older than five, Dries began to sneak out of the house and wander the streets. His absence did not seem to draw much attention in the large van Kuijk family. By this time, there were two more children for Maria and her daughters to look after. It was easy for one of them not to be missed.

As retribution for having impregnated his daughter, Johannes Ponsie and his wife moved in with Adam and his family. When Dries's Grandmother Ponsie died in 1907, two years before he was born, Adam moved Johannes into a Catholic charity home for the elderly. Dries visited his grandfather regularly. Johannes regaled his grandson with the glamour of life on the road. He told of taking tattered Bibles thrown away by the church and making slipcovers for them and selling them as new. Johannes Ponsie was full of the spirit of the con man. He passed this on to Dries.

Dries learned how to con people to get what he wanted early in life. He demonstrated to his friends that his fast talking could get him almost anything that he wanted. On one occasion, Dries and two friends were standing outside the Breda soccer stadium. As it is throughout Europe, soccer is the most popular sport in Holland. Dries's friends were lamenting the fact that they did not have the money necessary to buy tickets to the soccer match. Dries quickly concocted a plan to get them in.

They would gather up some clothes and pretend that they had been asked to bring them to one of the players. The other boys didn't give the plan a prayer of working. However, they each went back home, got some clothes, and met at the stadium. Dries walked up to the ticket taker and spoke to him for a couple of minutes. To his friends' amazement, Dries turned and motioned for them to come along. They were going in. This scheme worked for several games until the man at the gate finally caught on.

A talent that Dries quickly developed was the ability to make money, which he always earned and never stole. Dries frequented a local candy store and invariably had money to buy candy. The shop owner began to wonder where such a little boy was coming up with money on such a regular basis. Was he stealing from his mother or father? Dries assured the shop owner that he had earned the money, and the owner accepted the young boy's word.

Very early on, Dries established the principle of never doing anything for free. There was no such thing as an act of kindness to be rewarded with a thank-you. If Dries van Kuijk helped an old lady with her groceries, he demanded to be paid for it.

The third Sunday of October was a day that the children of Breda looked forward to all year. This was when the carnival came to town. The carnival officially began after the city's church services were over. Dries was always one of the first to run to the carnival grounds.

His favorite part of the carnival was the Bonbever Family Circus. He developed a relationship with the circus and worked for it every year. One of his jobs was to ride around town on a bicycle with a giant front wheel and a small back wheel carrying a billboard on his front and back advertising the circus. This was Dries's first exposure to being a promoter.

One of his favorite acts was the trained horses. On Sunday afternoons, Adam van Kuijk played in a regular card game. In his absence, Adam placed Dries in charge of the stable. To alleviate the boredom, the boy decided to make the horses in the stable into his own circus act. Over the next few weeks, he trained the them in secret. Finally, he was ready to give a performance. He gathered together his brothers and sisters and a few neighborhood children one Sunday afternoon. They watched in amazement as Dries cracked a whip and the horses began to trot in a circle. He cracked the whip again, and they switched directions. Another crack and the horses reared up on their hind legs. Soon Dries was a minor celebrity among the local children.

Dries proved to be a better animal trainer than he was a student. He did poorly in school and failed to even show up on a regular basis. In desperation, his parents placed him in a Catholic school known for its strict discipline. Most of his classmates were orphans or from extremely poor families.

But Dries was more interested in playing practical jokes than he was in his studies. No matter how severely the monks at the school punished him, he continued his pranks. Oftentimes, Dries played hooky. If there was a circus or a carnival in a nearby town, he would go there rather than to classes. On other occasions, he would spend all day staring at ships, perhaps dreaming of where they might carry him one day. No matter how severely his father or the monks punished him, Dries demonstrated that he couldn't be controlled. He always had to win.

It is unclear if Dries ever made it through the sixth grade. A friend said that he and Dries both dropped out after the fifth. His brother Ad said that Dries was sent to a boarding school after the fifth grade because he had become such a discipline problem. If Dries ever attended that school, his name somehow did not make it into their permanent records. What is certain is that by the time Dries became a teenager, he was out of school and floating from job to job.

He first worked for a grocery store, but routinely failed to show up for work and was fired. Next he became the shaver in a barbershop. His career as a barber was short lived. He had a habit of wandering out of the shop when something in the street caught his attention.

His brother Joseph helped him get a job in the jam factory where Joseph worked. Dries was bored at the factory and soon quit. He then asked his father's permission to move to Rotterdam to live with his uncle, Jan Ponsie. His plan was to find a job at the harbor. Once in Rotterdam, Dries cut himself off completely from his family in Breda.

The same year that Dries moved to Rotterdam, his sister Marie became a nun and went to live in the convent. When she was officially made a member of the convent, Dries was the only one in the family not to attend. He sent money to his mother regularly, but had no other contact with her.

On July 6, 1925, Adam van Kuijk died. The van Kuijk family was now without a breadwinner. They had to give up their home to make way for Adam's replacement as stable keeper.

On January 17, 1926, a judge appointed Jan Ponsie legal guardian of Dries and his minor brothers and sisters. Despite this, Dries was the one who lived with his uncle. The rest of the family remained in Breda with their mother.

Rotterdam was a large international port, and Dries saw ships that sailed all around the world. He noticed that there were several young men his age working on these ships. If the story that he told his uncle Jan is to be believed, Dries soon joined their ranks. He returned home one day and informed his uncle that he had a job working for the Holland/America ship line. He went on to say that he had to go on a trip. He packed his belongings and left.

A few days later, a trunk arrived at the house of Dries's mother. Inside were most of his belongings and personal papers. Dries van Kuijk had left for America without saying a word to his mother.

Dirk Vellenga investigated to see if Dries actually worked for the Holland/America line for his book *Elvis and the Colonel*. He was unable to find any mention of Andreas van Kuijk in the company's records. However, if Andreas had been a temporary employee, his name would not have been entered into the records, according to historians familiar with the company's practices.

Of course, Dries might not have been a member of the Holland/America crew at all. He might have been a stowaway. Perhaps he made friends, while working at the port, who let him aboard and concealed him for the eleven-day journey to America. Or maybe Dries saved up a little money and bribed his way onto the ship. All that is known for sure is that he made it to Hoboken, New Jersey, where he got by U.S. Customs and Immigration and set foot in America for the first time.

Dries settled in immediately in the home of a family of Dutch immigrants living in New Jersey. It is unknown how he became acquainted with this family. They were in no way related to him. Perhaps the same sailor who helped Dries get to America made the introduction.

Dries lived with the family for several months, not once letting his own family in Holland know what had happened to him. The American family kept pressuring him to write home that he was safe. Dries finally relented to a degree. He said that they could write a letter to his family if they wished. However, rather than giving them his mother's address, he gave them the Ponzies' address.

A few weeks later, the Ponzies received a letter from a Dutch family in the United States that said Dries was okay and staying with them. The letter added that Dries was "such a nice boy."

The Ponzies exchanged several letters with the American family. Then came one informing them that Dries had left without saying good-bye or leaving a note. The American family speculated that he might have joined the army as he had discussed doing.

Dries did not join the army. He returned to Holland. The next time his family heard from him was on September 2, 1927, his mother's birthday. That evening there was a knock at the van Kuijk door. The door was opened, and there stood long-lost Dries. He was would not talk about how he got to America, what he had done while he was there, or how he made it back to Holland.

During the fall of 1927, Dries took a job loading and unloading cargo from barges on the canal. He then took a job on a boat that traveled between Breda and Rotterdam carrying cargo. Dries eventually moved into an apartment in Rotterdam and saw very little of his family after that. He never once visited the Ponzies, but did get in touch with one of his boyhood friends, Cees Frigters. They talked at length without Dries once mentioning his trip to America.

In July 1929, again a trunk belonging to Dries arrived at his mother's house. The trunk had been sent by Dries's employer in Rotterdam. He had left, and they didn't know where he had gone. Inside the trunk were most of Dries's belongings including unopened birthday presents from his family.

Dries was returning to the United States, if somewhat indirectly. First he would stop in Curaçao, a Dutch colony in the West Indies.

He did not need papers to enter. Dries then hopped a freighter bound for Mobile, Alabama. From there, he traveled to Fort McPherson, Georgia, where he enlisted in the U.S. Army under the name of Andre van Kuijk.

Joining the army was a way to establish an American identity. It was an easy matter to enlist in those days as long as you could speak English and didn't have any serious medical problems. It was particularly easy if you volunteered to be stationed in Hawaii. Hawaii at the time was not a popular assignment. It was very difficult getting home on leave because of the distance and expense.

Dries, who was now Andre, completed basic training and was sent to Fort Shafter, a few miles outside of Honolulu. He was assigned to the Sixty-fourth Regiment, which was in charge of the antiaircraft guns protecting the naval bases at Pearl Harbor.

Upon arriving at Fort Shafter, Andre met with Capt. Thomas R. Parker. This Tom Parker was from Nebraska. Andre told Parker that he was an orphan with no living relatives and had worked for several years as a sailor. Parker did not fall for Andre's story about not having any family. He explained it was the army's policy to deduct a portion of a soldier's pay for his nearest relative. If Andre would give him the name of his nearest relative, he could arrange for the payments to be sent. Andre relented and gave his mother's address. However, Maria van Kuijk would not be able to use the checks to locate her son since they were all sent from Washington, D.C.

Now that Captain Parker was aware of his Holland connection, Andre set about making sure that the captain liked him. He didn't want Parker, in a fit of anger, sending him back to Holland. Andre's fellow soldiers said that he was constantly brown-nosing the captain. He volunteered for extra duty on his off time and generally did anything that he thought would impress Captain Parker.

The van Kuijk family didn't hear from Dries for some time. Finally a letter arrived. It was obvious from the content that Dries had written it. However, the strange thing was that the letter was written in English not Dutch. Even more peculiar was the signature at the bottom. It was not signed "Dries van Kuijk," (and they, of course, knew nothing about "Andre"), rather Dries had signed the letter "Thomas Parker." He gave no explanation for his name change nor did he reveal why he had gone back to America without telling his family.

It stands to reason that Captain Parker was the source of Dries's adopted name, Thomas Parker. Dries substituted an A for the R as his middle initial. The A supposedly stood for Andrew, though it might have been inspired by Dries's real first name, Andreas.

"Tom Parker" wrote his family several more letters over the following months. They were vague and had no return address. He retained the secrecy of what he was doing in America throughout his correspondence. He sent a few snapshots, but never commented on them. The family was left to draw its own conclusions from the pictures. In one of them, Thomas Parker was standing next to a large car. In another, he posed next to a swimming pool. The family came up with the idea that perhaps he was working as a chauffeur for a rich family.

Tom Parker did give his family a subtle clue to his whereabouts in one of the pictures he sent them from Hawaii. In it, he was sitting on a bucket. On the bucket was painted A-64. This stood for the Sixty-fourth Regiment, which was part of the Hawaiian Coast Artillery, where Tom was stationed.

In January 1930, the army had started sending money to Tom Parker's mother. Seventeen checks were sent between then and February 1932. Each was for five dollars. Then the checks and letters abruptly stopped. The final letter said,"Mother I don't have much news." The family kept waiting for Dries to return, but he never did. Maria van Kuijk died in 1958 not knowing the whereabouts of her son. The van Kuijk family was not to know what became of Dries or Tom Parker for twenty-nine years.

In the fall of 1931, Captain Thomas R. Parker was transferred to Washington, D.C. At about that same time, Tom's two-year stint in Hawaii was up, and he was transferred to Port Banancas in Pensacola, Florida. A few months later, Tom was out of the army, his enlistment time over.

Tom Parker knew where he wanted to work when he got out of the army. He would try his hand at his boyhood love, the carnival. Tom had never gotten that out of his system. Calling himself Thomas A. Parker, he signed on with the Johnny J. Jones Exposition.

Chapter 2

Step Right Up

When Tom Parker hooked up with the Johnny J. Jones Exposition, it was a shadow of its former self. It had been one of the largest carnivals in the United States. At its peak, it required sixty-four railroad cars to transport the show. A combination of the Great Depression and the death of its founder devastated the quality of the carnival. With finances faltering, its size was pared to reduce expenses. By the time Tom Parker came along, the Johnny J. Jones Exposition had been reduced by two thirds. Much of what was left was in disrepair.

This was not exactly a glamorous start for Tom Parker's show business career. Nonetheless, it was a job in a field to which Parker was attracted. An immigrant with no real identity and no experience had to start somewhere.

Near the end of 1933, the Johnny J. Jones Exposition was purchased by E. Laurence Phillips. Phillips owned a string of movie theaters. He had enough money to help restore the carnival to its former glory. One of his first moves was to hire a new advance man, Peazy Hoffman. Peazy was short and fat and always wore a white hat. He looked quite a bit like a cartoon character. However, Peazy's skill as a promoter was anything but a joke. He had worked as an advance man for some of the largest operations in the business.

The job of the advance man was to travel to a town a few days before the carnival was due to hit and generate publicity. It was his responsibility to make sure that the crowds came when the carnival got to town. He used a variety of promotional tactics to accomplish this. He would blanket the town with handbills advertising the carnival. He would go on the radio hawking the show, place advertisements in the local paper, and if he was effective in stroking a reporter, a short news piece would appear announcing the forthcoming appearance of the carnival.

Peazy agreed to take Tom Parker on as his assistant. Tom quickly found his niche in promotion. In the carnival world, to promote and to con were synonymous. Parker came up with a clever con to draw crowds. When the carnival got to town, he would spread the word that a special event would be taking place on Saturday night. The special event was a marriage on the Ferris wheel. The catch was that the marriage was a phony. Parker played the groom and another carnival worker played the bride. When the ceremony was set to begin, everyone was cleared off the Ferris wheel except for the bride, groom, and "reverend." All the lights of the carnival were turned off except for those that were on the Ferris wheel. As the wedding march played, the car containing the wedding party was taken to the top of the wheel where the ceremony was conducted. Afterwards, the crowd dispersed to spend money on rides, food, and what have you. This process was repeated in town after town.

When winter arrived, the carnival went on hiatus. The winter headquarters for the Johnny J. Jones Exposition was DeLand, in east central Florida. However, most of the other carnivals' winter headquarters were across the state in Tampa. This was where the action was and that was where Tom Parker spent his off-season.

Tom had to come up with ways to earn some money over the winter. He did a little promotion work for department stores. Most of his ideas were gimmicky, such as having a couple lay in a bed in a store under a sign saying that they were conducting a sleep-endurance contest. At Christmas, he would dress up like Santa Claus and lure children into the toy department.

One of Parker's other off-season ventures was to run a pony ride outside department stores. In the winter of 1935, Parker went to Ranaldi Printing in Tampa to get some tickets made up for his pony ride. Parker was familiar with Ranaldi because it did the printing for the Johnny J. Jones Exposition. He did not have enough money to pay in advance. The company's owner, Clyde Ranaldi, agreed to let Parker pay off the five dollar charge at one dollar a week. Parker never forgot Ranaldi's help. Years later, he would make sure that Ranaldi got printing jobs from RCA for Elvis Presley items.

An associate of Parker's in the Johnny J. Jones Exposition said that Parker told him that he wanted to be the biggest promoter in the business. He had complete confidence in his abilities. It wasn't a question of if he would rise to the top, the only question was how long it would take. The top of the carnival world was a job with the Royal American Shows.

The Royal American Shows was founded by Carl Sedlmeyer in 1921. Sedlmeyer started traveling with a carnival after being orphaned in his early teens. He worked his way up the ranks and ended up with one of his own. His Royal American Shows was the first carnival to take thrill rides such as the roller coaster outside the confines of an amusement park and into rural America. In addition to its rides, it featured a variety of performers, ranging from vaude-ville to minstrel to jazz.

The Royal American Shows billed itself as having "the world's largest midway." It was a self-contained city and employed more than one thousand people. It was prosperous enough that it traveled by private train, seventy cars long, rather than by truck. The Royal American Shows generated its own power to operate fifty-two rides. Its generators could create enough electricity to illuminate a city of fifty thousand. It even had its own traveling neon-tube factory.

The Royal American Shows started out the year in Tampa and then traveled throughout the United States and Canada. Its stops would coincide with large fairs around North America, the first always being the Memphis Cotton Carnival in May. By the time the Royal American made its way back to Florida, it was November.

Parker's first position with the Royal American Shows was working on the "pie truck." The pie truck was the carnival's mess hall. He also ran a "mitt camp" for reading palms. He was almost psychic, that man, all in a humorous spirit, of course.

Carl Lucas, a fellow carnival worker, told of the time that Parker stepped out of the kitchen to offer some advice to management. A meeting of the carnival staff had been called to discuss lowering the admission price from fifty to twenty-five cents to stimulate attendance. Tom Parker spoke up and said that he had a better idea. He wanted to post advertising signs around town reading, "Admission $1. One-half your money back if not satisfied." Although skeptical, the management gave the scheme a try. Just as Parker had predicted, the crowds increased and almost no one took them up on the refund offer.

After the success of the admission gimmick, Parker was surprised to learn that the Royal American didn't have a place for him as a promoter. When he realized it wasn't ever going to use him in that capacity, he took to working with the Johnny J. Jones Exposition on the side. He didn't want to break his ties with the Royal American completely so he continued spending time doing various jobs for them.

While the Royal American didn't do anything for Tom Parker's career as a promoter, it had a profound impact on his love life. In 1935, the Royal American Shows made its annual appearance at the Florida State Fair in Tampa. Parker was there working one of the concession stands.

He loved smoking cigars, especially when they were free. Each year the Hav-a-Tampa cigar company would set up a booth at the fair. When Parker visited it in 1935, he got more than a cigar from the girl manning the booth. She struck him as being unusually attractive. Upon striking up a conversation, he learned that her name was Marie Mott.

Marie Mott was born in Florida in 1905. She was one of six children. Her father was a not-so-successful blacksmith. There was never much money in the Mott household. To try and make a better life for herself, Marie married Robert Ross in 1925. Ross, a photographer by trade, spent as much time trying to charm the ladies as he did taking pictures. Within two years, Marie and Ross had a son they named Robert, Jr., and were divorced.

In 1933, Marie married Willet Sayre. Sayre could never hold a job, and Marie was forced to work to support the family. The marriage lasted a little more than a year. After the divorce from Sayre, Marie and Robert, Jr., moved in with Marie's parents.

Marie was not a particularly pleasant woman. It was hard to mention anything that she said that she didn't hate. She also was obsessed by her health. People who knew her never made the mistake of asking her how she was feeling. This would launch her into a dialog about her aches and pains. Apparently Tom overlooked these faults and fell in love with her.

As luck would have it, she was single. Later in 1935, they were married. Parker jokingly referred to his new wife as "Miz-Ree." The newlyweds worked together on the pie truck of the Royal American Shows. In the winters, they would move in with Marie's parents.

There is no reason to doubt that Thomas Parker loved Marie.

They remained married for forty-five years until her death, he called her every day they were apart, and there was never any hint of either of having affairs. Nonetheless, Parker could not have been ignorant of the fact that a marriage to an American woman would strengthen his role as an American. If his Dutch origin ever became an issue, he could use his American family as a defense to remain in the U.S.

Curiously, there are records of Marie Mott's first two marriages in the Tampa courthouse, but there is no record of her marriage to Thomas Parker. Even Marie's brother, Bitsy Mott, wasn't exactly certain of the details of his sister's marriage to Parker. He knew that they did not have a wedding reception of any sort. He speculated that they were married at the courthouse. Perhaps they were married on the road while on carnival or perhaps they simply declared themselves to be married and never went through the formality of a ceremony. Or maybe Tom Parker didn't feel that he could provide necessary identification to obtain a marriage license.

Tom Parker's mentor in the Royal American Shows was a man named Hoxie Tucker. Tucker was known to be a tough businessman who was an expert in manipulating people. He took Tom under his wing and taught him everything he knew. Tom learned much from Tucker in the art of gimmicky promotion. An example of this was when Tucker had all the trucks painted bright purple so the carnival could be spotted from miles away.

In the era in which Tom Parker worked in the carnival, the larger operations would often feature well-known country-and-western singers. In the late 1930s, Royal American bought a traveling show called the Billy Ray Comedians. The star of the show was a singer named Gene Austin. At the suggestion of Hoxie Tucker, Austin hired Tom Parker as his manager in 1939.

Gene Austin was one of the first famous pop singers in America. His 1927 recording of "My Blue Heaven" sold five million copies. It set a sales record that stood until the mid-1950s when the rock era began. Austin went on to become a major star. He even had a short career in Hollywood. By the time the Colonel met him, his heyday was well behind him, and his appeal was limited to being an oldies act.

Parker made Austin believe that he knew everybody that mattered in the South and impressed him with his spirited enthusiasm for the job. With people not exactly beating down his door to promote him, Austin was willing to give Parker a shot.

There are more similarities between promoting country musicians and carnivals than first meet the eye. Both usually perform in traveling shows that require tremendous amounts of advance publicity to be successful, publicity that has at its root the notion that everyone is susceptible to a con. While promoting the carnival, Tom Parker had indeed met influential people throughout the southern United States.

As the advance man for the carnival, he would arrive in a city a few days ahead of the show. Among his duties was attaining the necessary permits to cover the town with posters and flyers and arranging for newspaper and radio advertisements. By the time the rest of the group got to town, the local citizens were chomping at the bit to lay down their money.

Parker used the only approach and method with Gene Austin that he knew, the same one that he had used with the carnival. He even copied the slogan that he had used with the Johnny J. Jones Exposition. Instead of saying, "Johnny's coming" on his promotional items, he said, "Gene's coming." He used both elephants carrying billboards to promote Austin as well as stationing midgets outside concert auditoriums to draw a crowd.

Parker booked Austin the same small southern towns he had become familiar with while traveling with the carnival. He would prime the town with bills and advertising, just as he had done with the carnival, and fill the small concert halls. Although his days as a headliner were over, Austin still had a large base of fans. The small-city and town people were impressed with having him perform even if he wasn't making records anymore.

Austin was excited about playing in front of full houses again. He thought maybe Parker could help him return to his former glory. Austin proposed that Parker move with him to Nashville. Being in one of the music capitals would make it easier to try for a new recording contract. To Austin's dismay, Parker turned him down. He said that he wasn't ready to leave Tampa.

What could have possibly possessed Tom Parker? He was so close to reaching his stated goal of becoming a big-time promoter. If he didn't go to Nashville with Austin, he would have to start all over again. Perhaps he wasn't ready to uproot Marie and her son. Maybe he didn't have faith that Austin would be a success again and didn't want to be associated with a failed attempt.

Tom Parker's next career move was even more bizarre than his decision to give up Gene Austin. He took a job with the Hillsborough Humane Society in Tampa, but not as a dogcatcher, as has been falsely repeated over the years. He replaced H. C. Gordon, who was retiring as the society's field agent. This meant that Parker was responsible for fund raising and drives to encourage people to adopt stray animals. He was still a promoter, only now he was promoting animals instead of people. On occasion, he would also investigate complaints of cruelty to animals. In the records of the humane society are reports filed by Parker on a "pony beating," "boys shooting birds," and a "goat without water."

Working for the humane society had several perks. One was a rent-paid apartment. Another was a result of his putting a cage in his car and calling it an animal ambulance. For this, he was rewarded with free gasoline. When World War II started, Parker received special rations of gas and tires to be used on the "ambulance."

Parker also found a way to feed his family for free. He went to stores all over Tampa soliciting food for dogs at the shelter. He was so successful that the donated food far exceeded the animals' capacity to eat it. Then Parker hit upon the idea of trading the excess food to different stores for human food for him and Marie. Taking this one step further, he persuaded stores to donate hamburger and even steaks to give the poor animals a treat. The food went straight into the Parker larder.

By all accounts, Parker was very good at his job at the humane society. He developed a relationship with *Tampa Tribune* reporter Paul Wilder. His picture appeared in the *Tribune* in the act of "rescuing a dog." Marie Parker was also in the picture. In the background was the Parker's car on which he had painted "ambulance." Wilder frequently published tear-jerking stories fed to him by Parker in his column, "In Our Town." Without fail, the featured animals would be adopted.

One of these columns about a puppy at Christmastime generated more than one thousand requests for the dog. For once the humane society had a greater demand for animals than it had animals. Tom Parker dressed like Santa Claus and would give away the dogs to people who came looking for their Christmas puppy.

Parker couldn't resist playing a practical joke now and then on the pet adopters. His favorite was when someone said they wanted a puppy that would always be small enough to keep inside the house. He would intentionally give them one that he knew would grow into a giant within a year.

One scam Parker worked was placing a large barrel in the humane society lobby with a sign by it indicating that donations were urgently needed for the animals. The real benefactor of the donations was Tom Parker. When he saw someone putting money into the barrel, Parker would often insist that they take a dog or a cat as a token of his appreciation.

Some years later in an interview, Parker said, "We used to make a pretty good production on any dog or cat we gave out to impress the responsibility on the adopter. And at times, we even screened the people for their personalities on dogs."

To earn extra money while working for the humane society, Parker helped stores with their grand openings. He would borrow elephants and tigers from circus friends to create a minizoo. He also worked as a department-store Santa Claus. Years later, he would dress up like Santa for the Christmas cards that he and Elvis sent out each year.

Parker's next scheme was to set up a pet cemetery in the back of the humane society. He quickly learned how distraught people would become when their pets were hit by a car or met their demise in some other way. Parker had a teenage assistant at the humane society named Bevo Bevin. He had Bevo clean the weeds and trash from behind the building. Next, he erected a tombstone engraved "Spot" and placed it on an imaginary grave. His cemetery was now ready for customers. The fee for a plot was ten dollars. Bevo made doggie caskets that were included in the burial fee.

To take advantage of the mourners, Parker began selling tiny dog tombstones. He bought them for fifteen dollars and resold them for fifty. He also made a deal with the local florist to get flowers that were ready to be discarded in exchange for hauling them away. Parker sold the flowers to many of his tombstone customers.

In setting up the pet cemetery, Parker ignored the fact that the land did not belong to him. Humane society officials couldn't have helped noticing the business he was running in their backyard. However, they were acutely aware that the financial state of the society had vastly improved under Parker's direction. They chose to ignore the side deals that he worked for himself in exchange for his expertise in raising money and finding homes for dogs and cats.

While Parker was working for the humane society, MGM came to Tampa to film *A Guy Named Joe* starring Spencer Tracey and Van Johnson. Several dogs were required for the movie. MGM went to the humane society to obtain the necessary animals. Tom Parker was the man with whom they dealt. Each day he would bring the dogs to the set. He stood around watching the filming. This would not be the last time that Tom Parker would be on a movie set. One day he would be calling the shots, not following around a pack of dogs.

In 1941, Tom Parker found a new side job. Circumstances brought on by World War II helped him restart his career as a promoter. He began promoting local country-and-western concerts for the Grand Ole Opry as the advance man for Tampa and other cities in the middle and southern portions of the state.

By rationing gas and tires, the federal government virtually stopped leisure travel. As a result, the crowds traveling to Nashville to see the live performances of the Grand Ole Opry diminished greatly. The Opry decided to take its show on the road and rely on local promoters to hype it.

Early on Parker demonstrated a talent for having someone else pay for his acts' advertisements. One of his favorite methods was to enlist the sponsorship of a grocery or department store in the city in which his show was to appear. He would place a discount ticket coupon in the local newspaper at the store's expense. The coupon was redeemable when purchasing a ticket at the store in question. The store benefited through the increased traffic of ticket buyers coming in. While this method is fairly common today, Parker was a pioneer in lining up sponsors to promote a concert.

During this time, he met some of the biggest names in country music. People like Roy Acuff, Bill Munroe, and Minnie Pearl. According to Minnie Pearl, Tom Parker did an excellent job promoting the shows. "He tied our show in with chains like Kroger, and it was smart promotion because it filled the house several times," she said.

Roy Acuff was impressed enough with Parker to ask him to go to Nashville to work for the Grand Ole Opry. Parker told Acuff that he would only be interested in being his manager. This would have necessitated Acuff leaving the Grand Ole Opry's Artist Service

Bureau. He wasn't ready to abandon the Opry and declined the Colonel's proposal.

Performers in the Opry didn't have individual promoters and managers. They were all booked by WSM Radio's Artist Service Bureau. This was the same WSM that owned the Grand Ole Opry on which they performed. Parker realized that the performers couldn't possibly have been receiving the best deal when the organization handling their booking was owned by the same company with which they contracted for personal appearances. Basically their representation was negotiating with itself. Tom Parker reasoned that if some of these performers had representation independent of WSM, they stood to make a lot more money. As did the man who represented them.

One year later, another traveling show came to town and provided Parker with the opportunity he had been looking for. Among the groups that he booked was Pee Wee King and the Golden West Cowboys. What Pee Wee King remembered most about Colonel Parker was his tremendous energy. He was never satisfied. He always wanted more. Everything was negotiable with the Colonel. He would dicker over radio and newspaper ad prices. He did not hesitate to ask anyone for anything. He would ask auditorium owners for a share of their refreshment sales. "Regardless of how big the crowds or advance sales were, he always tried to get a bigger crowd." The vocalist for the group was a young man who seemed to have a promising future. His name was Eddy Arnold.

Tom Parker had found the artist that he had been looking for.

Chapter 3

Eddy Arnold

Eddy Arnold was born on May 5, 1918, in Hendersonville, Tennessee, the youngest of eighteen children. Like most people in Hendersonville, the Arnold family earned their living by farming. In the evening after dinner, Eddy's mother would entertain the children by singing and playing the guitar.

Eddy soon fell in love with music. Much of his free time was spent sitting in front of the radio, dreaming of being a singer. His musical taste was diverse, ranging from Jimmie Rodgers to Bing Crosby, but his favorite was Gene Autry. His mother sat patiently many evenings teaching Eddy to pick out chords on her worn guitar. For his birthday one year, he received his first guitar, a Sears and Roebuck "Silvertone Model."

Eddy's first performance in front of a large crowd was in a high-school talent show. A classmate of Eddy's, Kathy Miller, remembered his professionalism as compared to the other would-be stars.

"Most of us knew that Eddy could sing and play the guitar, but we had no idea how talented he really was. His guitar playing wasn't all that good, but his voice was something special. All the girls were after him from there on," Kathy said.

While playing in talent shows got Eddy dates, it didn't earn him the money to pay for them. He decided to drop out of high school so he could have more time to work on the farm. He soon tired of being a full-time farmer. If he could find a job away from the farm, he could support himself and help contribute much needed cash to the family.

In 1936, eighteen-year-old Eddy decided to focus all his efforts on establishing a career as a professional musician. He and a friend, Speedy McNatt, left Hendersonville for Jackson, Tennessee. They put together an act that consisted of Eddy singing and playing the guitar with Speedy accompanying him on the fiddle.

The duo played a seemingly never-ending series of dates in small Jackson nightspots. Their pay ranged from fifty cents to a dollar a night plus tips. Performing in these juke joints was dangerous work. The singers were treated with little respect. On one occasion, a man grabbed Eddy's guitar out of his hands and emptied his mug of beer into it.

Even though he was supporting himself singing, Eddy wasn't satisfied. He wanted to be something bigger than a saloon singer. He wanted to make records. However, he knew that he would need to establish connections with people who were better connected in the music business than barkeepers if he was to realize his dream.

As an interim step to becoming a solo act, Eddy decided to try and land a spot with an established group. He recorded a demo of him playing and singing which he sent to Joe Frank, the manager of his idol, Gene Autry.

Frank was not able to offer him a spot in Gene Autry's band. However, he did offer him a position with another one of his clients, Pee Wee King. Eddy was disappointed at not getting to play with Autry, but he was excited about the opportunity to play with King.

In January 1940, Eddy joined Pee Wee King's band, the Golden West Cowboys, at a salary of twenty-five dollars per week. His role was to sing harmony and play rhythm guitar. Life with the Golden West Cowboys wasn't as glamorous as Eddy Arnold had imagined it would be. Reliable transportation was always a problem for the group. They traveled in a caravan of cars only one step removed from the junkyard. Even though Pee Wee was a "star," his car was no better than the rest. On one occasion, the Golden West Cowboys were late to a performance because the transmission had fallen out of Pee Wee's car at a stoplight.

Pee Wee King was better known for his on-stage antics than he was as a singer. Eddy added a new dimension to the group. He drew people who would not otherwise pay to see Pee Wee clown around. With this young crooner on the bill, Pee Wee was able to land the Golden West Cowboys a spot on WSM Radio in Nashville, the center of the country-music world. Its powerful fifty-thousand-watt signal allowed it and its Grand Ole Opry to be heard as far away as New York.

When the Opry took its show on the road during World War II, Camel cigarettes sponsored the tour which lasted for nineteen months and spanned the United States. The Golden West Cowboys were a part of the tour. In addition to performing with Pee Wee King, Eddy was given a solo spot on the show. It was during this time that the Grand Ole Opry's George Haig gave him the nickname, "The Tennessee Plowboy." This nickname came from his farm origin, not his singing style. Eddy's voice had little of the southern twang prevalent in country music. His style had more in common with Frank Sinatra than it did Hank Williams.

When the Camel Caravan ended, Eddy lost his opportunity to perform as a solo artist. It was obvious to him that the applause the Golden West Cowboys received was directed as much toward him as it was toward Pee Wee King. By 1943, his potential as a solo artist could no longer hide among Pee Wee's band members. Nudged by his wife, Sally, who he met during an extended radio job at WHAS in Louisville, Arnold approached Harry Stone, the manager of WSM, for his own spot on the station.

Stone agreed to give him a job doing two fifteen-minute shows a day. One was in the morning, and the other was at noon. Eddy would receive fifty dollars a week, double what he was getting from Pee Wee King. Eddy also continued to play in clubs at night, where he could earn another fifty dollars a week. The Arnold family enjoyed the newfound prosperity.

The only goal that Eddy had not accomplished was landing a recording contract. In 1943, Nashville was not the recording capital that it is today. However, most record companies sent scouts to the Opry looking for new talent. On his own, Eddy met with all the record representatives who came to Nashville, trying to persuade them to sign him, without success. Finally, he turned to Harry Stone for help.

During a convention at the National Association of Radio Broadcasters, Stone sold his friend, Fred Forster, on Eddy's talent. Forster was the owner of the Forster Music Publishing Company. He agreed to speak on Eddy's behalf with Frank Walker, an executive with RCA.

RCA was an unlikely prospect for a young artist like Eddy Arnold. It had very few country artists on its roster. In fact, it was one of the few record companies that did not bother to send representatives to Nashville. However, Fred Forster was a good friend and business associate of Frank Walker. Willing to take a chance on Eddy based on Forster's assessment of his talent, Walker agreed to offer Eddy a recording contract without an audition. The Tennessee Plowboy was ecstatic when he received a telegram asking him if he would like to come to New York to make a record. His enthusiasm was soon doused by an unlikely source.

The musicians union went on strike against the record companies. The strike was called by union boss James Petrillo, who feared that the spreading of records on jukeboxes and over the radio would put instrumentalists out of business. The strike meant that no new records would be made. Eddy's new career was put on hold until the strike could be settled.

It was in 1944, during the wait for the strike to end, that Eddy hired Tom Parker as his manager. He first met Parker several months earlier in Tampa when he was still with Pee Wee King. At that time, Parker had offered his services as manager. Eddy was impressed with his connections in the music industry and was also a fan of Tom's one-time client, Gene Austin. However, regretfully, Eddy turned down Parker's offer. He just didn't think that he could afford to give him a percentage of his earnings.

But the record contract changed things. Eddy's anticipated greater income meant he could afford Parker. Also his need for a manager had become much greater with the knowledge that he would now be negotiating with savvy music executives rather than tavern owners.

Tom Parker persuaded Arnold that he could propel him to stardom. According to Eddy, Parker used a line that he would continue to use with slight variation over his entire managerial career. "Let me handle the business, you do the yodeling," he said.

Once again, it was up to Parker to work a town into a frenzy before his act arrived. This time, not only did Parker write press releases, he wrote entire feature articles about his client and left them, along with photographs, at the local newspapers.

But Parker knew his shortcomings. His background was strictly in promotion. He had never negotiated a record contract, a movie contract, or a radio deal. With very few contacts in the entertainment business, he realized that he would need help if he was going to take Eddy Arnold to the big time. He needed someone who could introduce him to the establishment of bigwigs and then help negotiate contracts with them. If you wanted to be on top, you had to associate yourself with the top organizations. The William Morris Agency was the logical choice.

William Morris was the leading talent agency in the business. Parker developed a relationship with Harry Kalcheim of the Morris agency's New York office. He got Kalchiem to take on Eddy Arnold as his client. Tom Parker would maintain strong ties with the William Morris Agency throughout the remainder of his life.

Tom Parker also established strong ties with Steve Sholes, the head of RCA Records' small country-music division and Gene and Julian Aberbach, the owners of Field and Range music publishers. He would make use of these relationships when he began to pursue Elvis Presley some years later.

Since his client couldn't get into a recording studio, the only way to generate income was for Tom Parker to line up personal appearances. He put together a staff to assist him in promoting Arnold which consisted of his brother-in-law, Bitsy Mott, and Bevo Bevin, who had worked for him at the humane society. The managerial crew traveled from city to city in a Studebaker with a trailer behind it carrying posters and other supplies. On the side of the car was painted "Eddy Arnold, the Tennessee Plowboy."

At first Parker was forced to promote Eddy on a shoestring budget. Bevin served as advance man for Eddy's concert appearances. He made sure that the tent that Eddy was to perform in was set up. Also, he blanketed the town with posters advertising that Eddy Arnold was coming. So tight was the budget that Bevin had to go around town collecting the posters after the show was over.

Bevin made it tough on Parker to keep the few props that he had. Bevin's one weakness was a near-obsession with women. He would stretch the truth and tell them that he was Eddy Arnold's manager. A few times, he met girls and ran away with them for two to three weeks, taking all the posters with him. Bevin always came back, and invariably Parker would yell at him for a while and tell him that it had better never happen again. In the end, he would pat Bevin on the back and tell him to get back to work. Parker had a soft spot for his con man.

Later, as Eddy became more successful, Parker expanded his staff by hiring Tom Diskin. They met in Chicago where Diskin was managing his two sisters in an act billed as the Dickins Sisters. He and Parker became acquainted when the sisters were booked on several of Eddy Arnold's tours. It was not long before Diskin was working for Parker. Diskin would remain the number one assistant for the remainder of Parker's managerial career. At first Diskin helped in the office. He was then assigned the task of carrying out much of the organizational work for artist tours.

There was no question in Eddy's mind that Parker was totally dedicated to advancing his career. "When Tom is your manager, he is all you. He lives and breathes his artists. I once said to him, 'Tom, why don't you get yourself a hobby, play golf, go boating or something?' He looked me straight in the eye and said, 'You are my hobby.'" He said that Parker would stay up into the wee hours of the morning working on his next plan.

At the time, most managers relied on local promoters to take care of the details of their artists' appearances. Everything would be handled from the manager's office or by telephone. According to Gabe Tucker, the bass player in Eddy Arnold's band, Parker arranged Eddy's concert appearances with a meticulous, hands-on approach. He would visit a venue prior to the concert date, among other things to verify the number of seats in the auditorium. He would use this information to determine how many songbooks to bring to the concert.

Eddy described Parker as appearing uneducated to those who did not know him. Parker relied upon horse sense rather than formal education. He had a funny way of pronouncing certain words that could make him sound unintelligent (in reality, this was due to his Dutch origin). Parker would play upon this image to lull his negotiating opponents into a false sense of security. Before they knew it, the deal was done, and he had the upper hand.

Tom Parker would take advantage of any possible opportunity to promote Eddy Arnold. On one occasion, he was driving through Tampa when he noticed a crowd gathering around a group of singers in a grocery-store parking lot. Parker wheeled into the lot, jumped out of his car, and made a beeline for the stage. As soon as the group finished the song that they were singing, Parker walked on stage and grabbed the microphone. He asked how many people had heard Eddy Arnold's latest single. He then hyped Eddy's upcoming performance at the state fair. He invited them all to come see Eddy. With that, he replaced the microphone, left the stage, got in the car, and headed on his way. The shocked band did not know what had hit them.

When Parker took over as Eddy Arnold's manager, he began personally selling Eddy's souvenir pictures at concerts. This didn't set well with the members of Arnold's band who had been doing it previously. They had earned extra money from selling the programs. Parker also had the band on salary. They had been receiving a percentage of the earnings.

On one occasion, a venue manager told Parker that he would have to give him a percentage of the souvenir sales generated at the concerts. Parker said, in that case, he wouldn't be selling any souvenirs that night. Also, there would be no intermission during Eddy Arnold's concert. Therefore, the venue manager did not need to worry about selling any Cokes, popcorn, or hot dogs. The manager gave in. He wouldn't take a percentage of the souvenir sales if Parker would have an intermission.

On another occasion, Eddy was booked into an auditorium where the manager was failing to pay the acts until after they performed. Parker told Eddy not to start until he waved at him. Showtime came, but no show. Naturally, the manager sought out Parker to ask what the problem was. Parker explained that his act didn't perform until he waved at them. "I only wave when I get paid." The manager got the message and promptly handed over Eddy's share of the box office receipts. Parker waved, and the concert began.

The musicians' union finally settled its strike in December of 1944. After a fifteen-month delay, Eddy could at last get into a recording studio. Parker prevailed on Steve Sholes, whom he had met promoting the Grand Ole Opry shows, to personally handle Eddy for RCA. It was unusual for Sholes to take on a novice like Eddy, but he did so out of his respect for Parker's judgment.

It was agreed that Eddy would first be featured as a mainstream country artist. Parker planned to develop Eddy into a performer with a broad market appeal. He would establish him in the country field, and then he would ease him into the pop market.

At Eddy's first recording session, "Mommy, Please Stay Home" was chosen to be released as a single on RCA's budget label, Bluebird. Bluebird records sold for thirty-five cents. When an artist became established, he was moved to the RCA label where they were sold for fifty cents. The pressing of "Mommy, Please Stay Home" was limited to eighty-five thousand copies because of a shellac shortage created by war rationing. Bluebird sold all eighty-five thousand copies.

In early 1945, Eddy was back in the studio to record "Each Minute Seems a Million Years." While the song only stayed on *Billboard*'s country chart for two weeks, it went all the way to number five. His next single, "All Alone in the World without You," did not continue Eddy's hot streak. It sold only thirty-five thousand copies.

Parker kept the pressure on disc jockeys to play Eddy's records. One year he brought an elephant to the annual D.J. convention in Nashville. He draped the animal with a giant blanket reading "Never Forget Eddy Arnold" and paraded it back in forth in front of the hotel where the D.J.'s were staying.

In 1946, Eddy got back on track. He recorded "That's How Much I Love You." The song was a stylistic departure from his previous records. It was an up-tempo song with a sort of country blues feel and was a hit. It went all of the way to number two and stayed on the country chart for seventeen weeks.

Eddy Arnold was a hot property. Tom Parker took advantage of this to negotiate an improvement in his position with the Grand Ole Opry. He got Eddy a host position on a portion of the Opry, which meant that Eddy would introduce other acts as well as perform himself. Being granted a host position was an advancement up the Grand Ole Opry ladder. It signified that you were not just a performer, you were a star.

Parker was also able to upgrade the size and quality of the venues in which Eddy performed. At last, he was able to leave the juke joints and move on to the tent shows and an occasional auditorium. This meant bigger crowds, which meant a bigger take for them. Money was much more important than ambiance to Tom Parker when he selected where Eddy Arnold would perform.

In his autobiography, Eddy tells the story of a promoter offering to book him into a very elegant chain of theaters that he owned. But the promoter wanted a percentage of the sales of souvenir programs in addition to the fee for the use of the theaters. Parker snapped back that it would be fine as long as he got a share of the popcorn and soda-pop sales.

Eddy's recording career accelerated in 1947. His first release of the year, "What Is Life without Love," went to number one, as did its follow-up, "It's A Sin." In August, Eddy had his first gold record with "I Will Hold You in My Heart Until I Can Hold You in My Arms." It stayed on the Billboard country music charts for forty-six weeks including twenty weeks at number one, setting a country record. "I Will Hold You in My Heart" also became his first song to reach the pop charts where it peaked at number twenty-two.

By 1948, under the guidance of Tom Parker, Eddy Arnold had

fifteen hit records under his belt. Gone were the days of traveling in Parker's beat-up old Studebaker. They now traveled by chartered airplane. It was then that Parker decided he could no longer effectively conduct business living in Tampa. He would relocate to the capital of country music, Nashville. As was his style, he relied on someone else to provide his housing in Nashville. He and Marie Parker moved in with Eddy Arnold.

Arnold had a four-bedroom house in Madison, just north of Nashville. Parker quickly wore out his welcome in the Arnold household. He set up his office in their family room and expected Arnold's wife, Sally, to wait on him and Marie. After a few months of this, Sally Arnold insisted that something had to be done. To get Parker out of his house, Eddy Arnold gave him another house that he owned in Madison. The Parkers were the proud owners of their first home . . . at no cost.

In addition to a new house, Tom Parker received an addition to his name in 1948. He was made an honorary colonel in October 1948 by Louisiana Gov. Jimmy Davis. Davis was a former country singer who wrote the classic song, "You Are My Sunshine." He and Tom Parker met while Parker was traveling with the carnival. From the moment he received his title, Tom Parker insisted on being addressed as "the Colonel."

After the Colonel picked up his title, he exploited it to his advantage. It was not unusual for governors in the 1940s South to appoint campaign helpers with "colonel" before their names. It signified that you were a friend of the governor and could be very useful for things like getting out of speeding tickets. When he had problems obtaining a hotel room, Parker capitalized on his "rank" to create an opening for himself by making the clerk think he was a military colonel.

Armed with still another identity, Colonel Tom Parker decided to take on the powerful Grand Ole Opry. The Colonel got Eddy a nationally syndicated radio show, the *Checkerboard Square Show*, sponsored by Ralston-Purina. It was broadcast weekdays at noon over the Mutual Broadcast System and lasted for fifteen minutes. Now that Eddy had his own radio show, the Colonel did not see a need for him to continue on the Grand Ole Opry. The only reason that he wanted Eddy on the Opry to begin with was exposure. The money they had received was peanuts compared to that from his record sales and personal appearances. But the Colonel knew Eddy would not leave the Opry unless he was prodded. He decided to make a demand of the Opry that he knew had little chance of being accepted. He could then go to Eddy and say that he had given them a chance, but they turned him down.

The Colonel went to the Opry's Jim Denny and demanded a share of the box office receipts in return for his client continuing to perform on the Opry. No one had ever had the audacity, or for that matter guts, to make such a demand. In those days, the Opry was *the* power in country music. Its booking agency literally controlled the booking of country artists in the United States. The agency had the ability to freeze an artist out of its concert tours. The agency also controlled an artist's access to performing on the Grand Ole Opry. The average promoter was petrified of upsetting the agency. However, the Colonel was not an average promoter.

As expected, his demands were turned down by Denny, who was not about to give any performer a percentage of the gross. Denny was more comfortable with the notion of him receiving money from an artist than giving money to one. It has been rumored that a borderline artist could improve his chances of getting on the Opry by making a "audition payment" to him.

The Colonel dutifully reported to Eddy that he could not work out an agreement with Denny. Eddy would have to leave the Opry. It was not an easy decision for him to make. He had wanted to be a part of the Opry for so many years, he was emotionally attached to it. Furthermore, fellow Opry performers Roy Acuff and Minnie Pearl had become his close friends.

It took a lot of persuading for Tom Parker to get Eddy to leave. The Colonel argued that the Grand Ole Opry wasn't worth the 15 percent of his gross earnings that they took in exchange for booking his live performances. And besides, there just was not enough time for national tours, his *Checkerboard Square* radio show, and the Opry. Eddy drove as much as 700 miles in one day to make a Saturday-night Opry performance. If he wanted to continue his upward climb, something would have to go. The Colonel made him see that the Opry was the most expendable of the three.

Besides, Parker contended, the Opry wasn't needed to sell records. He was right. In 1948, an Eddy Arnold song was number one on the country charts for all but three weeks. He had two one-million sellers, "Anytime" and "Bouquet of Roses."

On the strength of the record sales, the Colonel negotiated a royalty rate for Eddy Arnold that was the highest at RCA. The contract contained a clause that said that no other RCA artist could have a royalty rate higher than Arnold's. If the company wanted to pay someone more than Eddy Arnold was making, it had to raise Arnold's royalty rate so that it was equal.

With the huge record sales, the Colonel had no trouble getting bookings. To make certain that the Opry could not use their influence to lock him out, he offered promoters better deals than they could get through the Opry. It has been reported that the Colonel also paid Jim Denny not to book Opry performers in a venue within two weeks of one of Eddy's concerts. The Colonel did not take chances. He made sure that he had every number covered before he spun the roulette wheel. Soon he set up a successful agency booking other acts in addition to Eddy.

Now that he had triumphed over the Opry's agency and could book his acts at any arena in the country, the Colonel set his sights on the new target to conquer, Las Vegas. Vegas appealed to the him for two reason. First, a performer could earn more money performing in Las Vegas than anywhere else. Second, if there was anything that the Colonel loved more than money, it was gambling with it.

He was able to get Eddy an engagement at the El Rancho Vegas, one of the poshest hotels in town. Eddy had never performed in a major nightclub before and was a little nervous about how he would be received by audiences much more sophisticated than his usual ones. Also, most shows in Las Vegas, even then, were lavish productions complete with orchestral accompaniment. His act was no frills. Just him and a couple of bandmates. His fears proved ungrounded. He played to a full house every night. Standing ovations were plentiful. The Colonel was right again.

In 1949, Eddy made his national television debut on *The Milton Berle Show*. Milton "Mr. Television" Berle was the biggest star in the early days of the medium, and his program was the highest rated. Eddy's popularity at the time was so great that Berle centered the show around him. Eddy sang three songs, "Anytime," "Cattle Call," and "Bouquet of Roses."

Tom Parker was a man who displayed little emotion. He inspired fear in others with his matter-of-fact, tough negotiating style. An incident that happened while *The Milton Berle Show* was being produced is the only time on record that the Colonel showed fear.

He was a firm believer in the importance of punctuality. If you arrived for a 12 o'clock meeting for him at 12:05, you would find that he had already left. As was his custom, he showed up fifteen minutes before rehearsals for the Berle show were scheduled to start. When he walked into the studio, all of the lights were out. He called out to see if anyone was there. The lights came on and standing a few feet in front of him was the Frankenstein monster himself, Boris Karloff, in costume. Karloff was scheduled to appear on the same broadcast as Eddy. He had arrived even earlier than the Colonel for rehearsal. When the Colonel saw "the monster," he jumped out of his shoes. For days after, he would say to anyone who asked him about the incident, "How would you feel in a dark hall with Boris Karloff, with no lights on and nobody else there?"

While television provided the exposure that the Colonel wanted for his artist, it wasn't where the real money was. The big money was made on the other side of the country, in Hollywood. Hollywood was unfamiliar territory to the Colonel. He realized that he would need help getting in the door. The logical choice was the William Morris Agency, still the most powerful agency in the world, with a client list that included a majority of the actors in Hollywood. Parker engaged William Morris to seek a movie deal for Eddy.

The Colonel neglected to mention any of this to Eddy, who was shocked to learn he would be making not one, but two movies in the space of three months. The singer-soon-to-be-actor wanted to know how it was possible to make two movies so quickly. The Colonel had to admit that they would be a little short on budget and quality, but gave assurances that they would be acceptable. All Eddy had to do was what he knew how to do—sing and play the guitar—and the whole country would get a chance to see the Tennessee Plowboy larger than life. Being in the movies would help further his music career. More importantly, it would make money.

So Eddy went to Hollywood and made *Feudin' Rhythm* and *Hoedown*. True to the Colonel's word, they only took three months to complete. Both films were one step less sophisticated than the *Beverly Hillbillies* television program. They were released in 1950 to highly critical reviews. Eddy was no actor, and he knew it.

The movies did fairly well at the box office thanks to the star's large fan base. However, Eddy expressed concern that the bad reviews would be damaging to his career. The Colonel told him not to worry and was again proven right when a song from *Hoedown*, "There Is No Wings on My Angel," went to number six on the country chart.

If Eddy wasn't going to set the movie world humming, there was always television. There he could be presented doing what he did best, singing. There would be no need to fill the gaps between songs with a nonsensical story as there was in a movie.

In July 1952, *The Eddy Arnold Show* premiered on CBS as a summer replacement for the vacationing *Perry Como Show*. It aired on Monday, Wednesday, and Friday evenings for fifteen minutes in the format of a miniconcert. In 1953, the show was moved to NBC as a summer replacement for *The Dinah Shore Show*.

Just when everything was going right with Eddy Arnold's career, he decided to make a drastic change. In late 1953, there was a knock at the Colonel's door. When he opened it, a young man handed him a telegram. It was from Eddy Arnold. The telegram read, "Your services are no longer required. From receipt of this wire, consider yourself dismissed."

The Colonel never commented on the reason behind his breakup with Eddy Arnold. Arnold had little to say himself. The most he would say was that their personalities didn't mesh. "Tom and I had conflicting personalities."

To this day, Eddy is contacted on a regular basis by people who say they are writing a book about Colonel Parker. He refuses to discuss the reasons behind the split. He also will not say anything negative about the Colonel. Eddy refers to the Colonel as a good manager and a wise man who knew how to get things done. The Colonel was a decision maker, not an order taker. And, according to Eddy, that is what made him a good manager. As close as Eddy will come to criticizing Parker is to characterize his manner as very aggressive.

Albert Goldman interviewed Eddy Arnold for his Elvis biography. Goldman said Arnold was very generous with stories about the Colonel's publicity stunts. The mood changed when Goldman asked him why he fired Parker if their relationship had been so good. Arnold answered, "It was simply a matter of temperaments.

Tom is a very flamboyant man. I am a very conservative man." With that, the interview was abruptly ended.

Without direct explanation from the Colonel or Eddy, other inside sources provide the only clues to the reasons for the split. Two of the Colonel's closest associates at the time tell similar versions of the breakup.

The most popular theory is that Colonel Parker wanted to continue working Eddy harder and harder while Eddy was ready to slow down. The Colonel kept him on an exhausting tour schedule. At times he would book Eddy in two cities in one day, 100 miles apart. They began spending more time trying to smooth out their personality differences than they did advancing Eddy's career. As Eddy became a bigger star, he grew tired of Parker's flamboyant promotional manner. He wanted something more dignified, and he wanted to spend more time with his family.

The Colonel's brother-in-law and assistant, Bitsy Mott, confirmed that Arnold got tired of what he considered to be tacky promotions. The event that finally pushed Eddy over the edge, according to Mott, was an advertisement that the Colonel placed in the entertainment trade magazine, *Variety*. The ad read, "Eddy Arnold sold out for a year." This was a fabrication on the Colonel's part. He knew that he would whet arena managers' appetites if they thought that Arnold was booked solid for a year. They would try to get the Colonel to squeeze in a date for them. The advertisement worked as planned. The phone rang off the hook with people wanting to book Eddy. Mott said that Arnold found this gimmick distasteful and that he did not want to trick people into booking him. It led to the firing.

According to another one of the Colonel's assistants, Oscar Davis, the final straw occurred during an appearance date in Las Vegas. When Eddy dropped by Colonel Parker's suite unexpectedly, the Colonel hurriedly stuffed some papers into a drawer. Curious, Eddy asked to see the papers, but the Colonel refused.

Eddy grabbed them and saw that they were plans for a national tour to promote his upcoming record release. He was upset that the Colonel never consulted him before conducting a promotional campaign. He couldn't stand the Colonel and his carnival style any longer. He was afraid that his reputation would be harmed. In short, Davis said that Arnold was unwilling to put up with the Colonel's low-brow style now that he was a huge star and didn't think he needed him anymore. Davis said that the two agreed to stop doing business together the day that the Colonel got Eddy's telegram.

At first, it did not seem that the absence of the Colonel or a more relaxed schedule were going to have any negative impact on Eddy's career. His next release, "I Really Don't Want to Know," went to number one on the country charts and spent a total of thirty-seven weeks there. However, over the next couple of years, his chart success gradually slowed. By 1957, he had only one chart song, and it only went to number twelve. The next year there were no Eddy Arnold songs on the charts.

From 1955 to 1963, Arnold was in a semiretirement. His record sales declined, there were few TV spots and few concert tours. His career was stagnant until he hired Jerry Purcell as his manager in 1964. Purcell changed his image from bolo tie to tuxedo. His idea was to move Eddy away from being strictly a country artist and move him towards a mainstream wider audience. This was the same idea that Colonel Parker had when he first became Eddy's manager. With the help of the enterprising Purcell, Eddy was one of the most popular country acts of the late 1960s. After his big comeback hit, "Make the World Go Away," Arnold charted seventeen country hits, and all but two crossed over to pop charts.

Despite their breakup, the Colonel and Eddy Arnold remained on good terms. Eddy says that the Colonel would call and wish him happy birthday every year. For his part, Eddy called the Colonel every couple of months. Both seemed to be sentimental about their time together. As a part of their breakup agreement, Colonel Parker was retained as Eddy's booking agent in the mid-South area and remained so until 1965.

While Eddy was able to continue his career without the Colonel, the reverse wasn't true. The Colonel found himself in the position of being a manager without an artist. Locating a new client wasn't easy. The Opry's Artists Service Bureau still controlled virtually all the major acts.

For a short while, the Colonel found a new type of client to promote. He assisted with publicity in Frank C. Clement's campaign for the governorship of Tennessee. Clement won the election. As a token of appreciation, he made Parker an honorary colonel of the state of Tennessee, making Parker a colonel two times over.

After the campaign, Colonel Parker tried a couple of other avenues with limited success. He investigated the possibility of starting and managing an artist service bureau for the Louisiana Hayride to help it compete with its rival, the Grand Ole Opry.

After the Hayride project was dropped, the Colonel resumed his search for a client. Ernest Tubb, Cowboy Coppas, and Red Foley were without a manager since the death of Joe Frank in 1952. The Colonel approached each of them, but none were interested.

The Colonel began hanging out in the lobby of WSM Radio. He did this for two reasons. One was that the station was the center of the country music world. Posting himself in the lobby, he was certain to see and be seen by everyone who was anyone in the business. The second reason was that there were free telephones in the lobby. The Colonel would use them to conduct his business. He abused using the phones so much that they were finally removed.

By late 1954, the Colonel had bounced back. *Billboard* magazine heralded his return in its November 6, 1954, issue. It announced, "Tom Parker has signed a pact with Hank Snow to handle the latter exclusively on personals. After the first of the year, he'll take over management of Hank Snow Enterprises which includes radio, TV, film and recording commitments."

Hank Snow had promoted his own tours for years. However, he had dreams of creating a larger organization that could book the tours of other country artists. He looked to the Colonel to help him accomplish that goal.

Chapter 4

Hank Snow

★
★ ★ ★

*H*ank Snow was born Clarence Eugene Snow on May 9, 1914, in the small town of Brooklyn, Nova Scotia in Canada. He was the fifth of six children born to George and Marie Snow.

When Clarence was seven, his mother and father were legally separated. The court prohibited his mother from obtaining custody of any of the children because she was judged to be economically unfit to support them. Clarence's paternal grandmother was made his legal guardian. The rest of the Snow children were dispersed among several foster families.

On the eastern coast of Canada, fishing was the major industry. When Clarence was twelve, he signed on with one of the ships as a cabin boy. He functioned as a servant to the fishermen. In return, he received food, a place to sleep, but no pay. In his spare time, he was allowed to fish. He could sell his catch as his only source of income.

It was aboard the ship that Clarence heard a radio broadcast for the first time. The few stations that the ship's radio could pick up mostly featured weather reports. Occasionally, they would play a little country music. Clarence fell in love with what he heard.

With the money that he had saved from selling fish, Clarence ordered a $5.95 T. Eaton Special guitar. His first performances with the guitar were held in private. He would listen to the radio and play along. Eventually he got up the nerve to sing in front of the crew. To his surprise, they applauded. Thereafter, Clarence was the ship's main source of entertainment.

In 1933, at the age of 19, Clarence decided to pursue a singing career. His goal was to land a radio spot on CHNS radio in Halifax. CHNS was a small 1,000-watt station with a range of about 250 miles. Most Canadian radio stations at the time had a few singers giving regular live performances on the air.

In March 1933, Clarence wrote a letter to the manager of CHNS radio, William Barrett, asking for an audition for a performing position with the station. A couple of weeks later, he received a rejection letter. It said that all the performers who appeared on CHNS were paid by the sponsors who advertised on their programs. CHNS could not use Clarence unless a sponsor requested him.

While Clarence was discouraged, he didn't give up. He decided that he would go to Halifax and try and meet Barrett in person. In order to finance the trip, he took on the backbreaking work of stripping and repainting a ship. He received thirty-two dollars for his efforts.

Once in Halifax, Clarence called CHNS and spoke with Barrett's secretary. He talked her into making an appointment for him for an audition. The next day, after walking the four miles from where he was staying to CHNS, Clarence was introduced to Cecil Landry. Landry doubled as station announcer and chief engineer. Clarence was led into a studio and positioned in front of a microphone. For his audition, he chose two songs written by his idol, Jimmie Rodgers.

Landry was quite impressed by the performance. He told Clarence to come back at seven that night, and he would put him on the air for fifteen minutes. Clarence couldn't believe his luck, but there was one thing that worried him. Landry had instructed him to have a "theme song" ready to lead off his performance. He had no idea what a theme song was. Luckily, he found someone who filled him in. Clarence decided that he would use Jimmie Rodgers's, "The Yodeling Cowboy."

A few days after his performance, the station let him know that he had received a large amount of fan mail. He was offered a fifteen-minute show to be broadcast every Saturday night. Clarence billed himself as "The Cowboy Blue Yodeler," in imitation of Jimmie Rodgers who was known as "The American Blue Yodeler." Not long after that, at Cecil's Landry's suggestion, Clarence changed his name to Hank because "Hank Snow" had a nice western ring to it.

Now that he had an established radio career, Cecil Landry told Hank to contact RCA Victor's Montreal division about an audition. He wrote to A. H. Joseph, RCA's artist and repertoire man for its Montreal office, the person who signed new talent and picked the songs to be recorded. In October 1936, he got an appointment with Joseph. Packing what clothes he had into his beat-up suitcase, tying a rope around it to prevent the faulty latch from falling open, he headed for Montreal.

When Hank arrived at Joseph's office, the two men made small talk for a while. Finally, Joseph got down to business and asked him if he had written any original songs. Hank had ignored the part of the letter Joseph had sent him stating RCA was only interested in original material. He had not written anything. Not wanting to ruin his big chance, he lied and said that he had two good songs that he had only recently written. So Joseph arranged an audition for the next day. If both his singing and his songs passed muster, RCA might be interested in hiring him as a singer/songwriter.

Amazingly that night in his hotel room, Hank was able to write two songs, "Lonesome Blue Yodel" and "The Prisoned Cowboy." The next morning he recorded them. Both songs were Hank's attempt at writing like his idol, Jimmie Rodgers. After the session, Hank couldn't judge from Joseph's reaction whether to be encouraged or discouraged. Joseph promised to study the recordings. Depending on how they sounded, he might consider them for release on RCA Canada's Bluebird label.

For several weeks, Hank went to the mailbox every day looking for some news from Joseph. Finally a letter came. RCA would release Hank's record. Unfortunately, the first record brought more excitement than money. When Hank's first royalty check was for only $1.96.

In November 1937, Joseph invited Hank back to Montreal for another session. One of the eight songs that he recorded, "The Blue Velvet Bird," became a minor hit in Canada. Now that he had a hit song, Hank was ready to go on the road performing. As a relative unknown, with little money, he would promote his tour himself.

He began by taking out a map and picking several towns as possible stops on his tour. He then wrote letters to auditoriums in these towns inquiring about the possibility of renting the facility for a one-night performance. After securing several venues, Hank ordered advertising posters. He couldn't afford to have his picture printed on them. The posters were generic, blocked letters with a blank space in which to write the location and time of a particular appearance.

In the meantime, new Hank Snow records continued to be released. No new recording session was necessary in 1938 since RCA was still drawing from his 1937 session. In 1939, Hank returned to Montreal to record six more songs. By 1940, he was an established recording artist in Canada. The royalty checks got bigger as did the crowds at his concerts.

Over the next four years, Hank repeated the cycle of recording and touring. However, his success was limited to Canada. None of his records had been released in the United States. Nor had he performed there. His opportunity to crack the U.S. market came in mid-1944 when he received a letter from Philadelphia promoter Jack Howard. Howard had been given Hank's name by a Canadian acquaintance and was offering to book some dates for him in his area.

Hank traveled to Philadelphia in July 1944. His first performance was for a group of five thousand servicemen. He also was part of a package show that performed in Delaware. After his mini-concert tour was over, Hank went to West Virginia to visit a country artist known as "Big Slim." Big Slim was a star performer of radio station WWVA in Wheeling. WWVA's signal carried all the way into Canada. Hank listened to Big Slim's show on a regular basis. He had written Big Slim and began a regular exchange of letters.

During the visit, Big Slim said that he could probably get Hank a spot on WWVA if he came back later in the year. Hank took up Big Slim's offer and returned to Wheeling in December 1944. He was given two shows a day at WWVA.

If there was anything that Hank wanted to be more than a singer, it was a singing cowboy. He hoped to follow in the footsteps of Gene Autry and Roy Rogers. In mid-1946, Hank headed for Hollywood. Making the rounds of the movie studios, he met some nice people and even a few movie stars, but had no luck in persuading them that he was destined to ride across the silver screen. However, as he had done before, he turned a failure into an opportunity.

While walking down Hollywood Boulevard, he spotted an office with a sign that read, "Frank Foster Booking Agency." Hank went in, spoke with Foster, and learned that he booked country acts in the area. Hank accepted Foster's offer to book shows for him.

After a six-engagement tour in Washington and Oregon, Foster counseled Hank to take out ads promoting himself. Hank agreed that it was a good idea, but he didn't have the money. Foster then suggested he consider selling his songs to a publishing company and using the advance money to finance the ads.

After an unsuccessful visit to one music publisher, Hank walked a few blocks to another one, Hill and Range. Hill and Range was owned by the brothers, Julian and Gene Aberbach. Hank spoke to Julian and told him he needed money and would be willing to sign the rights to publish all of his future songs to them. Julian asked how much advance money he needed. Hank said $300 would be okay. Julian offered a thousand. Hank signed an exclusive song-writing agreement with Hill and Range on the spot.

After his success with Hill and Range, Hank turned his attention to getting his records distributed in the United States. When Hank first came to the States in 1944, he was able to get an appointment with the head of RCA's New York office, Frank Walker. Hank hoped that he could talk Walker into releasing some of his Canadian records in the United States. Hank waited for Walker for two hours past their scheduled meeting time, but Walker never showed up.

Shortly after Hank's trip to California, he learned that Frank Walker had left RCA. He started a letter-writing campaign to Walker's replacement, Steve Sholes, asking for a U.S. recording session. RCA Canada's A. H. Joseph also lobbied Sholes on Hank's behalf. Finally, in March 1949, Sholes invited Hank to a recording session in Chicago. During the session, Hank played four songs that he had written. Sholes like all four. Hank had saved a fifth song for last that he thought was his best. Hank had high hopes for, "I'm Movin' On," but Sholes wasn't interested. The next day, in a three-hour session, Hank recorded the four songs that Sholes liked. Two weeks later, Sholes called with the news that "Marriage Vow" and "Star Spangled Walls" had been chosen for his first U.S. release.

In late 1949, Hank received a call from his friend Ernest Tubb saying that Jim Denny wanted him to join the Grand Ole Opry. Hank's first performance on the Opry was January 7, 1950. He sang his first U.S. release that night. On the strength of the audience's response, Denny hired Hank as a regular at a salary of seventy dollars a week.

On March 28, 1950, Steve Sholes was in Nashville for Hank's second recording session. The first song recorded was "I'm Movin On," which Sholes had turned down only a few months earlier. Apparently he had forgotten the song or Hank gave a better performance this time because Sholes loved it.

In April 1950, "I'm Movin' On" backed by "With This Ring I Thee Wed" was released. It shot to number one on the country charts and held that position for twenty-nine weeks. Incredibly, it remained on the chart for fourteen months. "I'm Movin' On" went on to become the most played country song of all time.

With the number one song in the country, personal appearance requests poured in. Hank was relieved not to have to worry about promoting his own shows anymore. Having signed with the Grand Ole Opry and its artist bureau meant that Jim Denny took care of that. The bureau booked shows and subsequent radio spots and other advertising. Hank was paid $500 a night for performing on the Opry tours. He couldn't believe that he was actually making that much money.

On one of these tours in 1951, he met a man who in time would become the only real enemy he ever had. Having finished six nights at the Hippodrome Theater in Baltimore, Hank caught an American Airlines flight home. On board, he met Eddy Arnold and his manager, Colonel Tom Parker, for the first time. The three men had what Hank called "a nice visit." The Colonel had a car waiting at the airport and gave Hank a ride home. Tom Parker impressed Hank as being a thoroughly pleasant man. Events of five years later would drastically alter his opinion of the Colonel.

In the meantime, Hank continued to enjoy his remarkable success. His follow-up to "I'm Movin' On," "The Golden Rocket," went to number one on the country chart. Over the next five years, he had sixteen top-five songs. He was voted the number-one country star in the world in 1950, 1951, and 1953.

In 1954, Hank started down a path that later he would very much regret taking. That fall, he began to search for a new manager. He wanted someone to handle all facets of his career including booking concerts, creating radio and television appearance opportunities, and negotiating contracts. As part of his search, Hank interviewed several candidates.

Several people recommended that he speak with Colonel Tom Parker who was no longer handling Eddy Arnold. Hank arranged to meet with Parker to discuss his managerial needs. The meeting was held at the Colonel's house only a few blocks from Hank's own home in Madison, Tennessee. The Colonel's office was located in a corner of his detached garage.

According to Hank, when he addressed the Colonel as "Tom," Parker shot back, "At all times, from here on out, you refer to me as Colonel Parker." Despite this reprimand, their meeting lasted two hours. The Colonel spent most of it recounting all the great things he had done for Eddy Arnold and promising to do the same for Hank. Hank failed to ask the Colonel why he and Eddy Arnold had broken up, seeing that the Colonel was doing so many great things for him.

There were several more meetings at which the Colonel focused on what he had done since he and Eddy Arnold had parted. For one thing, he had formed a booking agency, Jamboree Attractions, and had a client list that included Charlene Arthur, Cowboy Coppas, the Davis Sisters, Whitey Ford (professionally known as the Duke of Paducah), Mother Maybelle and the Carter Sisters, Tommy Sands, and Slim Whitman. He also had a music publishing house, Jamboree Music.

Hank was convinced that the Colonel was his best choice for a manager. He agreed to a contract that would pay the Colonel a flat fee of $2,500 for the remainder of 1954, in exchange for "special services rendered to start handling Hank Snow's personal management." Beginning January 1, 1955, a new contract would go into effect that would pay the Colonel a percentage of Hank's earnings.

A few months later, the Colonel suggested that Hank acquire 50 percent interest in Jamboree Attractions and Jamboree Music. He felt that Hank's prominent name would draw performers and songwriters to the respective companies. In addition, as a songwriter with experience in music publishing, the Colonel thought that Hank could contribute to the administration of Jamboree Music. The Colonel placed a value on the combined assets of Jamboree Attractions and Jamboree Music of five thousand dollars. Colonel Parker's assistant, Tom Diskin, owned 25 percent of the companies and under the Colonel's proposal, would be bought out.

The new partnership was named Hank Snow Enterprises/ Jamboree Attractions. Hank had no doubt that a successful booking agency would come out of the combination of his name and Colonel Parker's promotional talent.

The organization with the Colonel at the helm proved very successful. Within a year, Jamboree Attractions was booking Faron Young, Ferlin Huskey, the Carter Family, Onie Wheeler, and Hank's son, Jimmy Rodgers Snow. It was soon one of the largest independent booking agencies in country music.

Several package tours were put together by the partners. A forecasting of the type of music in the Colonel's future came when he suggested that they book a tour with rock-and-roll star Bill Haley sharing the bill with Hank. He and Snow agreed to place fifteen thousand dollars each in an escrow account for promotional and operational expenses.

The show hit eighty cities in the Midwest and was a sellout everywhere. It was, therefore, something of a shock to Snow when after the tour, the Colonel presented him with a crude-looking financial report that had the tour barely breaking even despite the packed houses. Hank suspected the Colonel had neglected to put up his fifteen thousand dollars or had prepared a fraudulent financial statement. However, for some strange reason, he did not question the Colonel.

Colonel Parker gave Hank the same confusing, sloppy financial statements for subsequent tours. Hank received no other statements with which he could judge the success of Hank Snow Enterprises/Jamboree Attractions. He felt that he had no choice but to accept the accuracy of the Colonel's statements. He was too busy to perform his own review of the partnership's books what with performing 250 dates per year, appearing on the Grand Ole Opry, and making records.

The arrival of a young performer in early 1955 was to confirm Hank's uneasiness about the Colonel's trustworthiness. The young performer's name was Elvis Presley.

Chapter 5

Elvis Presley

Elvis Presley's musical career started on January 4, 1954. On that day, he visited the Memphis Recording Service for the purpose of cutting a two-sided demo. Elvis paid four dollars to record the songs "I'll Never Stand in Your Way" and "It Wouldn't Be the Same without You." Elvis hoped to catch the attention of the owner of the Memphis Recording Service, Sam Phillips, who also owned the Memphis-based Sun Record Company.

In a real-life fairy tale, Sam Phillips was impressed and signed Elvis to a recording contract. Phillips teamed Elvis with two Memphis musicians, Scotty Moore and Bill Black. Moore played lead guitar, and Black played stand-up bass. On July 5, 1954, the trio recorded their first single, "That's Alright, Mama," backed with "Blue Moon of Kentucky."

On July 7, 1954, Dewey Phillips played "That's Alright, Mama" on his WHBQ radio program *Red Hot and Blue* at approximately

9:30 P.M. By 11:00 P.M., Phillips had played the song seven times. During the show, he received fourteen telegrams and forty-seven phone calls. Dewey called Elvis's home from the station to request an interview, but Elvis was at Suzore's Number Two Theater. Elvis's father went to the Suzore, collected Elvis, and took him to WHBQ for the interview.

On July 12, Scotty Moore became Elvis's manager. Eighteen days later, Elvis, Scotty, and Bill made their first concert appearance. The show was held at the Overton Park Shell in Memphis. Slim Whitman was the headliner.

Soon after, Elvis, Scotty, and Bill became regulars at a small Memphis nightclub called the Eagle's Nest. Elvis in particular quickly developed a strong local following. This was reflected in his record sales. On August 28, 1954, *Billboard* magazine listed "Blue Moon of Kentucky" as the number three country-and-western song in Memphis.

Elvis's success caught the attention of Bob Neal, a popular Memphis disc jockey. In addition to being a D.J., Neal promoted country-and-western package shows in the city. He also promoted the Grand Ole Opry and Louisiana Hayride shows locally and in Arkansas and Mississippi cities in the range of his radio program. He had been wanting to get into artist management, and Elvis Presley looked like the ideal start.

After watching Elvis a few times at the Eagle's Nest, Neal asked Sam Phillips if Elvis had a manager. Sam Phillips told him that Scotty Moore had been handling things. However, Scotty would be happy to go back to just playing the guitar. With that, Bob Neal got in touch with Elvis and Scotty and asked if they would be interested in him booking their personal appearances. Both Elvis and Scotty were agreeable. Bob Neal called his new venture Elvis Presley Enterprises and opened an office at 160 Union Avenue.

Since Elvis, Scotty, Bill, and Bob Neal all had day jobs, weekday concerts had to be within close driving distance of Memphis. Also,

Neal was operating on a shoestring budget, relying on his popular early morning radio show to promote the concerts. This meant that Neal booked them in Tennessee, Arkansas, and Mississippi. His wife, Helen, was in charge of ticket sales at the door.

Bob Neal often traveled with Elvis, Scotty, and Bill. Red West, a high-school classmate of Elvis's, went along as a bodyguard. West said Bob Neal "was a real good ole boy, a straight shooter. He seemed to be more in it for the fun than for the money. He was a pretty funny dude who might have made it as a stand-up comic if he had worked at it. Sometimes Bob would go out and warm up the crowd before Elvis and the boys came on."

In the beginning, Bob Neal's comedy was as popular as Elvis's music.

Elvis got his first shot at the big time on October 7 when he made an appearance on the Grand Ole Opry. He was on during the segment hosted by Hank Snow and sponsored by Kellogg cereals between 10:15 and 10:30 P.M. By all accounts, Elvis received a polite applause at best. Some accounts have suggested that the Opry's Jim Denny told Elvis that he "should go back to driving a truck." Elvis was not invited to perform on the Opry again.

He did not stay down for very long. Two weeks after his Opry failure, he appeared on the Opry's biggest competitor, the Louisiana Hayride. Hank Williams got his start on the Hayride, which was broadcast every Saturday night on KWKH radio in Shreveport, Louisiana. The show ran from eight to eleven thirty. Part of the broadcast was heard on a network of 190 CBS radio stations in the South and Southwest.

Sam Phillips drove with Elvis, Scotty, and Bill to their first Hayride performance. Elvis was on a part of the show devoted to newly discovered singers, sponsored by Lucky Strike cigarettes. He sang "That's Alright, Mama" and "Blue Moon of Kentucky." The audience responded warmly to Elvis, and he was asked to become a Hayride regular.

Because Elvis was a minor, his parents, Gladys and Vernon Presley, accompanied him to Shreveport on November 6, 1954, to sign his contract with the Hayride broadcast. The contract required Elvis, Scotty, and Bill to make fifty-two consecutive Saturday night appearances on the Hayride, for which they would be paid according to union scale. Elvis would receive eighteen dollars per show with Scotty and Bill receiving twelve dollars each. Full of confidence, the trio all quit their day jobs to concentrate on music.

It didn't take Elvis long to rise to the top of the pecking order of the Hayride. A *Billboard* magazine article in the December 11, 1954, issue said, "The hottest piece of merchandise on the Louisiana Hayride at the moment is Elvis Presley, the youngster with the hillbilly blues beat."

In the fall of 1954, Scotty Moore wrote a letter to Colonel Parker's assistant, Tom Diskin, at his office in Chicago, using an address he found in *Billboard*. He inquired as to whether they might be interested in booking some dates for Elvis. Scotty had forfeited some of his duties managing Elvis in favor of Bob Neal, but he thought that he could demonstrate his value to the group by securing a booking for the Blue Moon Boys, which is what Elvis, Scotty, and Bill were calling themselves, in a big city outside the South. It's likely Scotty was feeling somewhat insecure at this time, since the Sun recording contract was with Elvis, not the Blue Moon Boys. What's more, the Louisiana Hayride contract had specified Scotty and Bill as Elvis's backup musicians.

On January 13, 1955, Diskin regretfully informed Scotty that there was no place in Chicago where he could book the group. In his letter, he said that there were few opportunities for "hillbilly entertainers" in the area. What Diskin did not say was that the Colonel was already aware of Elvis. In fact, thanks to his assistant, Oscar Davis, he would meet Elvis in less than one month to discuss booking him on a Hank Snow tour.

Scotty Moore's management of Elvis officially ended on January 1, 1955. On that day, Elvis signed a contract naming Bob Neal as his manager. Neal was to receive 15 percent of Elvis's gross earnings. The signing was announced in the January 8 issue of *Billboard*.

While Elvis was popular throughout the South by early 1955, he was still unknown in the capitals of the entertainment business, New York and Los Angeles. Bob Neal wanted to expand Elvis beyond his regional following. To do that, he needed to get him national exposure. Neal knew that the best way to accomplish that was through television. He arranged an audition for Elvis on *Arthur Godfrey's Talent Scouts* in New York.

Because their schedule was full, Elvis, Scotty, Bill, and Bob Neal flew to New York rather than taking the train. It was the first time that they had flown and the first time that they had been to New York. They were very optimistic about finally being on the brink of making it.

When they arrived at the studio, Arthur Godfrey wasn't present. One of his assistants conducted the audition, which did not go well. Although Elvis and company did the identical act that was starting riots across the South, it was received with a stony silence instead of shrieks. The lady conducting the interview remained completely expressionless. It was clear by her "We will call you if we are interested" response that they wouldn't be meeting Arthur Godfrey any time soon.

They were all disappointed, especially Bob Neal. He had been saving for the trip for months. He had seen the show as Elvis's—and his—shot at the big time. Now who knew if there would ever be a big time? Little did Neal know that stardom was just around the corner for Elvis. However, he would reach the top under the management of Colonel Parker, not Bob Neal.

It was Oscar Davis who brought Elvis to the Colonel's attention. Davis first met Colonel Parker in Tampa when Davis was managing

Ernest Tubb. Colonel Parker and Oscar Davis's personalities were vastly different. Davis's negotiation style relied heavily on charm. The Colonel leaned toward intimidation. Davis threw money around like it was nothing. The Colonel was a professed penny pincher. Even their appearances were like night and day. Davis dressed like an English gentleman, wearing expensive suits, a perfect tie, and a flower. The Colonel would go to a meeting with the president of the United States wearing a short-sleeve shirt with the tails hanging out and no necktie. Davis confided to his associates that the Colonel embarrassed him.

Like the Colonel, Davis was a personal manager. His most famous client was Hank Williams. Davis was the Colonel's equal when it came to creating gimmicks to make his client money. He came up with the idea of charging admission to Williams's wedding to Billie Jean Jones. This was despite the fact that the two were already married.

The ceremony was held at the 14,000-seat Municipal Auditorium in New Orleans. The "wedding" was a complete sellout so Davis added a matinee performance. Total ticket sales for the day were thirty thousand dollars. In addition, advertisers donated "wedding gifts" in exchange for being able to place advertisements in the municipal auditorium.

Oscar Davis was more adept at making money than he was at keeping it. When Hank Williams died on January 1, 1954, he found himself with no job and no money. Davis would get one more chance at the big time when he became Jerry Lee Lewis's manager in the summer of 1957. Lewis, for a while, rivaled Elvis as the king of rock and roll. Davis dropped the Killer after the flamboyant rocker destroyed a promising career by marrying his thirteen-year-old second cousin, Myra Gale Brown.

Before hooking up with Lewis, Davis worked with other managers as an advance man. One of his principal employers was Colonel Tom Parker. While at WMPS Radio in October 1954 promoting a Red Foley show, Davis ran into Bob Neal and asked him if there was any promising local talent. Neal played a record for him by a Memphis kid named Elvis Presley and suggested Davis accompany him to see the kid at the Airport Inn that night. When Davis saw the excitement that Elvis generated, his wheels began to turn.

Oscar Davis waited for Neal to leave before approaching Elvis and Scotty Moore on his own. Introducing himself as the man who had managed Hank Williams, Davis expressed an interest in working with Elvis. According to Davis, Elvis was a big Hank Williams fan and was excited by the possibility of having the same manager.

Elvis accepted an invitation from Davis to attend an upcoming Eddy Arnold show at Ellis Auditorium. Appearing with Arnold as secondary headliners were Minnie Pearl and Hank Garland. Elvis was particularly impressed by the quartet backing Arnold, the Jordanaires. Backstage after the show, Davis introduced Bob Neal and Elvis to Eddy. Just when Elvis was starting to warm up to Arnold and the Jordanaires, Oscar Davis pulled him and Neal off to the side and suggested that they go across the street and have some coffee. As they were leaving the backstage area, they passed a heavy-set man smoking a cigar. Elvis asked Davis who the man was. Davis answered that it was Colonel Tom Parker.

For weeks, all Davis would talk about with the Colonel was this kid Presley. He kept pestering the Colonel to meet Elvis. Finally the Colonel gave in, but first he would send someone he could trust to see what was going on. For his mole, he chose Hank Snow's son, Jimmy Rodgers Snow.

Jimmy Snow was following in his father's footsteps as a performer. The Colonel arranged for Jimmy Snow to be booked at the Cotton Club in Lubbock, Texas, on the same bill as Elvis. He gave Jimmy instructions to observe Elvis both on and offstage. When Jimmy Snow came back with an ecstatic report on Elvis, the Colonel went to see Elvis perform himself. He stayed in the rear of the auditorium and did not speak to Elvis or Bob Neal. A few days later, the Colonel arranged to meet them in Memphis to discuss booking Elvis on a Hank Snow tour.

The get-together was set for February 6, 1955, between Elvis's afternoon and evening performances in a Faron Young show at Ellis Auditorium.

When Elvis and Scotty arrived at Palumbo's, a restaurant near the auditorium, there was tension in the air. Tom Diskin was in the middle of trying to explain to Sam Phillips that the Colonel hadn't meant to insult him. The Colonel simply was pointing out that a small company like Sun didn't have the distributing power of a major record company. The Colonel said nothing as Diskin rattled on and Sam Phillips seethed. Scotty Moore decided that this was not the time to mention the rejection letter from Tom Diskin that he had received less than a month earlier.

Then it was Oscar Davis's turn to smooth Sam's ruffled feathers. Colonel Parker, Davis said, could actually help Sun. He would book Elvis in cities that he had never appeared in before. The concertgoers, in turn, would buy Elvis's and Sun's records.

The Colonel, however, was not there for Sam Phillips, Scotty Moore, or the rest. He was there for Elvis Presley, and that's who he addressed as he fired the first salvo in his campaign to win him over. He needed to plant the seed of change in Elvis's mind, the change the singer would have to make to become a star, the change that was Colonel Tom Parker. Elvis needed to play larger arenas. He needed a bigger record company that could get him into every record store in the country and on every radio station.

Elvis had never considered that Sun might be holding him back. The way he saw it, Sun and Sam Phillips had given him his big break. The short meeting ended with the Colonel holding out the enticement that maybe he would be able to book Elvis on one of his tours, sometime.

Bob Neal stayed behind with the Colonel, talking up Elvis,

telling of the excitement he was creating and the full houses he was drawing. The Colonel played it cool. In light of Sam Phillip's attitude, he might be better off sticking with the young singer that he was already handling, Tommy Sands. In fact, the Colonel thought that he would write to Steve Sholes and tell him about Sands. Bob Neal urged the Colonel to attend Elvis's evening performance at Ellis Auditorium and see for himself the audience's response. Finally, Parker agreed. His reference to Tommy Sands was probably just a game the Colonel was playing to make Bob Neal nervous. (Sands, without the Colonel, would go on to a succesful singing and acting career, marry Frank Sinatra's daughter, Nancy, get divorced, and then more or less fade into oblivion.) The Colonel wasn't as lukewarm about Elvis's prospects as he pretended to be. Before he left Memphis, it was agreed that Elvis would be booked on one of Hank Snow's tours of the Southwest.

Naively, Bob Neal viewed his relationship with the Colonel as a partnership from the beginning. He had no intention of giving up Elvis. Bob Neal had grand visions for his discovery. He hoped to get him into television and movies. He saw the Colonel as a means to that end.

Elvis's first appearance with Hank Snow was on February 14, 1955. It was a benefit for the Roswell, New Mexico, Fire Department. Elvis was well received for a relatively unknown performer. As the tour swung through western Texas, Elvis's confidence grew nightly as did his applause. The Colonel was impressed enough to book him on Snow's upcoming May tour.

This tour began in New Orleans and ended in Florida. As the headliner, Hank closed the show. Elvis gradually worked himself up the bill to the position immediately proceeding his. Hank quickly found that following Presley was an unenviable position. He began to suffer the embarrassment of walking out on the stage to applause that was asking for Elvis's return. Being no fool, Hank went to the Colonel, and they agreed that Elvis should close the first half of the show. This would give the crowd time to calm down before the "star" Hank Snow went on.

If one day has to be singled out as the beginning of the legend of Elvis Presley, that day would be May 13, 1955, when he appeared at the Gator Bowl in Jacksonville, Florida. Gladys and Vernon Presley were in attendance. As Elvis closed the first half of the show, he thanked the audience and uttered the words that started an avalanche. "Girls, I will see you backstage." With that invitation, many of the females in the audience surged after Elvis, who took off at a run for the locker room that was serving as a dressing room. Some 100 girls managed to push their way inside before the door could be shut. They attacked Elvis, tearing off his clothes. Elvis climbed on the top of a bathroom stall until police could clear the mob. When Elvis was finally escorted to his car, he found it vandalized with the names of many of his female admirers.

Somewhere near the now-calm stage, the Colonel stood smiling. He had seen his future, and his name was Elvis Presley. But wanting Elvis and getting him were two entirely different things. Elvis already had a manager, Bob Neal. To make matters worse, Bob Neal's wife, Helen, was good friends with Gladys Presley. Gladys Presley wore the pants in the family. It would be tough to sell Elvis on dumping Bob Neal if Gladys wouldn't go along.

The Colonel had already figured out that the fastest way to Elvis's heart was through his wallet, and he wanted to be the one to fatten it. The Colonel had to make certain that Elvis's earnings stayed relatively low while he was with Neal. With that in mind, he negotiated the lowest deal possible with Bob Neal for Elvis to appear on the Colonel's Hank Snow package shows. He wanted to put the idea in Elvis's head that he could never make much money as long as he was with Neal.

Bob Neal did not accompany them on the May tour. According to Scotty Moore, Colonel Parker took advantage of that to butter up Elvis, telling him that he deserved better than he was getting.

Every night after the show, the Colonel would slip Elvis extra money. (One story that has circulated over the years is it was an extra $200 a night.) Elvis was a little confused about why he was getting money from the Colonel and not from Bob Neal. The Colonel made no attempt to disguise his intent. He told Elvis that he was giving him the money because that is what he should be making. If he signed with the Colonel, he would be making that much and even more.

It didn't take long to win over Elvis. He thanked the Colonel at every opportunity for everything he had done for him. Elvis even began asking the Colonel his opinion of his stage attire. However, the Colonel had to do more than bamboozle Elvis. Elvis was still a minor. Gladys and Vernon Presley would have to give their consent.

Elvis was talking about Colonel Parker to anyone who would listen, including his girlfriend, Bob Neal, and his parents. Vernon cautioned Elvis that he really didn't know anything about the Colonel. He also reminded Elvis that he already had a manager. Elvis countered that he knew plenty about the Colonel. He knew what he had done for Eddy Arnold, he knew that he had important friends in the music business and in Hollywood. Bob Neal didn't. Nonetheless, Elvis assured his parents that Neal would be a part of any deal that he made with the Colonel.

Vernon was won over fairly quickly by the barrage of telephone calls and telegrams from Colonel Parker. He fell under the hypnotic spell of the promoter's promises of riches for Elvis and his family. The things the Colonel said began to make sense to him. Sun Records wasn't big enough for Elvis. Sun needed Elvis, but Elvis didn't need Sun anymore.

Moving in for what he hoped was the kill, the Colonel visited Gladys and Vernon Presley at their home in Memphis. What started out as a short visit ended up being an all-out sales pitch. But Gladys proved a much tougher sell than Vernon had been. Among other things, she wanted to know which church the Colonel attended. Since organized religion was not part of the Colonel's repertoire, he was forced to dance around the question.

However, he sensed an opening when Gladys mentioned that she thought that Elvis was already working too hard. He saw a way to score points with her by suggesting that as Elvis's manager, he would have her son working "smarter," not "harder." The gambit backfired. Gladys was not about to abandon her friend, Helen Neal, who came by the house to visit her on a regular basis. The Presleys and Neals went on picnics together. Elvis ate dinner at the Neals' house. The Colonel, on the other hand, struck her as being very big city. Big city to Gladys Presley was a distinct negative, and she was offended by the Colonel insulting Neal's ability to handle Elvis.

Then there was the business of the fans going beserk. Elvis's second appearance in Jacksonville had nearly resulted in another riot. A short article about the concert, written by the Colonel, appeared in *Cash Box* magazine. He emphasized that Elvis's clothes had literally been torn off after the show. When Gladys Presley mentioned her concern over such melees, the Colonel tried another tack.

He, too, worried about Elvis's safety. He certainly didn't want to see any more riots, and he agreed that Elvis was overworked. If he could earn more money for his appearances, then he could cut down on his schedule. They could all use the money and the time off to take a nice vacation. With all that said, the Colonel sensed it was time to back off. There was no need to sign any contract then. He could wait until Gladys Presley was more comfortable.

The Colonel went looking for reinforcements and enlisted an old friend, country comedian, Whitey Ford, better known as the Duke of Paducah. The Colonel knew that Gladys listened to the Grand Ole Opry on the radio every Saturday night. He also knew that the Duke was one of her favorite performers.

The Colonel invited the Duke over to his home and played a

couple of Elvis's records for him. After the records were finished, the Colonel told him that he would book him on Elvis's next tour. In return, he asked the Duke to keep an eye on the young performer. Of more importance to the Colonel was that Gladys and Vernon Presley would be in attendance when Elvis appeared in Little Rock and that Gladys Presley would be keeping an eye on the Duke, who had a reputation as being a religious man. The Duke would work kind words about the Colonel into his conversations with Gladys.

Elvis was scheduled to appear in Little Rock on August 3. The day before the show, the Colonel met with the Duke to rehearse his lines. He told him that it was almost certain that Gladys and Vernon Presley would stop by their son's dressing room, so the Duke should be there before the show. After Gladys and Vernon arrived, Elvis was to say, "Now Mama, the Duke here has been with the Colonel for a long time. He knows him from A to Z." That was to be the Duke's cue to lay the praise on thick for the Colonel.

The scenario played out exactly as the Colonel had envisioned. Gladys and Vernon Presley arrived in the dressing room as anticipated. The Colonel made small talk with them for a few minutes and then excused himself. Out went the Colonel and in went the Duke.

After some getting-acquainted time, the Duke launched into his prepared spiel. Oh, he had known the Colonel for years. He had seen firsthand the Colonel's contribution to Eddy Arnold's success. Colonel Parker could make Elvis a star. He could help him earn more money than he could ever spend. The money part sold Vernon Presley. Gladys, however, raised the issue of Elvis's contract with Bob Neal and Sam Phillips as obstacles to Colonel Parker working with her son. The Duke promised her that if she and Elvis wanted the contracts undone, Colonel Parker could make it happen. Why, the Colonel knew everything about making an artist successful.

Gladys repeated to the Duke what she had told the Colonel. She just didn't see any reason to make changes right then. Elvis was extremely disappointed. Later, the Colonel reassured him that everything would work out. Just give it some time.

The Colonel picked up his efforts after the Little Rock rejection. He called the Presleys almost every day and had the Duke do the same. He also kept selling Bob Neal on the deal, telling him that he would benefit from the arrangement as much as Elvis would. Finally he decided to bring in Hank Snow to take on the formidable, immovable Gladys.

But first he would have to prime Snow. After the first Jacksonville concert, the Colonel had brought up the idea of signing Elvis to a managerial contract. According to Hank, by that time the Colonel was aware that two performers had become friends and that Elvis would respect Hank's advice on career decisions. The Colonel suggested that Hank "baby-sit" Elvis and try to persuade him to dump Bob Neal in favor of Hank Snow Enterprises/Jamboree Attractions.

It was now Hank's turn to visit the Presley home. With Vernon in the bag, his focus was Gladys. In his sales pitch to the Presleys, Hank told them that the Colonel would not be managing Elvis alone. He and the Colonel would be doing it together through their joint company. Elvis had unlimited potential with proper management. Colonel Parker had achieved great success for Eddy Arnold. He and Hank had big plans for Elvis, including television and radio. He also would hook up Elvis with a larger record company that would be better equipped to promote and distribute his records. Hank Snow's visit eased Gladys's mind quite a bit. Even Bob Neal assured her that he had reviewed the contract and had no problems with her signing it.

Gladys Presley finally gave in. On August 15, 1955, Elvis signed a contract with Colonel Parker that named him "special advisor" to Elvis and Bob Neal. Although the contract was for the Colonel to represent Elvis, its primary focus was on what Elvis would do for the Colonel. Most of it was dedicated to requiring Elvis to appear on Colonel Parker-promoted shows at a cheap rate. There was also a clause that said that the Colonel was to negotiate all the renewals on Elvis's existing contracts. This effectively made the Colonel Elvis's manager.

At about the same time, Bob Neal informed Scotty and Bill that they were being put on a salary of $200 a week when they were working and $100 a week when they were not. Up to that point, money earned had been divided with 50 percent to Elvis and 25 percent each to Scotty and Bill. The two immediately blamed Colonel Parker for the change. Little did they know that if it had been up to him, Elvis would have dropped them and used Hank Snow's band as his backup. If the Colonel was ready to cut loose Scotty and Bill, was anyone secure?

Bob Neal seemed to have come to the same conclusion. He turned over most of the decision making to the Colonel. The last contract of any consequence that he negotiated for Elvis was a one-year renewal with the Louisiana Hayride broadcast. Elvis was to be paid $200 per week rather than the original $18. Behind Neal's back, the Colonel urged Vernon not to sign the contract, maintaining it committed Elvis to too many performances at too small a price. Vernon ignored the Colonel and signed anyway.

When the Colonel took over Elvis's management completely in 1956, one of the first items on his agenda was to get out of the Hayride contract. He viewed it as constricting, just as he had Eddy Arnold's involvement with the Grand Ole Opry. He didn't like that the contract required Elvis to be in Shreveport every Saturday night. This precluded making national tours. It made no sense for Elvis to appear on the Hayride for $200 when he could generate several thousand dollars a night on his own.

The Colonel bought out the remaining six months of the Hayride contract for ten thousand dollars and one final charity performance. In later years, he would mistakenly be given credit for getting Elvis on the Louisiana Hayride. He was quick to deny this. "Boy, I got him off the Louisiana Hayride," he would say.

With Elvis under contract, the next step in the Colonel's plan was to get him away from Sun Records and signed with a major company. Sun Records' small size and weak finances made it impossible for the company to generate record sales at the level that the Colonel wanted for Elvis. Sun had virtually no promotional budget. For example, it was common practice for record companies to take out advertisements in *Billboard* magazine and other music publications promoting artists and their latest single. It wasn't until Elvis's recording of "Baby Let's Play House" hit the country charts in July 1955 that Sam Phillips advertised an Elvis record in the trade papers.

To the Colonel's surprise, Phillips seemed willing to accommodate his wishes. In early summer 1955, Sam Phillips put the word out through Bob Neal that Elvis's contract was for sale at the right price. Phillips was having financial problems. He had used what remaining money he had to buy out his brother Judd's share of Sun Records. His distributors were not paying him on time. He was even behind on royalty payments to some of his artists, including Elvis.

Bob Neal in turn asked the Colonel to help him get a buyer for Elvis's Sun contract. The Colonel did not waste any time going to work. Decca Records producer Owen Bradley was vacationing in Daytona Beach. He ran into Colonel Parker at the dog track. The Colonel asked him if he had ever heard of Elvis Presley. Bradley said that he had not. The Colonel proceeded to tell Bradley how no one wanted to follow Elvis on stage because they would walk out to cheers of "We want Elvis." They did not want to hear the supposed "star," they just wanted Elvis.

Elvis was a hot property that Decca could use. With Elvis's Sun contract up for sale, the Colonel would help Decca sign Elvis in exchange for Decca helping him buy out Bob Neal's managerial contract.

When Bradley returned to Nashville he spoke with Decca's artist development chief Paul Cohen about Elvis. Cohen agreed to find out from Neal what it would take to get Elvis's Sun contract. When Neal said eight thousand dollars, Cohen told him he was crazy. As the weeks went by, both Bradley and Cohen got more and more reports of Elvis stealing shows. Cohen decided that maybe eight thousand dollars was not as bad as it had seemed. He phoned Neal again and was told that the price had gone up to twenty thousand dollars.

Offers were coming in from virtually every major record label. At first Sam Phillips wasn't very serious about selling. His asking price was constantly fluctuating. He would throw out a number like fifteen thousand dollars. If someone accepted, he would say that he had changed his mind and the price was now twenty thousand.

The Colonel saw that he needed to help Sam definitely make up his mind to sell. He worked Sun's distributors to nudge Sam into selling the contract. He told them that Elvis's contract was for sale, which made them reconsider ordering more Elvis records. Sam Phillips found out about this and confronted the Colonel. Phillips blew off steam while the Colonel denied any bad intentions.

In November 1955, Sam Phillips formally empowered Colonel Parker to solicit offers for Elvis's contract. The Colonel and Sam finally worked out a deal where for five thousand dollars, the Colonel would get an exclusive option to sell the contract. Phillips's asking price was thirty-five thousand dollars plus the five thousand dollars that he owed Elvis in back royalties. This was the highest price ever asked for a recording contract. He gave the Colonel until December 1 to find a buyer or the option would expire, and Sam would keep the five thousand.

The Colonel immediately went to work. Among the first companies he met with was Columbia Records. On the advice of Wesley

Rose, Columbia had decided to make a serious offer. Rose was the owner of the Acuff-Rose music publishing company. He was the first person to exploit the publishing of country songs with great success. Rose was able to persuade friends in the business like Mitch Miller, the head of artists and repertoire for Columbia Records, that many of these songs would be excellent material for noncountry acts. Because of Rose's urging, Mitch Miller had Tony Bennett record the Hank Williams's tune "Cold, Cold Heart."

When Rose told Mitch Miller that this kid Elvis Presley was worth taking a look at, Miller sent a couple of representatives to the annual disc jockey convention in Nashville to talk with Colonel Parker about buying Elvis's recording contract. Elvis had a little more than a year left with Sun. It only made sense for Columbia and the other companies to sign Elvis to a long-term contract, and that meant negotiating with Colonel Parker.

The Columbia representatives met with the Colonel in the lobby of the Jackson Hotel and began their sales pitch. It was widely known that RCA was the Colonel's front-runner. The Columbia people told the Colonel that their sales force and distribution was far superior to RCA's. Columbia was the most prestigious record company in the world and on and on.

The Colonel suggested that they meet again the following day, and he would bring Elvis along. The next day, when they got together in a hotel coffee shop, Elvis was given the Columbia grand speech that Colonel Parker had received. After some brief chitchat, the Colonel dismissed Elvis with "All right Elvis, let me talk some more to the boys."

When Elvis had left, the Colonel cut to the chase, telling the Columbia executives that he had already been offered a lot of money. The Columbia executives quickly responded that they had been authorized to offer a forty-thousand-dollar advance. The Colonel chuckled and said that they were way off base. But he promised that he would get back with them. The next time

Columbia's Owen Bradley saw Colonel Parker was at WSM Radio. The Colonel and RCA's Steve Sholes were standing together in the hallway. The Colonel told Bradley that Columbia had waited too long. Elvis had been sold to RCA.

There was no doubt in the Colonel's mind from the beginning that RCA was where he wanted Elvis to be. He had worked with RCA and Steve Sholes for ten years. He felt comfortable with the company. However, the Colonel did not want RCA to take it for granted that they were the front-runners. He continued to work several record companies to get the money high enough for Sam Phillips to consider. He made them all think that they had a chance if their offer was right, even while he was focusing most of his efforts on selling RCA on Elvis.

The Colonel even put aside old grudges in his quest to win over the company. In 1954, the Colonel had managed a tour for RCA called the RCA Country Caravan. An RCA publicist arranged to have both *Life* and *Look* magazines cover the caravan's Jacksonville show. The Colonel was enraged when he wasn't interviewed by either magazine. He felt that his work was responsible for the tour's success, and accused the publicist and RCA country promotion manager, Chick Crumpeter, of deliberately steering the reporters away from him. Crumpeter, he claimed, wanted all the glory for himself. Crumpeter protested his innocence, but the Colonel threatened to have his job.

The Colonel was not successful in removing Crumpeter from his position. One year later, they ran into each other in Richmond, Virginia. Crumpeter was in town to meet the local D.J.'s. Parker was there with Hank Snow, Elvis, and the rest of the troupe for a concert.

Crumpeter bumped into the Colonel backstage before the show. To his surprise, the Colonel acted like he was a long-lost friend. Naturally, there was a purpose behind the Colonel's civility. He was eager for Crumpeter to see Elvis perform. The Colonel knew that if Crumpeter liked what he saw, he would report it back to Steve Sholes. If the reward merited it, the Colonel could put aside a grudge.

Crumpeter attended the show that night and was amazed at what he saw. The next morning, he had breakfast with the Colonel, Hank Snow, and Elvis. Crumpeter took all four of Elvis's Sun singles back to New York with him for Steve Sholes to hear. According to Crumpeter, Steve Sholes had his sights on signing Elvis the moment he heard them.

Sholes went to see Elvis perform in person and right away felt he would be a star. But Sholes knew that most RCA executives viewed country and western as a stepchild and were ready to dismiss Elvis as a flash in the pan.

It took a long while before he was able to get the top brass at RCA to buy Elvis's contract. His records had really not sold very many copies, and Sholes was asking them to pay more for Elvis's contract than anyone had ever paid before. Finally, in 1955, when "Baby Let's Play House" made it to number ten on the country charts, Sholes had some evidence to throw at his bosses.

On October 28, 1955, a telegram arrived at Colonel Parker's home office in Madison. The sender was W. W. Bullock, manager of RCA's singles division. The message: the highest that RCA would go for Elvis's contract was twenty-five thousand dollars.

The next day, the Colonel and Tom Diskin drove to Memphis to meet with Sam Phillips and Bob Neal. They arrived to find Sam in a meeting with Hill and Range Music Publishing representatives. Hill and Range was negotiating a deal to produce an Elvis song folio and handle Sun's catalog in Europe. As part of the deal, Hill and Range would promote the recordings of the songs in the United States.

Hill and Range owners, brothers Gene and Julian Aberbach, were Austrian Jews who had worked in the music publishing business in Europe before fleeing the Nazis in 1940. Upon arriving in

America, they worked five years for Chappell Music before starting their own publishing company. Hill and Range was the first New York publishing company to recognize the potential of country-western music. Hill, short for Hillbilly, was chosen to represent country. Range represented the western.

Hill and Range came up with an ingenious plan to build their publishing business. They allowed their singer/songwriters to participate in 50 percent of the publishing income. This had never been done before. Sharing the wealth enabled Hill and Range to attract name acts such as Bill Munroe, Ernest Tubb, Bob Wills, and Hank Snow.

The Aberbachs had worked with the Colonel on publishing both Eddy Arnold and Hank Snow. He enlisted their help in wresting Elvis's contract from Sam Phillips. The Colonel got the Aberbachs to make the sale of Elvis's recording contract part of their deal with Sun Publishing. Because Hill and Range had been sending a lot of good material to RCA, the Colonel knew that they also would be powerful allies in selling RCA on Elvis.

After the Hill and Range meeting, Sam joined the Colonel and Tom Diskin at the Holiday Inn restaurant The Colonel began by asking Sam again how much he wanted for Elvis's contract. Sam reiterated the thirty-five thousand dollar price. The Colonel said that he didn't know if anyone would go that high. The most that RCA was willing to pay was twenty-five thousand. Tom Diskin chimed in and asked Sam Phillips how much money he had made from Elvis. Sam told him to shut his mouth, he wasn't interested in hearing from him or talking to him.

On November 10, the Colonel and Elvis attended the disc jockey convention in Nashville. At the convention, *Billboard* magazine presented Elvis with an award for being the "most outstanding new country star." *Billboard's* rival, *Cashbox*, made him "Up and Coming Star of the Year." Jumping on the bandwagon, *Country Music Jubilee* magazine gave him the "New Star of the Year" award.

The Colonel spent most of the time working on Steve Sholes. He made sure the RCA exec was aware of all the accolades Elvis was receiving. Just in case that wasn't enough, the Colonel reminded everyone at RCA that he managed one of their biggest stars, Hank Snow. To emphasize his point, he had an elephant parade back and forth outside the convention site carrying a blanket that read, "Like an Elephant, Hank Snow Never Forgets." The inference was clearly that RCA stood to lose more than Elvis if they didn't buy his contract.

On November 11, 1955, Elvis performed. Afterwards Sholes agreed to Sam Phillips's asking price, but he had to personally guarantee that RCA's money would be earned back in a year. Sholes realized that he was taking a substantial risk in getting RCA to sign Elvis for so much money. "This boy could be the making of RCA, I thought, or the breaking or me," he said some years later. Sholes needn't have worried. During his first year with RCA, Elvis sold twelve million singles and three million albums.

Colonel Parker suggested that RCA purchase all of Elvis's Sun masters as part of the deal. When Columbia signed Johnny Cash, they neglected to buy the masters. As soon as Cash started having hit records on Columbia, Sun flooded the market with the Cash songs that they owned. As a result of this competition, the sales of Columbia Cash recordings suffered. By purchasing the masters, RCA would prevent Sun from issuing any more Elvis releases that would compete with their own. RCA took the Colonel's advice. It turned out to be a smart business decision.

On November 19, the Colonel telephoned Hank Snow with the news that RCA had agreed to buy Elvis's contract. It would be signed in Memphis the next day. He was taking a managerial contract along with him. If he had a problem getting Gladys and Vernon to sign that, he would call Hank and have him come to Memphis.

At about ten that same night, Hank received another call from the Colonel, telling him to be in Memphis the next day. Hank assumed from the serious tone of the Colonel's voice that he was having problems with the Presleys. In fact, the managerial deal was all but signed.

The next morning, Snow was met at the Memphis airport by representatives of both RCA and Hill and Range. They drove him directly to the downtown Peabody Hotel, where a combination luncheon/press conference was underway. In addition to RCA and Hill and Range representatives, in attendance were Elvis, Gladys and Vernon Presley, Colonel Parker, Bob Neal, Sam Phillips, and several members of the media.

Hank held the floor for the next hour and a half, his speech emphasizing the skills of Colonel Tom Parker. Gladys and Vernon Presley seemed to be paying particular attention, and Hank could tell by the expressions on their faces that they had been won over.

When Hank finished, the signing of the contracts began. The first was Elvis's recording contract. RCA was paying Sun Records forty thousand dollars to bow out, five times what they could have had it for a few months before.

The Sun buyout agreement was only two pages long. It required Sun to turn over all the taped recordings of Elvis Presley in its vaults. It also required it to stop selling Elvis Presley records by December 31, 1955. In return, Sam Phillips received thirty-five thousand dollars. RCA also agreed to pay Elvis back royalties of five thousand dollars.

Elvis's royalty rate with RCA was 5 percent as compared to the 3 percent he had been receiving from Sun. This didn't amount to very much in real dollars. Elvis would receive an extra eighteen thousand dollars for every million records he sold.

The second contract was a publishing agreement between Elvis and Hill and Range. Under the deal, Hill and Range set up two companies for him, "Gladys Music" and "Elvis Presley Music." Elvis owned 50 percent of these companies, and the Aberbachs owned 50 percent. By getting a publishing company for Elvis, the

Colonel effectively increased his royalty per record sold by 50 percent. This was because he would be receiving 50 percent of the broadcast royalty and mechanical royalties (which is what publishers receive for allowing a song they own to be recorded) that were normally paid to the publisher of the song. Hill and Range received the right to control the publishing on at least one song on every single that Elvis released.

After the contract signing, there was a photo session. Partners Colonel Parker and Hank Snow flanked Elvis in one of the pictures. Another definitely posed picture has the Colonel with his hand on Gladys's shoulder while Vernon looks on.

After the photo session, they stopped by for a short visit with Mary Keisker on her radio program. According to Keisker, Hank Snow said, "I'm very proud this boy made his first appearance on the national scene on my section of the Grand Ole Opry." Keisker was a little upset at Hank trying to take credit for something she didn't think he deserved. She shot back, "Yes, but I remember you had to ask him what his name was."

Hank waited all afternoon for the paper that he was most interested in to be signed, his and the Colonel's managerial contract with Elvis. At five o'clock, he still had seen or heard nothing about it. Finally at six, he approached the Colonel who said that he was getting ready to drive back to Nashville. He asked Hank to join him so that they could discuss the contract.

In the car, the Colonel said he had gone to Memphis with two managerial contracts. He carried one in each pocket. The one he gave the Presleys would depend on their reaction to what he said during negotiations. Hank interpreted this to mean that one of the contracts had more favorable terms for Hank Snow Enterprises/Jamboree Attractions than the other.

He was surprised to learn that the managerial contract had been signed before he got to Memphis. His assumptions about the nature of the contracts seemed to be confirmed when the Colonel told him that the Presleys signed the first one. The Colonel went on to say that some day they would be able to retire on the contract with Elvis. However, the Colonel did not discuss any of its details, and Hank was afraid to ask questions. Any sign of mistrust would throw the Colonel into a rage. Whenever the Colonel sensed a questioning of his honesty, he would shout, "What! Don't you trust the Colonel?"

Back in Nashville, Hank didn't really know any more about the arrangement with Elvis than when he left Memphis. He was uncomfortable with the situation and went to his attorney for advice. After filling in the attorney about his relationship with the Colonel, Hank produced the financial statements that the Colonel had given him. After reviewing them, the attorney had doubts about their validity. The revenues didn't seem to be nearly as high as Hank's accounts of the crowds indicated they should be.

Over the next few weeks, Hank's attorney conducted an investigation into the Jacksonville concert and the Colonel's financial report on it as a test. He obtained affidavits from several people who were involved in promoting and selling tickets for the show. This investigation indicated that Colonel Parker had altered the ticket sales to a figure much lower than they actually were, reported these artificially low gate receipts to Hank, and kept the extra money for himself. Even more damaging for Hank was the fact the Colonel had reported the low-ball number to the IRS. As part of the partnership, Hank could be held liable if these understatements of income were ever uncovered.

Hank's attorney persuaded him to go to Parker and demand that a corporation be formed immediately. This would help transfer some of the liability away from Hank to that corporation. He should also insist that the books of the corporation be open at all times to his personal accountant.

Hank invited the Colonel to his house, saying there was something important they needed to discuss. When the Colonel arrived,

Hank told him about his conversations with the attorney and what
the attorney had recommended about incorporating Hank Snow
Enterprises/Jamboree and opening the books for examination.

Colonel Parker exploded with an anger unlike anything Hank
had imagined. The Colonel insisted that they immediately dissolve
their partnership since it was obvious that they could no longer
work together. Hank thought for a few moments and asked what
would happen with their contract with Elvis if the partnership dis-
solved. The Colonel shot back with words that Hank had feared.
"You don't have any contract with Elvis Presley. Elvis is signed
exclusively to the Colonel."

It was suddenly all too obvious the true nature of the separate
contracts that the Colonel had taken to his meeting with Vernon
and Gladys Presley. The first contract named the Colonel as Elvis's
manager. The second contract named Hank Snow Enterprises/
Jamboree Attractions as manager. The Colonel only brought the
second contract along in case he needed to include Hank Snow to
pacify Gladys Presley. Vernon and Gladys had signed the first contract that made the Colonel Elvis's manager and omitted Hank.

Perhaps in an attempt to justify his underhanded dealings, the
Colonel reminded Hank that he had been against buying Elvis's
contract when the Colonel first suggested it. Of course, this was
ignoring the fact that the issue in the past had been Elvis's record
contract, not the one for managing him. The Colonel had wanted
their company to buy the record contract and then sell it to the
highest biddder. The Colonel would have had them pool their
assets, including Hank's recording royalties, to finance the purchase. Snow had no interest in doing that.

Hank asked his attorney about suing Colonel Parker for a share
of Elvis's contract. The attorney advised against it, saying the
Colonel could drag out the lawsuit forever. A few years later, after
his original attorney died, Hank approached another one about filing suit. This attorney's recommendation was also to walk away

from the Colonel. In the end, Hank decided that he had plenty of money and didn't need the aggravation. One wonders if he would have made the same decision had he known the tens of millions of dollars that the Colonel would make from managing Elvis.

After the split, Hank decided that he wasn't any happier with what the Colonel had done for him as a manager than he was about what he had done to him as a business partner. When Hank's contract with RCA had come up for renewal, the Colonel negotiated a new royalty rate of 3 percent. At that time, Hank was one of the top performing stars in the world. When that contract expired, he negotiated his own contract for double the royalty rate and three times the advance, even though his record sales were down. Hank was convinced that had he been negotiating five years earlier instead of the Colonel, he could have gotten the higher royalty rate then.

Faron Young has a slightly different version of the falling out. He maintains that Hank Snow and the Colonel's problems began before the dispute over the Elvis contract. Snow was upset because the Colonel was devoting more attention to Elvis. Young also claims that Snow did not try to sue the Colonel until a year after Elvis's contract was signed when it was obvious how much money he was missing out on. It was then that he decided to try and get back half of the company and Elvis's contract. He couldn't get an attorney to take the case.

While Hank Snow desperately wanted to hang on to Elvis, Bob Neal had reached the point where he surrendered him without a fight. Neal had many personal reasons for stepping away from Elvis. He was still promoting concerts, and he owned a record store. He also had a wife and kids that he wanted to spend time with. He was exhausted from trying to juggle his job as a disc jockey with the responsibilities of managing Elvis. It could have been that he also realized that it was only a matter of time before the Colonel pushed him out of the way. It was obvious that he no longer had any real function. Elvis had to have realized this, too.

The Colonel and Bob Neal signed an agreement to act as Elvis's comanagers until March 15, 1956, when Neal's contract with Elvis expired. Neal had received 15 percent under his agreement with Elvis. The Colonel would get 25 percent. However, the two men would combine and split their shares equally until their agreement expired.

When interviewed later, Bob Neal said that he had no regrets about giving up Elvis. He had worked with him more for the fun of it than for the money. The traveling had gotten to be so much that it was becoming work. It was time for Neal to do something else.

Bob Neal had discussed the sale of Elvis's managerial contract with songwriter Mae Axton. He said that he felt that he had taken Elvis as far as he could. The Colonel had told Bob Neal that he was going to be getting a lot of money from RCA. When the RCA deal was done, he promised to give Neal a commission as part of his payment for walking away from Elvis. Neal said was planning on using the money to start his own booking agency.

In April 1956, Bob Neal did open a booking agency with Sam Phillips called Stars Incorporated. Johnny Cash formally signed with them in May 1956. In April 1958, Bob Neal got Cash signed with Columbia Records without informing Sam Phillips. This destroyed Neal's and Phillip's relationship. Stars Incorporated was disbanded. Bob Neal would continue to manage Cash. His first step after breaking with Phillips was to have Cash quit the Grand Ole Opry. Neal then took Cash to Hollywood, as Colonel Parker had done with Elvis. Neal soon learned that Cash was no matinee idol.

Chapter 6

Hitting the Big Time

★   ★   ★   ★

*A*s the Colonel planned for the upcoming year in Elvis's career, he wanted to get him the maximum amount of public exposure in the shortest amount of time. The Colonel knew that this would fuel record sales, concert tours, souvenir sales, and the pot of gold at the end of the rainbow, movies.

The Colonel put together a topnotch group of associates to help him achieve his goals. His chief aides were Abe Lastfogel and Harry Kalcheim of the William Morris Agency and Gene and Julian Aberbach from Hill and Range. It stood to reason they were all in the endeavor to make money for themselves, but the only way that would happen was for Elvis to succeed.

Once the Colonel picked his business partners, he stuck with them. In his entire career, despite managing several artists, he dealt with the same record company, RCA, the same music publisher, Hill and Range, and the same talent agency, William Morris. The

Colonel expected his loyalty to be returned by these organizations.

His standard of loyalty from William Morris was noninterference with his relationships with his artists. Agencies were known for trying to come between a manager and artist with the hopes of easing the manager out of the picture. Both William Morris and Abe Lastfogel knew that if the Colonel sensed that they were trying to move in on his act, they would be gone in a hurry. The Colonel and the agency had an understanding. The agency would never communicate directly with Elvis. Everything was funneled through the Colonel, who would pass on to Elvis what he needed to know.

The Colonel felt secure in his knowledge of the record business and conducting concert tours. However, he knew his limitations, and the world of Hollywood was, to a great extent, unfamiliar to him. If the Colonel was going to get help, he wanted the best. Unquestionably, William Morris and Abe Lastfogel were the best.

The Colonel and Elvis never had a written agreement with William Morris. An attorney, who investigated the Colonel's relationship with Elvis as a part of a lawsuit against the Colonel in 1982, attributed this to his need to preserve his complete authority over Elvis. If William Morris had no contract with Elvis, then its employment would be at the will of the Colonel. They would be forced to go along with the Colonel's plans for Elvis whether or not they agreed with them. In essence, they were working for the Colonel. This would prevent them from getting any ideas about edging the ole Colonel out and taking complete control of Elvis.

The first step in the Colonel's plan was to get Elvis's records into the stores. On December 2, 1955, RCA released Elvis's Sun single, "Mystery Train," backed with "I Forgot to Remember to Forget." This single was chosen because the Sun release was in the top ten at the time on the country charts. On December 30, RCA released the other Sun singles.

Soon after Elvis was signed to RCA, Steve Sholes told songwriter Mae Axton that they would be needing some new material for him. Mae used a line from a *Miami Herald* story about a man who had committed suicide as her inspiration. The man had left a one-line note. It read, "I walk a lonely street." She used this as her inspiration for "Heartbreak Hotel."

Sam Phillips was openly critical of RCA's use of Elvis. When Elvis recorded "Heartbreak Hotel," Sam told the *New York Post* the record was so bad that Colonel Parker and RCA were thinking of not releasing it. He called it "a morbid mess." Phillips was proven wrong. It became Elvis's first number-one record.

After Hill and Range made the publishing deal with Elvis, they established a pool of songwriters for him. Ben Weisman was one. He started out as a classical pianist. Irving Berlin introduced him to the Aberbach brothers, and soon he was writing country music for Hill and Range. Weisman first met the Colonel when he wrote "Mills of the Gods" for Eddy Arnold. Weisman and others in the Hill and Range pool were instructed to write songs for Elvis that would have popular appeal. The Colonel did not want Elvis pigeonholed as a country singer.

The Colonel also insisted that Elvis be given a piece of the songwriting copyright. This share would range from 25 to 50 percent. At first, songwriters were willing to do this because Elvis's record sales were so much greater than any other artist. They could give him a share of the pie and still make more money than they could with anybody else. Elvis ended up being listed as cowriter on several songs despite never having met his cowriter.

But Elvis wasn't comfortable with getting credit for songs he didn't write. So Hill and Range came up with another way to get a piece of the songwriter's royalty. Hill and Range drew up an agreement for perspective writers to sign that stipulated that one-third of their royalties would be assigned to Elvis, without actually crediting Elvis as a cowriter.

Most of Elvis's songwriters were never allowed to meet him.

Once, Jerry Leiber and Mike Stoller, who wrote "Hound Dog"

and several other big hits, visited Elvis in his Los Angeles hotel. Elvis told them that the Colonel wouldn't approve of his meeting with them alone. It was all part of the Colonel's desire to have complete control over what Elvis heard and didn't hear. He didn't need some songwriter whining to Elvis about being forced to give him a share of his royalties.

That Elvis only recorded songs published by Hill and Range didn't escape public attention. In fact, it was mentioned by entertainment attorney Seymour Lazar during his testimony to Congress concerning the disc-jockey payola scandal in 1958. "Songs that Elvis Presley records are primarily which his own publishing firm publishes," he said.

The Colonel had a couple of rules for songwriters besides the requirement that they never meet Elvis. Songs always had to be written in the first person so that the listener would identify it with Elvis. The language also had to be kept on the level of the audience. Finally, Elvis must win the girl in the end. His songs should always have happy endings.

Elvis's first album, *Elvis Presley*, was released in March. Within a month, it had sold 360,000 copies, making it RCA's first million-dollar album by a solo artist. It went on to become the biggest-selling album in RCA history.

The Colonel insisted that no one's name other than Elvis's was to appear on his RCA releases. Scotty Moore, Bill Black, and drummer D.J. Fontana were not mentioned anywhere. There were no producers or other studio personnel listed. Although it was highly unorthodox, RCA gave in to the Colonel's instructions. This set a pattern that would continue for the remainder of Elvis's career, that of the Colonel calling the shots. RCA did not do anything without his permission. According to marketing associates at RCA, the Colonel told them that they had done a nice job with Elvis so far, but they should sit back and let the Colonel handle things from then on.

On July 13, 1956, RCA released "Hound Dog/Don't Be Cruel." Eighteen days later, it had sold one million copies. Both sides of the single eventually went to number one. By September 1956, Elvis's sales were so great that RCA's pressing plants could not keep up with the demand. It had to contract with plants owned by Decca and MGM to press additional discs.

In 1956, Elvis accounted for two-thirds of RCA's total single sales. His ten million singles had earned him $450,000 in royalties. On October 30, press reports said that Elvis had agreed to a new payment structure with RCA whereby he would be paid one thousand dollars a week for twenty years instead of receiving royalties. According to the reports, this was to help him reduce his tax burden.

Colonel Parker was quick to deny the story. Elvis's contract with RCA had been extended with the royalty structure remaining the same. The original contract was for two years plus a one-year option. The new agreement was for five years with a five-year option. At the end of ten years, RCA had a ten-year option.

Over the next couple of years which saw most of Elvis's biggest single releases, RCA's biggest worry was getting him into the recording studio. The relationship between Steve Sholes and Colonel Parker was somewhat shaky. Parker knew that Sholes needed Elvis's product, and Parker controlled that product. For a man like Sholes, it was a humiliating position to be in and one that was exploited by the Colonel. Sholes had to plead for time to be made in Elvis's schedule for recordings. The Colonel wasn't stupid. He knew that Elvis had to release records to keep his fans happy and to continue making money. But, he just loved to keep everyone on edge.

Steve Sholes saw the Colonel's actions as disrespectful and a source of tremendous inconvenience. The Colonel made the situation worse by making Sholes the butt of his jokes. The RCA honcho took to creating excuses to avoid having his regular breakfast

with the Colonel, Tom Diskin, and Hill and Range's Freddie
Bienstock. When the Colonel sensed that Sholes was trying to
avoid him, he kicked up the humiliation campaign. The Colonel
made sure that Sholes had virtually no role in the recording studio.
Freddie Bienstock ran the show, and Elvis effectively was his own
producer. Having to endure this must have been demeaning for a
man of Sholes's status.

There was more to the Colonel keeping Elvis out of the studio
than simply his desire to be aggravating. He wanted RCA to always
be in short supply of material. This would add to his control of the
relationship. If they wanted more songs, it would be under his
terms. Giving them a backlog would take away his leverage.

To ensure huge record sales, the Colonel's strategy was to
unleash a blitz of exposure for Elvis. He knew that the best way to
reach the largest audience in the shortest amount of time was
through television. Bob Neal understood that also, but had failed
to get Elvis on television via *Talent Scouts*.

In late 1955, Colonel Parker mailed an 8 x 10 picture of Elvis to
Jackie Gleason. On the back, he wrote, "JG: This is Elvis Presley,
about to be real big, Colonel." Gleason took the picture to a production meeting. It was decided to sign Elvis for the Dorsey
Brothers' *Stage Show*, which was produced by Gleason and was a
lead-in to his *Honeymooners* show. On December 17, 1955, CBS
announced that Elvis would be appearing on *Stage Show* for four
consecutive Saturday nights beginning January 28, 1956.

Stage Show was filmed in New York. Elvis's second trip to the
Big Apple was in sharp contrast to his first. He didn't have to audition this time. On the morning of January 28, 1956, a dress
rehearsal was held at Nole Hall on Broadway. Jimmy and Tommy
Dorsey attended the rehearsal as did their mother. Tommy Dorsey
was no stranger to working with young singing stars. Frank Sinatra
rose to national prominence while singing for his band.

The broadcast took place at eight o'clock from CBS television studio 50. Elvis sang "Shake, Rattle and Roll" and "I Got a Woman." The show was watched by 18.4 percent of the viewing audience. It was number two to *The Perry Como Show*, but was still a respectable rating.

Elvis spent the week after his *Stage Show* appearance in New York. He went into RCA studios on Monday, Tuesday, and Friday for recording sessions. On February 4, he made his second *Stage Show* appearance, singing "Baby Let's Play House" and "Tutti Fruitty." The ratings were almost identical to the first broadcast.

Elvis spent the following week on a concert tour of Virginia and North Carolina. A snowstorm in Charlotte on February 11 almost made him late for his third Dorsey Brothers appearance. He arrived at the studio with only minutes to spare and sang "Heartbreak Hotel" and "Blue Suede Shoes."

The next week, Elvis was back in North Carolina for more concerts. At one in Wilson, two days before Elvis's last time on *Stage Show*, the Colonel was faced with the problem of the concert promoter selling twice as many tickets as there were seats. It would be bad PR to turn ticket holders away, and Elvis did not need the bad press right before going on national television. There would have to be two shows.

The Colonel attempted to turn adversity into opportunity. When he announced to the troupe that there would be an extra show, he said that he could not pay them any extra fee for doing it. Which, of course, was nonsense since he would receive the box office receipts from the second show. To the Colonel's surprise, the supporting performers revolted. They refused to do the second show unless they were paid. The Colonel capitulated.

For his final appearance on *Stage Show*, Elvis sang "Money Honey" and "Heartbreak Hotel." The ratings came in at 20.9 percent. The Dorseys couldn't upset Perry Como, but Elvis did give the show a boost.

Elvis received a surge in popularity after his television appearances just as the Colonel had thought he would. Elvis started receiving ten thousand fan letters a week. The requests to join his fan club exploded. Colonel Parker hired a public relations man named Charlie Lamb to run the club. Lamb had to hire twenty employees to handle all the requests.

The Colonel intuitively recognized the importance of Elvis Presely Fan Club members. He saw them as a tool for spreading the gospel of Elvis. They were the ones who would call radio stations requesting Elvis's newest release. They were the ones who would make sure that future Elvis movies were sellouts on opening night, something that would not go unnoticed by the newspapers. The Colonel stressed within his organization the importance of taking care of the club members. Every fan letter written to Elvis was to be answered. It did not matter if the letter was sent to Elvis's home, to RCA, or the fan club's Madison, Tennessee, headquarters. Personalized form letters were sent to the fans thanking them for writing and letting them know what was going on with Elvis.

With the *Stage Show* appearances on Elvis's résumé, the Colonel was ready to target a more popular program for his boy. Abe Lastfogel suggested *The Milton Berle Show* as the next step in the television exposure blitz. Berle was one of the biggest names on the small screen at the time. Lastfogel arranged for himself, Colonel Parker, and Milton Berle's agent, Ben Griefer, to have lunch at the Hillcrest Country Club in Los Angeles to discuss Elvis guesting on Berle's show. Afterwards Colonel Parker sent Milton Berle a film of Elvis on *Stage Show*.

After reviewing it, Berle agreed to book Elvis as a favor to Abe Lastfogel. Elvis's first Milton Berle appearance was broadcast April 3, 1956 from the *USS Hancock* in San Diego. Berle picked up Elvis and the Colonel at the airport. He sat in the middle of the backseat of the limo with Elvis on one side and the Colonel on the other. During the ride, Berle pulled out the contract for the show and started to hand it to Elvis. The Colonel snatched it out of his hand and growled, "Don't show that boy that contract!"

The show went smoothly. Elvis performed "Heartbreak Hotel" and "Blue Suede Shoes." He seemed more relaxed than he had been on *Stage Show*. Bill Black rode his bass like a horse during "Blue Suede Shoes." The Colonel later dressed him down for showboating. Elvis was the star. He did not want Black or anyone else detracting from that.

Elvis's second Milton Berle appearance took place on June 5, 1956. For the first time that year, Milton Berle beat *Sergeant Bilko* in the ratings. Elvis's bump-and-grind rendition of "Hound Dog" was the talk of America the next day.

Steve Allen caught the second Berle appearance and decided to book Elvis on his new show. Allen had the unenviable task of going up against the ratings powerhouse, Ed Sullivan. Elvis Presley might give him a shot at making a dent in Sullivan's audience. The Colonel negotiated a $7,500 fee with Allen for one appearance.

But controversy had arisen over Elvis's sexually suggestive rendition of "Hound Dog" on the Berle show and some pressure was being brought on Allen to cancel him, which he didn't want to do. If anything, the controversy would make Elvis more appealing and draw more viewers. NBC, however, was running scared. It announced that Elvis would appear on the show, but told him he would have to clean up his act. Steve Allen then came up with the idea of Elvis dressing in a tuxedo and tails and singing "Hound Dog" to a real live hound dog. Elvis would often look back on this performance as the most ridiculous one of his life.

Elvis was a guest on *The Steve Allen Show* on July 1, 1956. He sang "I Want You, I Need You, I Love You" and "Hound Dog." He sang the latter to a basset hound named Sherlock. The show received a rating of 22.2 percent, beating the top-rated *Ed Sullivan Show*'s 14.8 percent.

When he left the stage, Elvis found a William Morris representative waiting in the wings enthusing over how great the performance had been. According to a photographer who was there, "Tom Diskin was grinning like the Cheshire cat."

Two days later, Elvis returned by train to Memphis along with the Colonel, Tom Diskin, Scotty, Bill, D.J., and the Jordanaires, who had been hired by RCA to back up Elvis. Elvis liked their sound so much, he took them on the road with him. During the trip home, the Colonel wanted to pose at a typewriter for photographer Alfred Wertheimer. Wertheimer commented on his subject's poor typing skills. The Colonel fired back, "Wertheimer, I may not type very well, but they sure know what I mean up there at RCA."

On that same train ride, the Colonel played a practical joke on a couple of soldiers. He spotted them coming from the far end of the car. He told Alfred Wertheimer to address him loudly as Colonel when the soldiers got into hearing range. The Colonel pulled a newspaper in front of his face. Wertheimer barked out "Colonel" on cue. The two boys snapped to attention and saluted. Colonel Parker dropped his paper, smiled, and said, "At ease, gentlemen, at ease."

Elvis had a concert date in Memphis on July 4. That night the Colonel and Tom Diskin arrived at his new house on Audobon Drive at about nine with a police escort. The Colonel assigned Diskin to escort Gladys and Vernon Presley to the concert while the Colonel and Elvis rode together in the backseat of a police car.

Elvis took the stage at ten thirty. The show had started at eight with fourteen thousand fans in attendance. Dewey Phillips was emceeing. The Colonel donated five thousand souvenir programs to the concert, with the proceeds to go to charity. When he was asked why there was no prices on the programs, he responsed that you should never put a price on anything. The price would be determined when you found out what someone was willing to pay.

With successful outings on three popular television programs, the Colonel virtually had his pick of what would be Elvis's next appearance. The Colonel no longer had an interest in any but the highest-rated shows. The king of television variety at the time was Ed Sullivan. Sullivan once said that he would rather run a sixty-minute test pattern than put on Elvis Presley. He changed his mind when Elvis pushed *The Steve Allen Show's* ratings to the very top.

Ed Sullivan was on the telephone to the Colonel the day after Allen's show to discuss booking Elvis. He offered the Colonel three appearances for an unheard total of fifty thousand dollars, which was three times the previous record for a television appearance. Certainly the Colonel enjoyed having Sullivan at his mercy in light of the disparaging remarks he had made about Elvis.

Before the Colonel accepted Sullivan's offer, he gave Steve Allen the chance to match it. Allen didn't think he could afford the precedent of paying his guests such large sums and sent the Colonel and Elvis to Ed Sullivan with his best wishes.

On September 8, 1956, Elvis appeared on the cover of *TV Guide*. This coincided with his Ed Sullivan appearance on September 9. Actor Charles Laughton hosted the show that week as Sullivan was recovering from injuries sustained in a car accident.

NBC gave Steve Allen the night off when Elvis made his first appearance on the Sullivan show. Instead they ran a movie.

The program change proved to be a wise decision, avoiding a ratings' embarrassment for Allen. Eighty-three percent of the viewing audience tuned in to watch Elvis, a record that stood until the Beatles' first appearance on the show. The next day in the press, Ed Sullivan gave Elvis his due credit for the tremendous ratings he generated.

Through Elvis's television exposure, the Colonel was able to create a tremendous demand for concert appearances. In the spring of 1956, the Colonel started talking to his associates about finding an upscale concert venue suitable for a superstar like Elvis. In the

1950s, Las Vegas was the epitome of a glitzy, high-class, nightclub town. The Colonel found the New Frontier Hotel eager to have Elvis in its showroom. The hotel had just changed its name from the Last Frontier after an extensive remodeling job.

The vice president of the New Frontier, T. W. Richardson had been alerted to Elvis by family in his hometown of Biloxi, Mississippi. He felt Elvis would be ideal for the hotel's grand open-ing celebration. Elvis was against the idea because he knew that his teenage fans would not be able to attend his performances. The Colonel persuaded him that it would be good and impressive for his career to appear in one of the top hotels in Las Vegas. But more important still, the money was good. The New Frontier had agreed to pay Elvis $17,500 a week. The Colonel demanded to receive all the money in advance. "They got an atom-bomb testing place out there in the desert. What if some feller pressed the wrong button?" he joked to the press.

The opportunity for Elvis to appear in Las Vegas came about suddenly. There was little time for the Colonel to promote the event. The print ads that he was able to put together billed Elvis as "The Nation's Only Atomic Powered Singer." The Colonel thought that this was a clever takeoff on Nevada's role as the center of America's atomic bomb-testing program.

On April 23, Elvis opened in the Venus Room of the New Frontier. He was the closing act for Freddie Martin and his orches-tra. Martin specialized in creating pop versions of classical music. His show was big and glitzy. In addition to a seventeen-piece orchestra, he had dancers, twenty-eight singers, and even ice skaters in his show.

It soon became apparent that the Vegas audience had no inter-est in Elvis. For the first time in months, Elvis, Scotty, and Bill could hear every note that was played or sung. Elvis was so distressed by the poor reception that he couldn't remember Freddie Martin's name when he left the stage. After the first night's lukewarm response, Elvis was moved out of the closing spot. He kept his performances to an extremely short twelve minutes.

The only performance at the New Frontier that was a success was a special matinee show featuring Elvis only. The admission fee of one dollar got the teenager a ticket to see Elvis and a bottle of soda. If Elvis had any doubts, the bedlam at the matinee reinforced that he still had it.

The reviews of his Las Vegas performance were harsh. *Variety* said, "Elvis doesn't hit the mark. The loud singing of the tunes which rocketed him to the big time is weary and the applause comes back edged with it a polite sound. For the teenagers he's a whiz. For the average Vegas spender he's a fizz." *Newsweek* magazine likened Elvis to "a jug of corn liquor at a champagne party."

Initially, the Colonel was shaken. This was the first real failure in his handling of Elvis's career. However, he soon realized that Elvis was not the problem. It was the age of the casino audience. The Colonel predicted to William Morris that he and Elvis would be back to Las Vegas, and when they returned, it would cost the hotel ten times as much.

There were plenty of good headlines to counteract the bad. Elvis had a number one record with "Heartbreak Hotel." The advance order for his next single, "I Want You, I Need You, I Love You," indicated that it would be his second number one.

Elvis was not so quick to let the positive news make him forget Las Vegas. After that engagement, he visited his childhood friend, Buzzy Forbes, and complained about the New Frontier debacle. He was clearly upset with the Colonel and began to rebel against him for the first time by showing up late for concerts and addressing him in a rather sarcastic and belligerent manner.

According to Bitsy Mott, the Colonel considered selling Elvis's contract before Elvis had the chance to fire him. Mott says that the Colonel offered Elvis's contract to Oscar Davis for $100,000, but there was no way that Davis could come up with that kind of money. The Colonel had to have known that. After all, Davis was working for him as an advance man. Perhaps the Colonel thought that his offer would get back to Elvis and would get his attention.

When that ploy did not work, Colonel Parker took to his sick bed, claiming to have suffered a mild heart attack. Bitsy Mott recalled the Colonel saying he only had a short time to live. Despite the supposed life-threatening nature of his illness, the Colonel refused to go to the hospital. Perhaps this "heart attack" was dreamed up by the Colonel in an effort to gain Elvis's sympathy and get him back in line. In any case, within a few days, the Colonel had recovered, Elvis had forgiven him for Las Vegas, and everything was back to normal.

Now, more determined than ever to keep the sailing smooth, the Colonel decided he needed a mole to report on Elvis's every move. He wanted to know what Elvis was thinking and who he was talking to. This knowledge would give the Colonel time to step in and take corrective action if any problems popped up.

The chosen spy was his brother-in-law, Bitsy Mott. Bitsy became head of Elvis's security team, which gave him the excuse to be around Elvis at all times. He would report everything that went on to the Colonel.

When Elvis went back on tour in May, the Colonel doubled the ticket prices. As a result, about half the seats were empty. The teenage fans couldn't come up with the extra money. While the net income generated by sales of half as many seats at twice the price was the same, the Colonel didn't want empty seats. It was bad for the superstar image that he was trying to cultivate for Elvis. For the next tour, he lowered ticket prices, and the arenas sold out once again.

By the time of the May tour, the Colonel had turned Elvis's show into a potpourri worthy of the Royal American Shows. As his supplier, he used Al Dvorin, who had helped the Colonel round up some midgets when he was working on a promotion with Eddy

Arnold. Now Dvorin was called upon to put together a sort of vaudeville show to accompany Elvis. Included in the lineup were musicians, jugglers, dancers, comics, and even an Irish tenor.

Usually their individual names weren't even listed. They were simply called "Eight Great Acts." They were certainly not familiar names to Elvis's teenage audience. At first glance, it seemed crazy that the Colonel would have cluttered the bill with a string of "B" acts, however, there was a method to his choices. First, it is important to remember that audiences in those days expected the show to feature several acts. There was no such thing as a solo concert.

These sideshow performers had the distinct advantage of being extremely cheap to hire. Furthermore, they did absolutely nothing that could possibly have rivaled Elvis for the audience's affection. The Colonel had witnessed firsthand Elvis's embarrassing and then supplanting Hank Snow as the star when they shared the same bill. He wasn't about to take the chance of that happening with Elvis.

Lastly, the ridiculous lineup helped build the audience's anticipation and demand for the star. This demand built to a fervent pitch as the juggler was not followed by Elvis but by a ventriloquist who was not followed by Elvis but by a comedian. The Colonel would dangle the bait of Elvis coming out next then throw a tap dancer out on stage. When Elvis finally appeared, it was pandemonium.

According to Gabe Tucker, who worked on the Colonel's staff, the Colonel encouraged Elvis to exaggerate his onstage gyrations. Tucker remembered him telling Elvis, "I want you to shake your butt. It'll excite the girls. It's simply a turnabout of what striptease artists do in their act to excite men." Elvis confirmed this in a later press conference. "The Colonel made me controversial to get me going. But we haven't done anything bad. I trust him."

"My boy doesn't use any stimulants. He needs soothing syrup," Colonel Parker said, responding to a newspaper story claiming that Elvis's onstage gyrations were fueled by uppers. "I discovered the big secret that would send Elvis to the pinnacle of success. Female entertainers have been using it for years to turn audiences on. I just had Elvis do it in reverse."

Elvis didn't like the press saying that he was vulgar and contributed to juvenile delinquency. He detested the nickname "Elvis the Pelvis." The Colonel reassured him that the controversy was good for business. The more the preachers preached against him in their sermons, the more eager their parishioners would be to experience the evil for themselves.

"I don't care what they say about you, just as long as they spell the name right" summed up the Colonel's attitude.

A citizen of La Crosse, Wisconsin, definitely saw evil in Elvis. He wrote the following letter (brought to light years later through the Freedom of Information Act) to FBI Director J. Edgar Hoover to make him aware of the danger posed to America's youth.

May 16, 1956
Mr. J. Edgar Hoover,
Director, Federal Bureau of Investigations,
Washington 25 D.C.

Dear Mr. Hoover:

Elvis Presley, press agented as a singer and entertainer played to two groups of teenagers numbering several thousands at the city auditorium here Monday, May 14th.

As newspaper man, parent and former member of Army Intelligence Service, I feel an obligation to pass on to you my conviction that Presley is a definite danger to the security of the United States.

Although I could not attend myself, I sent two reporters to cover his second show at 9:30 P.M. Besides I secured the opinions of others of good judgment who had seen the show or had heard direct reports of it. Among them are Radio Station Manager, and former motion picture exhibitor, an orchestra player and a young woman employee of a radio station who witnessed the show to determine its value. All agreed that it was the filthiest and most harmful production that ever came to La Crosse for exhibition to teenagers.

When Presley came on the stage, the youngsters almost mobbed him. As you can judge from the article and picture enclosed from the May 15th edition of the La Crosse Tribune. The audience could not hear his "singing" for the screaming and carrying on of teenagers.

But eyewitnesses have told me that Presley's actions and motions were such to arouse the sexual passions of teenaged youth. One eyewitness described his actions as, "sexual self gratification on stage" another as, "strip tease with clothes on." Although police and auxiliaries were there, the show went on. Perhaps the hardened police did not get the impact of his motions and gestures like those of masturbation or riding the microphone. (The Assistant District Attorney and Captain William Boma also stopped in for a few minutes in response to complaints about the first show but they found no reason to halt the show.)

After the show more than 1,000 teenagers tried to gang into Presley's room at the auditorium. Then at the Stoddard Hotel. All possible police on duty were necessary for the hotel to keep watch on the teenagers milling about the hotel til after 3:00 A.M. the hotel manager informed me. Some kept milling about the city until about 5:00 A.M.

Indications of the harm Presley did just in La Crosse were the two high school girls (of whom I have direct personal knowledge) whose abdomen and thigh had Presley's autograph. They admitted that they went to his room where this happened. It is known by psychologists, psychiatrists and priests that teenage girls from the age of eleven and boys in their adolescence are easily aroused to sexual indulgence and per-version by certain types of motion and hysteria, the type that was exhibited at the Presley show.

There is also gossip of the Presley Fan Clubs that degener-ate into sexual orgies. The local radio station WKBH sponsors a club on the "Lindy Shannon Show."

From eyewitness reports about Presley I would judge that he would be both possibly a drug addict and a sexual pervert. In any case, I am sure that he bears close watch, especially in the face of growing juvenile crime nearly everywhere in the United States. He is surrounded by a group of high pressure agents who seem to control him, the hotel manager reported.

I do not report idly to the FBI. My last official report to an FBI agent in New York, before I entered the U.S. Army, resulted in the arrest of a saboteur (who committed suicide before his trial). I believe the Presley matter is a serious threat to U.S. security. I am convinced that juvenile crimes of lust and perversion will follow his show here in La Crosse.

I enclose article and pictures from May 15th edition of the La Crosse Tribune. The article is an excellent example of the type of reporting that describes the burlesque show by writing about the drapes on the stage. But the pictures, to say the least, are revealing. Note too that under the Presley article, the editor sanctimoniously published a very brief filler on the FBI's con-cern for teenage crime. Only a moron could not see the con-nection between the Presley exhibit and the incidence of teenage disorder in La Crosse.

With many thanks and with a prayer for God's special bless-ing on your excellent and difficult work for justice and efficiency,

Sincerely Yours,

{The name is blacked out}

Ironically, the *Christian Science Monitor* was one of the few publications to defend Elvis. An editorial was published in its June 7, 1956, issue entitled, "This Too Will Pass." "A good many parents are fearful for the future of American youth if it can see merit in Mr. Presley's aggravated assault on the musical idiom. We would remind such worriers of their own youth. Don't they recall their parents threatening to smash the loudspeaker or battery radio if Rudy Vallee megaphoned the main stein song through it again? Or fretting over juvenile appreciation for Cab Calloway's scat lyrics? But somehow the youngsters of their day grew up to be the responsible citizens of today. Brace up, parents of '56, in another twenty years, Elvis Presley won't seem so bad and your grown-up teenagers will be biting their nails over the entertainment sensation of '76."

The Colonel did not react with the lightheartedness he instructed Elvis to show when he found himself receiving public criticism. The incident that got the Colonel press that even he did not want revolved around a patent-medicine scandal.

Louisiana State Senator, Dudley J. LeBlanc, invented a potion in 1948 that was advertised to cure all sorts of illnesses. He named the elixir Hadacol. LeBlanc released a massive promotional campaign. Several stars were hired including Mickey Rooney, Minnie Pearl, and boxer Jack Dempsey. They were part of a road show that toured the country. Soon Hadacol was a multimillion dollar business.

Starting in 1951, Hadacol was banned from sale in several states. Its curative effects were attributed to its 25 percent alcohol content. In the middle of its controversy, LeBlanc announced that he had sold the product to a group of eastern businessmen. The product quickly disappeared from the shelves forever.

In 1957, LeBlanc was indicted by a federal grand jury for failure to pay taxes on Hadacol profits. That same year, columnists such as Louella Parsons reported that the Colonel had been involved with the product and even began referring to him as Colonel Tom "Hadacol" Parker. This rumor continued to plague him over the years. Usually the Colonel was pleased with stories that suggested he was good at conning the public, but not this time. He disavowed any connection to Hadacol. The only time he probably did have any connection to it was when he booked Minnie Pearl on the road show.

In August 1956, the Colonel set up a Florida tour. Elvis's girl-friend, June Juanico, accompanied him. He had met Juanico after a June 27, 1955, concert at Keesler Air Force Base in Mississippi. She was just one of Elvis's many girlfriends.

In the early days, the only time the Colonel ever got involved with Elvis's personal life was on the subject of marriage. He strongly encouraged Elvis to remain single. "Don't get serious with anyone because your career is taking off. You need to dedicate yourself to that." Nor did the Colonel want Elvis to have a steady girlfriend. When a girl was around him for very long, the Colonel did his best to make her feel uncomfortable by being obvious that he was trying to ignore her.

According to June, Elvis had asked her to marry him that July. He said that he had promised the Colonel that he wouldn't get married right away. They would have to wait a few years. The Colonel was afraid Elvis would lose his fans if he got married. Because the Colonel was responsible for him being a star, Elvis fig-ured he should follow his advice about staying single.

Elvis was scheduled to stop in Jacksonville on the tour. Judge Marion Gooding, determined to keep Elvis's act clean, met with the manager of the Florida Theater. He threatened to have Elvis arrested for contributing to the delinquency of minors if he put on the same show that he had put on in other Florida cities. The judge then met with Elvis, Colonel Parker, and the attorney for the Florida Theater and gave them the same message. He wanted a clean show without gyrations. The Colonel assured the judge that Elvis concede to his wishes. They didn't want any bad publicity.

Apparently Judge Gooding wasn't completely convinced. He attended the show himself, carrying with him three written arrest warrants. He had deputies stationed in the theater to carry out the arrest. As the show began, Elvis started to dance and then stopped himself in midmotion, telling the audience that he couldn't do that there. He stood completely still for the entire performance with the exception of occasionally wiggling his little finger. The Colonel grimaced when Elvis dedicated his final number to Judge Gooding, "You Ain't Nothing But a Hound Dog." Fortunately, the judge took it good-naturedly and tore up the arrest warrants, declaring Elvis fit for juvenile consumption.

The Colonel was a master at creating photo opportunities. On a couple of occasions on the Florida tour, he had auditoriums keep their doors shut right up until the time for the concert to begin. He had his photographers take pictures of the long lines that formed at the door to use for publicity. In the Colonel's version of the picture, the crowd had arrived hours in advance.

The tour stopped in Miami on August 3. A reporter there noticed June backstage and started asking questions. Her answers formed the basis of an article that appeared in the next day's newspaper. In it June stated that she was in love with Elvis, adding that unfortunately he was not ready for marriage. She also mentioned that she was accompanying him on his entire Florida tour.

Having elicited June's name and hometown, the reporter telephoned every Juanico in Biloxi, looking for information. Eventually he reached June's mother, May Juanico. Among other things, Mrs. Juanico stated that Elvis had asked her daughter to marry him.

When the Colonel read the story, he hit the roof. He barged into Elvis's dressing room and walked right past June. He told Elvis that he didn't need that type of publicity. He didn't even want to see in print that Elvis had a steady girlfriend. He had told him that the suggestion that marriage was even remotely possible was dangerous for his career. Finally, the idea that Elvis had an eighteen-year-old girl traveling with him was scandalous in itself. The Colonel told Elvis that he had to do something about it.

After that night's show, a reporter asked Elvis about the seriousness of his relationship with June Juanico. Elvis said he had twenty-five girls that he dated regularly, June was just one of them. The Colonel said that girls sometimes showed up eight at a time claiming to be Elvis's steady. Trying to make the whole thing seem like a joke, the Colonel said, "One girl even claimed that she was my daughter, and I don't have a daughter." The next day, the headlines read "Elvis Denies Beauty As His Steady." June Juanico stuck around for the rest of the tour. But when it ended in New Orleans, she headed back to Biloxi and Elvis went home to Memphis, their relationship over.

At a stop in Lakeland, Florida, the Colonel granted *Tampa Tribune* reporter Paul Wilder a lengthy interview with Elvis. This was unusual for the Colonel. He had shut off access almost completely to Elvis for interviews. An exception was made for Wilder because he had befriended the Colonel during his humane society days. It was Wilder who had featured the Colonel's exploits with the stray animals of Tampa on a regular basis in his column, "In Our Town."

Elvis and Wilder did not get along at all. The reporter spent most of the session asking Elvis insulting questions. Nothing was spared from Elvis's musical ability to his love life to his religion. By the end of the interview, Elvis was practically shouting at Wilder.

The reporter felt it was time to move on to the friendly face of Colonel Parker. He asked the Colonel about Elvis's future as an actor. The Colonel said, "Well Mr. Wilder, when we made the screen test for Mr. [Hal] Wallis in Hollywood, they tested Mr. Presley in a singing role, and also while he was there, they gave him a short story, a role play, whatever you call it, and Mr. Wallis decided after seeing the test that Mr. Presley was capable of starring in a dramatic production. When and how I don't know, but Mr.

Presley had no training in acting, and I saw the test, and if I was not his manager, I could not be more excited about a new personality than I am now being Elvis Presley's manager for his acting ability was the greatest. I think Elvis Presley could play any role he makes up his mind to play."

Wilder asked if Elvis would be making frequent appearances on television. The Colonel answered, "For many months, we were touring the country, and Elvis had never appeared on television, and the only way people could know about him was by his records. I have tried repeatedly to play his records and figure out someway where I could see him wiggle while listening to his records, which is impossible." However, the Colonel did not want too much of a good thing. "I think one of the main reasons that I don't book Mr. Presley on television more often is that to my way of thinking, many of the artists today are overexposed on television," he said.

According to Elvis's friend Jimmy Velvet, in 1956 the Colonel came up with a trick to increase Elvis's appearance fee. As the hottest act in show business, his fee already had increased from five thousand to ten thousand dollars per night. That didn't satisfy the Colonel. What he started to do when he got booking inquiries from promoters was to tell them that there were no openings in Elvis's schedule for the next year and a half. But, he could possibly cancel a date, and squeeze them in. However, they would have to pay Elvis an additional ten thousand dollars so Colonel Parker could get out of the cancelled contract. Of course, there was no "other contract." It was ploy to double Elvis's appearance fee.

Not everyone rolled over for the Colonel's tricks. On October 11, 1956, Elvis was in Dallas for a concert at the Cotton Bowl. Before it began, Elvis and the Colonel were served a summons by Dallas Deputy Sheriff W. R. Pike. Earlier, Deputy Pike had served actor Nick Adams with the summons confusing him with Elvis.

The summons accused Elvis and the Colonel of breaking a contract with R. G. McElyee that specified Elvis was to have made four appearances at the Fort Worth Coliseum at five hundred dollars per show. The contract was supposedly signed when Elvis appeared in Fort Worth on January 20, 1956. McElyee was demanding to be paid thirty-eight thousand dollars to settle his complaint, to which there was apparently some validity. The Colonel settled the dispute by hiring McElyee to promote a five-day Texas tour for Elvis in November 1956.

The concert went on, and 26,500 saw Elvis perform for thirty minutes. The stage was positioned on the football field's fifty-yard line. It was surrounded by an eight-foot tall chain-link fence. Ninety-five policemen were on hand to provide security.

Meanwhile Colonel Parker busied himself selling 8 x 10 glossies for fifty cents each. He kept all the proceeds for himself. He would sell as many as five thousand of these at a concert. Elvis knew about this and didn't mind since it gave the Colonel something to do.

The Colonel continued the concert tours in 1957. On March 28, 1957, Elvis appeared in Chicago at the International Amphitheater. It was the first date of a ten-day, eight-city trip in which he would give twelve concerts. The tour was promoted by Lee Gordon, an Australian who was hoping the Colonel would allow him to promote a tour of Australia for Elvis.

When Elvis came onstage in Chicago, he was wearing a gold-lamé suit. The suit heightened the frenzy of the audience. Several thousand of them rushed the stage. This went on throughout the first few songs. Finally a dozen teenagers made it to the stage. The show came to an abrupt end.

The Colonel had the suit created by Nudie Cohen, tailor to most of the country-music and movie cowboy stars of the day. It contained real gold leaf and cost $2,500. The Colonel was alarmed when he noticed that every time one of Elvis's legs hit the stage, gold dust fell off. After the concert, he asked Elvis to please not go down on his knees anymore. It was too expensive. As it turned out, Elvis found the gold pants restrictive and only wore them on a couple of other occasions.

The next tour was to Canada in April 1957. Not everyone was glad to have Elvis cross the border. Students at a Catholic girls' school were required to sign the following oath: "I promise that I shall not take part in the reception accorded to Elvis Presley and shall not be present at the program presented by him at the auditorium on Wednesday, April 3, 1957." Eight girls were expelled for violating this oath and attending the concert.

In Vancouver, a crowd of twenty-five thousand packed Empire Stadium. When only a handful of Canadian Mounties showed up, the Colonel protested that the security force was inadequate, to no avail.

The concert had barely begun, and the crowd already was pushing up to the edge of the stage. The Colonel pulled Elvis off and told him that the crowd was dangerous and security too light. He should not try and excite them anymore. The concert did not resume until they were back in their seats.

Elvis came back out and only got the "well" of "That's Alright, Mama" out before the crowd rushed the stage again. Colonel Parker ran out and grabbed the microphone. He told the crowd that if they did not start acting right, "Mr. Presley is not going to be performing." The Colonel then whispered to Elvis to do thirty-minutes instead of his usual hour. The crowd behaved until Elvis finished. But as soon as he left, they began destroying the stage taking everything that they could get for souvenirs.

During the Canadian tour, Oscar Davis decided to move in on a piece of the action. He was getting tired of doing advance work for the Colonel. Obviously approaching Elvis was out of the question. The next best thing in Davis's mind was Elvis's band and his backup singers. Davis approached Scotty Moore, Bill Black, and D. J. Fontana and the Jordanaires with the idea of him being their manager. He argued that with his guidance they could go on strike against Elvis and the Colonel. Davis was certain that the Colonel would cut them a better deal rather than losing everyone all at once.

Scotty, Bill, and D. J. were ready to sign with Davis. However, the Jordanaires were not interested. Scotty, Bill, and D. J. were making only $200 a week while Elvis had become a millionaire. Scotty and Bill knew that they were extra baggage to the Colonel, and given the opportunity, he would get rid of them. It was easy to understand their frustration. The Jordanaires, on the other hand, did not trust Oscar Davis anymore than they trusted the Colonel. Without the backup singers, Scotty, Bill, and D. J. were afraid that they would have not enough leverage with the Colonel. They backed out of the deal with Oscar Davis.

But they had complaints other than money. The musicians had been promised studio time at the end of Elvis's Christmas album session to record some instrumentals. When Elvis finished, Scotty, Bill, and D. J. got ready to do their numbers. Before striking the first note, Tom Diskin came in and announced that there had been a mistake. The studio was booked, and no time was available for them. However, the Colonel had given his word that they would be given time in the near future.

Scotty and Bill had heard this story before. They were tired of waiting and tired of working for peanuts. They went back to the hotel and wrote a resignation letter. They presented the letter to D. J. for him to sign, but he refused.

Bill Black was not about to give up. He got Scotty to go with him to ask for more money from the Colonel. They wanted a percentage of the profits just like they got when they first started out with Elvis. The Colonel told them that the financial arrangement would remain as it was whether they liked it or not.

Elvis returned to Memphis on September 11, 1957. The next day he called Scotty and offered to raise his and Bill's salary by fifty dollars a week. Scotty said that he needed ten thousand dollars in addition to the raise. Elvis said he would get back to him.

On September 21, Bill told Elvis that he and Scotty were leaving. A distraught Elvis called the Colonel with the news and asked what he should do. They would get a new band, the Colonel said, that's what they would do.

The next day Elvis was shocked to see a newspaper account of the resignation. Scotty Moore had been very frank about his disappointment at the way Elvis had treated him financially.

Elvis's side of the story ran the next day. He said that he would have worked things out with Scotty and Bill. However, since they had gone to the newspaper, he was not interested anymore. Elvis went on to say that people had been trying to talk him into dropping Scotty and Bill for the last two years (it was primarily Colonel Parker), but he had kept them around for sentimental reasons. He felt betrayed and was publically saying good-bye to them.

When Elvis arrived in Tupelo, Mississippi, on September 27 for a concert, he brought two new musicians with him. Hank Garland replaced Scotty Moore on guitar, and Chuck Wiginton took over for Bill Black on bass. They were fine musicians, but they just did not have the right feel for Elvis. A week after the Tupelo concert, despite the Colonel's protest, Elvis rehired Scotty and Bill.

On October 28, 1957, Elvis appeared at the Pan Pacific Auditorium in Los Angeles. There were many celebrities in the audience of nine thousand. None of the tickets were freebies. The Colonel made certain of that. The audience's response was hysterical as usual. However, the newspapers were especially vicious the next day. One account said that Elvis's performance reminded him of one of those screeching, uninhibited, party rallies that the Nazis used to hold for Hitler.

The Los Angeles Police Department told the Colonel that Elvis would have to tone it down for the next show. The police made the demand public knowledge. Reporters in turn asked the Colonel what Elvis's reaction was to the police. The Colonel said that it was really no big deal. Similar requests had been made a couple times before. The Colonel quoted Elvis as saying, "Well if I don't dance tonight, maybe I don't have to take a shower tonight."

With Elvis now a recording, television, and concert star, the Colonel decided that he could be merchandised just like Howdy Doody and Davy Crockett. Colonel Parker said to Jerry Brandt, an agent in William Morris Agency's music department, "Jerry, you give me all the popcorn in all the movie theaters across the USA, and you can shove Elvis up your ass. Merchandising, that's the secret."

The Colonel hired Hank Saperstein, president of Special Products, to manage the creation and merchandising of Elvis products. Only thirty-seven years old when he entered into the contract with the Colonel, Saperstein already had seventeen years of experience, having merchandised several television and movie characters such as the Lone Ranger, Lassie, and Wyatt Earp. Saperstein also originated the idea of putting prizes in cereal boxes as a sales gimmick. A *Look* magazine article about the Elvis merchandising phenomenon said that although the Colonel and Saperstein bore no physical resemblance, they had one identical trait, a love of money.

The Colonel gave Saperstein a piece of advice that he himself followed. He told him not to turn anyone down who came to him with a merchandising idea, he might need them for something else someday. Instead, the undesirable products could be weeded out by quoting a licensing fee so high that it would never be accepted. In this way, they would be turning you down rather than you rejecting them. You could then part on a friendly basis.

Saperstein did not need to come up with product ideas. The ideas came to him. Some of the proposals were too tacky for even the Colonel's taste. One such idea was an inflatable pillow modeled after Elvis's lips. If lipstick was applied to the pillow, Elvis's kiss could be reproduced on objects of the owner's choice. Saperstein turned down forty product pitches in one week.

One he did create was Elvis Lipstick. He got the idea after noticing that the wall of a concert hall in which Elvis was performing was covered with lipstick love notes. Elvis products were sold through Sears, Montgomery Ward, Woolworth, and a variety of other retail stores. Sales of Elvis Lipstick alone amounted to several million dollars.

Gross sales of Elvis products in the first six months they were on the market was twenty-six million dollars. Elvis received a royalty of between 4 and 11 percent of the wholesale prices of these products.

When Elvis decided to sell his house on Audobon and move to Graceland, a gum company approached him with an interesting offer. They would buy the house, tear it down, and turn it into two-by-three-inch chunks. These chunks would be given away as premiums in exchange for the wrappers from five packs of gum. The Colonel nixed the proposal because he had already signed an exclusive deal with a bubble gum company.

Saperstein also helped the Colonel to market Elvis himself. They both agreed that rather than try to diffuse the controversy surrounding the exuberant performer, they needed to exploit it. Saperstein fed the media juicy headlines about Elvis. He and the Colonel didn't care what the headlines said, they just wanted to make certain that they were on page one and in the largest type possible. Saperstein could even turn Elvis's prodigious spending into news. When Elvis went shopping for cars, the next day's headlines read, "Elvis in Spending Spree, Buys Three Cadillacs."

Saperstein traveled to Boston, which at the time was an extremely conservative city known for banning racy movies and books. He masqueraded as a "concerned citizen," contacting civic leaders to alert them to the danger of Elvis Presley. Once he succeeded in triggering their defenses, he took the story to the Associated Press. The headline read, "Elvis Is Banned In Boston."

The Colonel had seen his boy become the hottest item in the recording industry, on television, in mass merchandising, and on the concert stage. The only piece of the puzzle left was a movie deal. A telephone call from movie producer Hal Wallis in the early spring of 1956 brought the Colonel's final goal in sight.

Chapter 7

He Oughta Be In Pictures

★ ★ ★ ★

*H*al B. Wallis was one of the biggest producers in Hollywood. His résumé included *Jezebel*, *The Maltese Falcon*, *High Sierra*, and *Casablanca*, all made for Warner Brothers. Hal Wallis won Academy Awards for *The Maltese Falcon* and *Casablanca*. Now he was working with Paramount, most recently on Dean Martin and Jerry Lewis pictures.

It was an indirect route by which Elvis came to Wallis's attention. The producer's partner, Joe Hazen, called Wallis and told him to turn on *Stage Show*. A kid named Elvis Presley was performing. Hazen had been alerted to Elvis only minutes before by his sister-in-law who told him to turn on the show.

Wallis told Dick Vellenga for his book, *Elvis and the Colonel*, how he signed Elvis to a contract. "I first saw Elvis on the Dorsey Brothers' show. Early the next morning, I telephoned Tom Parker in New York and told him that I wanted to sign Elvis to a film contract. The Colonel was aware of me and my work and listened. Clearly counting the dollars in advance, he consciously revealed that Elvis would probably be out on the coast soon and would consider the possibility of a meeting."

The Colonel flew to Los Angeles to have dinner with Abe Lastfogel and Hal Wallis at the exclusive Hillcrest Country Club. The Colonel did not want to appear anxious to Wallis. Behind the scenes, he lay the groundwork for a favorable contract. He booked Elvis in a series of theaters owned by Paramount. In this way, the audiences' hysteria would be certain to get back to Wallis and the movie studio. He also had Elvis's fan club encourage a letter-writing campaign asking to see Elvis in the movies.

Three days after Elvis's second appearance on *The Milton Berle Show*, he performed at the Shrine Auditorium in Los Angeles. The Colonel wanted Hal Wallis to be there to witness the pandemonium that Elvis created. But when he called to invite him, he was told that Wallis was out of town. The Colonel flew into a rage and accused the secretary of lying to him and hung up on her.

The Colonel immediately called Abe Lastfogel and told him that Wallis was pretending that he was not in town to avoid attending Elvis's performance. After doing his best to calm down the Colonel, Lastfogel promised that he would look into the matter and get back to him.

Lastfogel couldn't imagine what reason Hal Wallis would possibly have for lying. He went ahead and called Wallis's office just so he could tell the Colonel that he had. The secretary explained that Wallis was out of town on a shoot, and she added that she would have explained it all to the Colonel if he had given her a chance. Lastfogel apologized on behalf of the Colonel and thanked the secretary for her help.

Being a peacemaker was a familiar role for Lastfogel. His easygoing demeanor was respected in Hollywood. He had to use his diplomatic skills on a regular basis, smoothing over tantrums thrown by one or another of William Morris's egotistical clients. Representing Elvis created a new twist to this. He found himself apologizing for the manager rather than the client.

Lastfogel played a pivotal role in Elvis's film career. In addition to making up for the Colonel's tantrum, he handled a great deal of the negotiations with the studios. When the Colonel decided to get Elvis into movies, Lastfogel was the one who knew the right people. His impressive list of clients, ranging from Marilyn Monroe to Frank Sinatra, gave him considerable clout in the business.

Lastfogel's first client had been Will Rogers. He rose up the ranks at the William Morris Agency to become the assistant to the agency's founder, William Morris, Sr. When the agency made a serious push to gain movie star clients, Lastfogel was sent to Hollywood to head up the West Coast branch.

Apparently the Colonel's tactics had the desired effect of intensifying Wallis's desire for Elvis. "I telephoned, telegraphed, and harassed Colonel Parker until he finally brought Elvis to Hollywood for a meeting and a screen test," Wallis said.

Colonel scheduled a screen test for Elvis to coincide with his trip to California for the Berle show. On March 27, 1956, Elvis and the Colonel arrived on the Paramount lot. Elvis performed a scene from Hal Wallis's next film project, *The Rainmaker*. Wallis would later compare Elvis's test to the first time that he saw Errol Flynn.

The first part of the screen test consisted of a lip-sync performance of "Blue Suede Shoes." Elvis used a prop guitar with no strings. He had expressed to the Colonel that he wanted to act in the movies, not sing. The screen test should have given Elvis a glimpse of what the future held for him.

Elvis then did two scenes from *The Rainmaker*. Burt Lancaster and Katharine Hepburn had been cast in the lead roles. Contract actor Frank Faylen played opposite Elvis in the screen test. Afterwards Elvis told Wallis that he did not think that the part was right for him, that he would find it easier to play a character who was more like himself. This was another nail in the coffin of Elvis as a serious actor. Wallis ran with the idea of him playing himself. Elvis would go on to play variations of Elvis in virtually all of his thirty-two movies. Of course, when Elvis played himself, he was a singer, not a serious actor.

Joe Hazen, Wallis's partner in movie production, was an entertainment lawyer. He handled the negotiations with the Colonel and Abe Lastfogel. Publically Hazen described the Colonel's business style as one of "intense and protracted negotiations." Privately he confided his much more blunt opinion to Hal Wallis. He said, "I wouldn't be a hundred feet from him. He's an obnoxious, terrible man. I have no rapport with him whatsoever. I have to deal with him."

The main point of contention in the negotiations was over Elvis's exclusivity with Hal Wallis Productions. The Colonel wanted Elvis to be able to make movies for other producers and studios in addition to Wallis. The final compromise allowed him to make one such movie per year.

Hazen had a contract prepared, but the Colonel put off signing it. He said he would take it with him to Elvis's final regular appearance on the Louisiana Hayride. After that, there would be a two-week tour of Texas and then on to Nashville for a recording session.

Lastfogel called Joe Hazen and gave him the news. He promised that he would send someone to wherever Elvis and the Colonel were to pick up the contracts when they were signed. Hazen remained in contact with William Morris for the next few days trying to find what it was going to take to get the Colonel to sign the contracts. In the meantime, Hal Wallis was busy looking for a script for Elvis's first movie when he finally signed. He had in mind a play called *Rat Race*. Wallis had tried to buy the rights to the story for a Dean Martin/Jerry Lewis movie, but the writer, Garson Kanin, refused to sell. Maybe he would be agreeable to selling it for Elvis's first picture if Wallis allowed him to write and direct the movie. He wasn't.

Finally the Colonel gave Elvis the okay to sign the contract, which was for seven years beginning June 1, 1956. Elvis would appear in one film per year under the contract. The salary was fairly modest. It would be $15,000 for the first movie and gradually rise to $100,000 for the seventh. The base salary was so low that Wallis and Hazen had to have the contract approved by the Screen Actors Guild. This was necessary anytime an actor was being paid less than $25,000 per year. The Screen Actors Guild ruled that the salary for the first two movies was too low and had to be revised.

Joe Hazen probably thought that his aggravation from the Colonel would be over once the contract was signed. He was wrong. During the negotiations, the Colonel had assured Hazen and Wallis that the only involvement he wanted in Elvis's movies was to make sure that he was well paid. He claimed ignorance about the actual act of making a movie and said that he would leave that to the experts. In fact, he did exactly the opposite. The Colonel tried to impose his will on every movie that Elvis ever made. He would continue to jab, poke, and prod both Joe Hazen and Hal Wallis for the next twelve years.

The Colonel would often show up at Hazen's office unannounced. At first, he would be extremely jovial, inquiring about Hazen's family and making other small talk. Suddenly he would segue into a new ridiculous demand such as reshooting scenes that had been completed for weeks. On other occasions, he would claim that they had breached the contract by failing to get his permission to use a picture of Elvis in promoting a film's premiere.

The Colonel would also issue outlandish demands that Hazen was forced to live with for fear of losing the cash-cow star. On one occasion, the Colonel arrived at Hazen's office carrying a wallet-sized photo of Elvis. He demanded that Paramount purchase

500,000 copies of the photos from him at three cents each to use as giveaways to moviegoers. Hazen grudgingly went along with the Colonel even though he could have purchased the same pictures from a commercial source for one cent each.

The Colonel liked to pretend that he was extremely conservative with the studio's money. Once he sent a check to Hal Wallis in the amount of $3.66 purportedly representing unused expense money. He attached a note saying that this should show Wallis that the Colonel stays on the ball.

When communicating with Hal Wallis and Joe Hazen, the Colonel was overly humble about his personal financial situation. In a letter to Wallis, he expressed his comfort in the knowledge that he had a good relationship with the Salvation Army in case his groceries ever ran low. Each year the Colonel would send Hal Wallis a Father's Day card from him and Elvis in recognition of Wallis giving birth to Elvis's movie career. The Colonel signed the cards "your two orphans."

Publically the Colonel downplayed his intellect and negotiating skills as compared to those of Hal Wallis and the Hollywood establishment. He cultivated an image of being an uneducated former carny with a phony title and clownlike appearance. It was part of his game to keep people from taking him seriously. Before they knew it, the poor dumb Colonel had gotten them to pay Elvis a million dollars for a movie.

Although Elvis's first movie contract was signed with Hal Wallis, his first movie was made with someone else, David Weisbart, who was producing a Civil War story, *The Reno Brothers*, for 20th Century-Fox. Three factors contributed to Weisbart beating Hal Wallis to the punch. First of all, Wallis was already busy with three movies. Second, he didn't have the right story to showcase Elvis's singing. And third, he was more than happy to sit back and see what succeeded and what failed with Weisbart's use of Elvis in *The Reno Brothers*.

In early 1956, the legendary Darryl Zanuck left 20th Century-Fox. His successor was Bud Adler. Adler was determined to quickly make a mark for himself at the studio and escape the long shadow of Zanuck. In the summer of 1956, he found himself face to face with Colonel Parker.

Adler probably thought that he would blow the Colonel away when he offered to pay Elvis twenty-five thousand dollars to appear in *The Reno Brothers*. After all, it was much more than the Wallis contract. He must have been shocked when the Colonel said, "That's fine for me. Now how much for the boy?" The Colonel proceeded to negotiate a side deal for himself to act as an "advisor" for the film. The amount that he received for this is unknown. The Colonel would secure similar deals for himself in the majority of Elvis's other films.

Elvis signed the contract for *The Reno Brothers* on August 14, 1956. Two days later, he had to report to Hollywood. Before leaving Memphis, he met with the pastor of the Assembly of God Church, James Hamill. According to Hamill, Elvis professed doubts from a spiritual standpoint about the course his life was taking. He was concerned that the world of Hollywood would lead him further away from the teachings of the church. Reverend Hamill suggested that Elvis contact the pastor of the Assembly of God Church in Los Angeles. He could meet with the pastor for spiritual guidance when he was in Hollywood.

Hamill learned later that Elvis never called the church in Hollywood. It seems that the Colonel learned of Hamill's advice. He told Elvis that he shouldn't get in touch with the pastor. It was okay if he wanted to sing religious songs, but he couldn't get so carried away with religion that it interfered with his career. He reminded Elvis that he had to live up to the contracts he had signed.

With *The Reno Brothers* being set in the Civil War era, Colonel Parker was faced with the difficulty of finding songs appropriate to 1865. The result of his search was three songs, two that were among the worst that Elvis had recorded to date and one that was among his best. "Poor Boy, We're Gonna Move" and "Let Me" were exercises in eating up screen time. The third song, "Love Me Tender," however, was a classic. Its power helped to carry an otherwise forgettable movie.

Originally there weren't going to be any songs in *The Reno Brothers*. Then Colonel Parker told Elvis that one song, "Love Me Tender," would be added. Its melody was lifted from the Civil War song "Laura Lee," making it more true to the film's time period than most people realized. Gradually, other songs were worked in.

Elvis appeared on *The Ed Sullivan Show* during the filming of *The Reno Brothers* and performed "Love Me Tender." Soon after, RCA had 750,000 advance orders for the single. Elvis performed the song again at a Tupelo concert, and the pre-orders rose to 860,000. The Colonel insisted that the name of the movie be changed to *Love Me Tender*. He thought that this would be an effective way to promote Elvis's new record and the movie at the same time. It was also his request that "Love Me Tender" be sung more than once in the film.

Adler granted the Colonel permission to be on the set at all times during filming. The Colonel sold Adler on this by claiming that Elvis would perform better with a familiar face around.

Colonel Parker set up his office in Elvis's dressing room.

The Colonel wasn't the only one that wanted to watch Elvis act. When word got out that Elvis Presley was on the lot, people from every department in the studio would drift in to watch the shoot. The crowd became so disruptive that Adler was forced to post guards to keep out anyone without a pass.

The Reno Brothers was scheduled to be completed in twenty-four days. For a movie on such a tight schedule, it was hopelessly disorganized. The casting of the one female and two male leads opposite Elvis still had not been completed one week before shooting started. Two days before shooting, the primary locations for the movie were still unsecured. When shooting did begin on August 23, there were still roles that had not been cast. Interviews continued for additional actors for three-quarters of the shooting.

It was no surprise that *Love Me Tender* fell behind schedule. To complicate matters, Elvis was booked on October 5 for a concert appearance. His contract with Fox said that he would be allowed time off to meet any previously agreed to commitments should the film run over schedule. Having Elvis gone would put Adler even further behind.

The Colonel used this crisis to put the studio honcho in his debt. He volunteered to cancel the concert. This would free up the entire week for finishing the movie. The Colonel wasn't just being a nice guy. He wanted something in return. He asked director David Weisbart for screen credit acknowledging his contribution to the film. Weisbart contacted Adler who was agreeable. Adler genuinely appreciated the thousands of dollars that the Colonel had saved him by canceling the concert and putting the schedule back on track. He agreed that the Colonel would be billed as "technical advisor." He also gave the Colonel gifts, including gold cufflinks, an office at Fox complete with secretarial help, and a limousine with driver. The total compensation for Elvis and the Colonel was also raised to $100,000.

More prints of *Love Me Tender* were made than any other film in 20th Century-Fox history. It opened in 600 theaters. The Colonel was at work for the November 15 premiere of *Love Me Tender* in New York. He had a forty-foot-tall cutout of Elvis placed on the roof of the Paramount Theater and walked around passing out "Elvis For President" buttons to onlookers. Fifteen hundred people were lined up when the Paramount opened its doors for the first showing at eight in the morning.

The Colonel advised theater owners to make sure that everyone left the theater after every screening. He was afraid that the teenagers would come for the matinee and stay for the next two shows. He did not want freebies taking up room that could be occupied by paying customers.

The Colonel instructed Elvis to leave Memphis before the premiere. He did not want Elvis commenting on the reviews of the movie when they came out. By leaving town, he would not have to make excuses to the media that tailed him everywhere he went when he was in Memphis. This was the beginning of the Colonel's new strategy of withholding Elvis from the world. He had wanted Elvis to be visible everywhere when he was in the creative stage of his popularity. Now that he had achieved stardom, it was time to push Elvis into seclusion to prevent overexposure.

The record release of "Love Me Tender" entered the charts at number two and quickly went to number one. It fueled ticket sales for a movie that would never make anyone's Top Ten list. When box office receipts were counted, *Love Me Tender* had earned six times its one-million-dollar production cost.

While the movie's box office was fantastic, the reviews were not. The *New York Times* said, "The picture itself is a slight case of horse opera with the heaves. Mr. Presley's dramatic contribution is not a great deal more impressive than one of the nags, but one thing you have to say for him, he certainly goes at his job with a great deal more zeal and assurance than the rest of the actors show."

Variety said, "Appraising Presley as an actor, he ain't. Not that it makes much difference." The *Los Angeles News* said that "without Elvis the film would be just an average, cheaply made western action movie but with him it is a box office bonanza." The *New Yorker* weighed in with "Mr. Presley whose talents are meager but whose earnings are gross excites a big section of the young female population as nobody never has done."

Even Elvis was harsh in his appraisal of the movie. He violated the Colonel's never-criticize-yourself-publicly order. While in Philadelphia for a concert, Elvis was asked by a reporter what he thought of *Love Me Tender*. "It was pretty horrible. Acting is not something that you learn overnight. I knew that picture was bad when it was completed," he said.

While in Hollywood for the filming, Elvis hung out with other young actors such as Natalie Wood, Sal Mineo, Dennis Hopper, and Nick Adams. The Colonel could not have been too happy with this side effect of Elvis's movie career. There was a risk that these new friends would start talking about managers and the percentages that they took. Elvis in one of these conversations might learn that the Colonel's 25 percent was above the norm. Elvis might even begin to question the Colonel's carny management style when he heard of the reserved nature in which most of these stars' managers conducted themselves.

According to Gene Aberbach, the Colonel deliberately isolated Elvis from the world because he was afraid of losing him. This even applied to people who didn't have any real possibility of threatening the Colonel. According to one of the Parker's William Morris associates, speaking to Elvis on a movie set or in the Colonel's office would cost you your job.

Officially, the Colonel's reason for isolating Elvis was that the more of a mystery that Elvis remained, the more people would be interested in him. However, the Colonel had other reasons for keeping Elvis sequestered that were a little more self-serving. He did not want Elvis exposed to people with ideas about how his business should be handled. He told Elvis that his job was to take care of performing and the Colonel's job was to take care of business. If anyone approached Elvis about anything related to business, he was to refer him to the Colonel.

The Colonel was very cautious about allowing anyone access to Elvis. He put people in a category of "us" and "them." If you were them, you were to be viewed with the utmost suspicion. According to those who were forced to deal with him over the years, the Colonel viewed anyone who tried to get close to Elvis with suspicion. He had a mistrust of people that was based in great part on his own deviousness. He knew how he operated and assumed that everyone else was doing the same.

The Colonel decided that he needed a mole in the group that Elvis hung out with in Hollywood. Bitsy Mott said that the Colonel hired actor Nick Adams for the job. Adams was part of the old James Dean group that Elvis had become friendly with.

When Elvis returned to Memphis from Hollywood, he confided to his parents that his new friends were critical of the Colonel. He was also tired of reading stories in the newspapers and in magazines where the Colonel took all the credit for discovering Elvis and making him a star.

Vernon chimed in and said that maybe they didn't need the Colonel anymore. After all, Elvis had Abe Lastfogel, who was the top agent in the business. He had a long-term movie deal with Hal Wallis. It seemed to Vernon that 25 percent of Elvis's money was an awful lot for doing nothing but promoting concerts. Despite the brash talk in the privacy of their home, Elvis and Vernon never acted upon any of this. Elvis soon became occupied with getting ready for his next movie.

After the success of *Love Me Tender*, the Colonel tried to renegotiate Elvis's contract with Hal Wallis. He took Harry Kalcheim of the William Morris Agency along with him to see Joe Hazen. Hazen went on the offensive, complaining that Elvis had never once arranged to have dinner with Hal Wallis while he was in Hollywood filming *Love Me Tender*. The Colonel countered that he was offended because neither Paramount nor Hal Wallis issued an invitation to Elvis or himself.

The Colonel related all the wonderful things that 20th Century-Fox had done for him, the office, the staff, the gold cufflinks, the salary for his help with the picture and Elvis. The Colonel hinted that Hazen should do the same. Joe Hazen made absolutely no response to the Colonel's hint.

The Colonel then got down to the original purpose of the

meeting, Elvis's contract. He began by saying that a Fox executive had offered Elvis seventy-five thousand dollars to sing two songs in one of their upcoming movies. The Colonel pretended that he was insulted by the offer. He offered to roll the dice with him for the salary, double or nothing. The Colonel had turned down the Fox offer because he didn't want Elvis making guest appearances. He was only interested in starring roles. However, the offer indicated to him that Elvis's market value had been considerably undervalued in his contract with Wallis. After listening to Parker talk in a similar vein for thirty minutes, Joe Hazen agreed to give Elvis an additional fifty thousand dollars for his first Wallis Productions film.

That wasn't the only time that the Colonel received an offer to hire Elvis to sing a song or two in a movie. Jayne Mansfield approached him about Elvis singing one song in her 1956 movie, *The Girl Can't Help It*. The Colonel told her that Elvis's fee was fifty thousand dollars. Mansfield thought the fee was out of line and decided to use her charms on Elvis. A few days after meeting him, she informed the Colonel that she and Elvis had worked everything out. The Colonel said that was fine with him, but the price was still fifty thousand dollars.

The Colonel couldn't resist one final dig at Hal Wallis. He sent him a card for Valentine's Day that pictured a high school graduate on the front with the words, "You Ought to Be in Television." The inside message read, "Cause You Are in a Class of Your Own." This was a deliberate play on Wallis's status as a producer. At that time, television producers were definitely the poor cousins of motion picture producers. To suggest that Wallis should be on television was an insult. This was an excellent example of the Colonel's "I'm only joking (but I'm really not)" way of insulting people. In his mind, to humiliate was to conquer.

This would not be the last time that the Colonel would use the "I have a better offer from other producers" tactic to renegotiate a contract with Wallis. In fact, he would repeat this throughout virtually every year of Elvis's twelve-year relationship with Hal Wallis.

Wallis and Hazen had put themselves in a difficult position by allowing Elvis to do outside pictures. Other studios would no doubt be eager to land the services of the hottest name in show business. As a result, they very well might offer the Colonel a considerably better deal than he got from Wallis. He could then use this as leverage to establish a new market rate for Elvis's services and try to renegotiate his contract with Wallis. This is exactly what happened.

In July 1956, Hal Wallis told the Colonel that he had just bought a story that would be the basis of Elvis's first movie for him. Hal Wallis conceived of the idea for *Loving You* after reading a short story in *Good Housekeeping*. The story centered around a runaway from a juvenile home who takes a new name from a cemetery headstone. A promoter later discovers that the young man has singing talent and helps him on his way to becoming a star. Wallis paid three thousand dollars for the rights to the story.

He asked Hal Kanter to write a screenplay for Elvis from the short story. Kanter began his career as a television comedy-skit writer. He then got into writing screenplays for Bob Hope and Dean Martin and Jerry Lewis. Kanter was reluctant at first, but agreed when Wallis said he could direct the picture despite Kanter's never having directed a movie before.

Having decided to write a screenplay that would be very close to Elvis's own story, Kanter wanted to spend some time with him in Memphis to get to know him better. The Colonel put up considerable resistance to allowing Elvis to meet with Hal Kanter. He wanted everything to go through him. It was only when Wallis got Abe Lastfogel involved that the Colonel gave in.

Kanter actually had most of the screenplay done when he got to Tennessee. His meeting with Elvis was designed to put some finishing touches on the story. At Hal Wallis's instruction, Kanter intentionally did not bring a copy of the script's draft with him. Wallis was afraid that if Colonel Parker got his hands on the script, he would want to edit it. He was not allowed to see the *Loving You* script until just before production began. When he did read it, amazingly he had no changes or criticism. He liked the life story of Elvis angle, and there were plenty of songs.

Hal Kanter accompanied Elvis to his final performance on the Louisiana Hayride, the extra one agreed to in the buyout arrangement. When they arrived at the auditorium, the Colonel and Tom Diskin were there waiting for them. Hal Kanter asked the Colonel what criteria he used to evaluate a potential script for Elvis. The Colonel responded that he counted the number of songs in it.

As they made their way through the back halls toward the dressing rooms, Elvis was bombarded by questions from reporters. After allowing a few, the Colonel jumped in and said that Elvis had answered all the questions that he would for free. Any additional ones would cost $100 each. Before anyone could respond to his offer, the Colonel had ushered Elvis into the dressing room and shut the door.

The Colonel left Elvis to his preparations and escorted Kanter into the auditorium. One of the opening acts had already begun to perform. The Colonel pointed out to Kanter the line of police that were standing guard in front of the stage. He told him that without the police, those innocent-looking girls would tear Elvis to pieces.

Each time an act left the stage and the announcer began to speak, the audience went wild. When a name other than Elvis's was announced, they would calm down. Finally the moment came when the star made his way on stage. The audience let forth a roar of screams as deafening as a cannon barrage. They did not stop for Elvis's entire twenty-five minute performance. Kanter said that he had never witnessed such hysteria before or since.

On January 10, 1957, Elvis left Memphis by train for Hollywood to begin filming *Loving You*. Two days later, he arrived at Union Station in Los Angeles. He was allowed to detrain in the railroad yard so that he could avoid the crowds waiting for him in the terminal. Later that day, he went to Radio Recorders for an RCA recording session.

Freddie Bienstock of Hill and Range oversaw the selection of songs for *Loving You*. The Hill and Range writers received copies of the script showing where songs were to be inserted. The staff writers would compete to come up with songs. Bienstock would listen to demos from the writers and decide which would be sent to Hollywood. Elvis and the movie people would then make their selections. Bienstock would usually send ten times more songs than they had spots.

The Hollywood establishment made a joke of Colonel Parker when he came to town. He was viewed as nothing more than a carnival pitchman who had stumbled upon a "golden child" of a client. However, Paramount took him seriously. The Colonel had an office on the lot throughout the filming of *Loving You*. It is unheard of for a manager to be given such a perk.

Hal Kanter noticed a pronounced change in Elvis's personality when the Colonel came on the set. He would be transformed from a fun-loving prankster into an all-business actor. Elvis would even stop signing autographs and posing for pictures when the Colonel was around.

According to Elvis's costar in *Loving You*, Lizabeth Scott, it was impossible to have a real conversation with Elvis because the Colonel stuck to his side and guarded him whenever there was a break in the shooting. Lizabeth Scott played Elvis's scheming manager in the movie. There were many similarities between Deke River's manager, Glenda, and Elvis Presley's Colonel Tom Parker. However, Hal Kanter created the character Glenda before meeting the Colonel.

Kanter threw a wrap party at Paramount Studios at the completion of *Loving You*. Colonel Parker managed to steal the credit away from him by warmly welcoming Kanter to his own party. He had a small booth erected in the middle of the room with a banner hanging across the top reading, "Elvis and the Colonel Thank You." Everyone congratulated him for throwing such a great party. To make matters worse, the Colonel sold raffle tickets with prizes being Elvis albums and a record player given to him by RCA. The proceeds went into his pockets.

Elvis's next movie was *Jailhouse Rock*. Originally, *Jailhouse Rock* was to be called *Jailhouse Kid*. Colonel Parker hated the title, but approved of the alternate choice.

Abe Lastfogel negotiated the deal for *Jailhouse Rock*. Elvis received $250,000 and 50 percent of the net profits plus the publishing rights to the songs. The Colonel turned down the offer for Elvis and him to review the script. The Colonel said that all he wanted to make sure of was that there were plenty of songs in the movie.

Jerry Leiber and Mike Stoller were hired to write the music for *Jailhouse Rock*. One day Elvis asked Stoller if he would write him a pretty ballad. A week later, Stoller came back with a demo of a song that he and Leiber had written called "Don't." Elvis wanted to record it.

When the Colonel found out what had happened, he was furious. He called Leiber and Stoller into his office and told them that they were not following the proper protocol for getting a song to Elvis. The demo should have first gone to Gene or Julian Aberbach. If it met their approval (if the songwriters agreed to give Hill and Range the publishing on the song), they would give it to Freddie Bienstock. Bienstock would then play it for Elvis. If they wanted to continue to have Elvis record their songs, they needed to start going through the proper channels, Parker said.

A few days later, Stoller was visiting Elvis at his hotel. The Colonel walked in and asked if he could speak with Elvis in private. When Elvis came back, he told Stoller that the Colonel was upset he was there, and he had better go.

In his dressing room on the set of *Jailhouse Rock*, Elvis was interviewed by columnist Joe Hyams. Hyams asked Elvis about the Colonel. "I have got an idea how to handle me better than anyone else has as far as keeping me in line," he said. "Colonel Parker is more or less like a daddy when I am away from my own folks. He does not meddle in my affairs. Ain't nobody can tell me you do this or that. Colonel Parker knows the business, and I don't. He never butts into record sessions. I don't butt into business. Nobody can tell you how to run your life."

Memphis D.J. Dewey Phillips dropped by the set of *Jailhouse Rock*. Elvis played a copy of his upcoming RCA single release "Teddy Bear" for him. Unknown to Elvis, Dewey took the record back with him to Memphis and played it on his radio show. Both the Colonel and RCA were livid. The Colonel told Elvis that this proved that he was right when he warned him about the dangers of some of his friends.

During filming, Elvis swallowed a temporary tooth cap. It lodged in his lung, and he was taken to the hospital accompanied by Colonel Parker. The Colonel was sent to the waiting room like an expectant father. Sometime later, a doctor came out and told him that the cap had been removed and that everything was fine. The Colonel cringed when heard how the cap had been removed. It seems that they went in the lungs by parting the vocal cords and using an instrument to fish out the cap. Colonel Parker definitely wasn't comfortable with someone touching his boy's vocal cords.

While Elvis was working on *Jailhouse Rock*, Hal Wallis completed a musical called *Hot Spell*. The Colonel became enraged when he thought that he heard a snippet of one of Elvis's songs playing in the preview for *Hot Spell*. He wrote Wallis demanding that the song be removed from the movie. The Colonel closed the letter by telling Wallis that if he did not feel that the Colonel was qualified to be with his organization, the Colonel would forward all his property to MGM. There was the threat of moving to another studio being used again.

When Elvis finished *Jailhouse Rock*, the Colonel went back to Joe Hazen to renegotiate the contract for Elvis's next movie with Wallis. He told him that 20th Century-Fox had agreed to pay $200,000 for the next picture that Elvis made for them. Hazen agreed to raise Elvis's salary for the next movie from $25,000 to $100,000.

Chapter 8

Private Elvis Presley

★ ★ ★ ★

Billboard magazine published a story in October 1956 claiming that Elvis would be drafted in December 1957. The source for the story was said to be a high-level Army official. The article went on to say that Elvis would go through six weeks of basic training and then would be placed in the special services. He would make public appearances on behalf of the army as part of his duty. In addition, he would be free to do projects for his personal benefit such as appearing on television and making records.

The article even claimed that the army would give Elvis leave to make a movie. It concluded by saying that the only people who knew the exact date of his induction were a small group of army officials and Elvis's closest business associates.

Even though the army immediately denied the story, Colonel Parker told Elvis that they could not just ignore it. It had created bad publicity by putting the idea in people's minds that Elvis was going to get special treatment. To counteract the bad publicity, the Colonel advised him to voluntarily report for a pre-induction physical at once. Elvis should also make it clear that he wanted to serve his time, if he were drafted, like any other solider. There would be no special services.

Elvis took the Colonel's advice and arranged with the draft board for a physical in January 1957. He passed and was classified 1A. Elvis later confided to one of his sergeants that he held Colonel Parker responsible for being drafted. He felt that volunteering for his pre-induction physical had caused him to be called into service.

It was almost inevitable that as a single young male, Elvis would get the call from Uncle Sam. There were three ways that he could have dealt with the draft. One was to take the route taken by many stars and enter the special services. There he would spend his time in the military entertaining troops. The second option would be to come up with some medical reason why he couldn't serve. The final option was to go in as a regular soldier.

Right before Christmas 1957, the army, navy, and air force all approached Elvis with special deals by which he could fulfill his military obligation. The air force offered to make Elvis a singing ambassador. His primary duty would have been to assist with recruiting. The other branches offered scenarios that would have had him entertaining troops.

Representatives of both the army and navy visited him at Graceland pitching their branch of the service. The navy went all out, saying he could perform in his free time, promising housing equivalent of an admiral's, and even offering to form a company made entirely of Memphis boys to accompany Elvis as his unit.

Elvis's military records confirm that the army was prepared to allow him to take the special services route with a tour of bases around the world. They would also let him continue his career by cutting records in his off time and making personal appearances.

The Colonel, Elvis, Vernon, and Gladys met at Graceland to discuss the offers. The option that most appealed to Elvis was not to serve at all. If there was no way out, the special services was his second choice.

One would think that the idea of Elvis being drafted would have frightened the Colonel as much as it did the singer. Amazingly, the Colonel did absolutely nothing to keep his meal ticket out of military, nor did he do anything to make Elvis's service easier. On the contrary, the Colonel recommended that Elvis serve his time like any other soldier. This despite that when he was faced with a similar situation, the Colonel had been no more eager to be drafted than Elvis was.

On January 8, 1942, Tom Parker had received a preliminary questionnaire from his draft board, the purpose of which was to obtain information to help in assigning a draft status for him. On the form, he put his birth date as June 26, 1909, his birthplace as Huntington, West Virginia, and that he was married with a dependent child. The last item gave him a draft deferment. He made no mention of his previous army experience. Oddly he listed his employer as Gene Austin of Hollywood, rather than the Humane Society. In January 1944, the government, desperate for troops, classified the Colonel 1A. However, he failed his pre-induction physical because of his weight and was reclassified 4F.

Perhaps the Colonel was afraid that if he tried to intercede on Elvis's behalf, someone would dig into his own military record and discover Andre van Kuijk. Or he might have been frightened off by the public outcry after the *Billboard* article. In reference to his decision to keep Elvis out of the special services, the Colonel said, "A sure way to debase your merchandise is to give it away." Vernon agreed with him.

Rumors have circulated since the 1950s that the Colonel actually was hoping that Elvis would be drafted. It remains somewhat of a mystery as to why the Colonel would have wanted him in the army at the peak of his fame. It has been suggested that the Colonel was hoping the army would rein in Elvis. Presley had commented to several people that what with his career skyrocketing, anybody could do his booking. It is almost certain that this got back to the Colonel. Perhaps Parker figured that after being out of circulation for two years in the army, Elvis would feel the need for someone to rebuild his career.

Elvis's longtime road manager, Joe Esposito, refuted that suggestion. He quoted Parker as saying, "What would a manager with thousands invested in his artist want to have that artist drafted? He would have to be crazy. No one could predict how two years in the army would affect Elvis's career. The public could have easily forgotten him."

During the middle of December 1957, the chairman of the Memphis draft board notified Elvis that he had been drafted. He wanted to give Elvis the opportunity to pick up his draft notice in person rather than having it mailed. He was certain that if it was mailed, someone would leak the news that Elvis had received a letter from selective service.

Elvis's draft notice was delivered by Milton Bowers, the head of the Memphis Selective Service Commission. It read, "Greetings: You are hereby ordered for induction into the armed forces of the United States and to report to room 215, 198 South Main Street, Memphis Tennessee, at 7:45 A.M. on the 20th of January for forwarding to an armed forces induction station." When Elvis said that he would accept the draft notice and be assigned to a combat platoon, all Gladys Presley could do was cry.

The next day, Elvis went to the Colonel's house in Madison. There he opened the back of the truck he had driven and backed out a red Isetta sports car. It was a gift for the Colonel. Reporters were on hand to preserve the gift-giving for posterity. Elvis and the Colonel posed for pictures sitting in the car. Within earshot of the reporters, Elvis said, "It is only a small, small way of showing my feelings for you." Tears could be seen in the Colonel's eyes.

That night attending the Grand Ole Opry with the Colonel and the Jordanaires, Elvis confided to one of the backup singers that he wished the Colonel had been more willing to get him out of his military service. At the Opry, they ran into many of the people who had shared the bill with Elvis in his country package-show days. Elvis talked with Johnny Cash, the Duke of Paducah, the Wilburn Brothers, and Ferlin Huskey, and he had a pleasant conversation with Hank Snow. However, Snow refused to get near, much less speak to, the Colonel.

While in Nashville, the Colonel told Elvis that his next movie for Hal Wallis would be based on a book by Harold Robbins called a *Stone for Danny Fisher*. The movie was to be called *King Creole*. The Colonel also had two more movies in the works for Elvis. One was for 20th Century-Fox, the details of which were not yet known. The other was a biography of Hank Williams that was going to be made by MGM. The Colonel told him not to worry about his draft notice. He would make sure that he had a deferment so that he could do *King Creole*. Elvis, however, was more concerned with his personal life than he was making a movie.

The Memphis draft board received a telegram from Paramount Studios requesting a sixty-day draft deferment for Elvis so that he could make *King Creole* for them. The appeal was made on the basis that Paramount would lose the $350,000 that it had already spent if Elvis was not permitted to complete the picture. The draft board responded that any requests for a deferment would have to be made by Elvis himself. Elvis duly made the request, and it was granted.

King Creole was scheduled to begin filming on January 13, 1958. On January 10, 1958, Elvis and the Colonel left Memphis by train bound for Hollywood, along with Tom Diskin, Freddie Bienstock, and a few of Elvis's friends. There were large crowds at each station stop. The Colonel had made certain that every city along the way had the exact schedule of the train. It pulled into Los Angeles on January 13. Two days later, a recording of the movie's soundtrack began at Radio Recorders.

Jerry Leiber and Mike Stoller supplied the songs. Leiber also pitched a Broadway musical to the Aberbachs that he thought would make a great movie for Elvis. Gene Aberbach told him to stick to what he had been hired for. If he tried to interfere with the plan laid out by the Colonel ever again, he would be finished with Elvis and Hill and Range.

Steve Sholes was in a panic. Elvis would soon be in the army and unavailable for recording. RCA, as usual, found itself with no songs in reserve. They needed a session that would give them product to release over the next two years. The Colonel identified February 1, 1958, as the only available date in the *King Creole* shoot for an RCA recording session.

Elvis wanted Jerry Leiber and Mike Stoller at the session. Tom Diskin relayed Elvis's request to Sholes, who in turn asked the songwriters to go to Hollywood. They were willing, but first they needed a contract for their services to be agreed upon with the Colonel.

The next day, a courier arrived at Leiber and Stoller's office with an envelope from Colonel Tom Parker. Their contract was supposed to be inside. However, there was nothing on the enclosed paper except for places for Stoller's and Leiber's signatures—and where the Colonel had already signed.

Jerry Leiber telephoned the Colonel to ask what the idea was sending a blank contract. The Colonel told him not to worry about it. They should just sign the paper and send it back to him. He would fill in the details later. Leiber hung up on the Colonel. He never spoke to the Colonel or worked with Elvis again.

The session went on without Leiber or Stoller. It was a disaster. Elvis was upset that his request had not been met. He only recorded two songs. This reinforced the Colonel's commitment to keep songwriters away from Elvis. He didn't need them messing up the boy's head. Again the Colonel instructed Bitsy Mott to keep an eye on who was coming in contact with Elvis. Under no circumstances should any songwriters or other people who might try to interfere in their business be allowed access to Elvis's hotel room. After a couple of weeks to cool down, Elvis told the Colonel that he wanted to go back into the studio. The Colonel wouldn't let him, seeing that as an admission to Steve Sholes that the first session wasn't handled appropriately.

In early February, the cast of *King Creole* traveled by train to New Orleans for location shooting. A regular blackjack game got going during lulls in the filming. Walter Matthau and the Colonel were always the first to sit down at the table. On one occasion, Matthau ran out of money and wanted to continue playing on credit. Everyone in the game was agreeable except the Colonel. If Matthau wanted to play cards with the Colonel, it would be strictly on a cash basis. It didn't matter that he knew Matthau was good for the money. He wouldn't bend. Matthau got someone to lend him some cash and stayed in the game.

While in New Orleans, one of Elvis's entourage met a young man whose father was a tailor. A deal was struck whereby the young man would supply seven matching blazers for free in exchange for being able to advertise that Elvis and his friends wore clothes from his father's store. The next day, the blazers were delivered to the set. On being handed his, Colonel Parker knew that something was wrong and hit the roof when he found out that a deal had been made behind his back. He screamed that Mr. Presley had never endorsed anything, and he wasn't about to start now. The young man was so frightened by the Colonel that he told him to keep the jackets anyway.

Hal Wallis threw a wrap party for *King Creole* on the studio lot. The Colonel had hundreds of helium-filled balloons with "King Creole" printed on them for the occasion. He handed out bunches of them to everyone who entered the party. Then, on his command, all the balloons were released to the ceiling.

In general, *King Creole* received positive reviews. The *New York Times* called it "a surprisingly colorful and lively drama." Elvis was credited for "some surprisingly credible acting."

On the train trip back to Memphis, the Colonel created another publicity opportunity. He telephoned disc jockeys in every city along the route to let them in on a "secret," which was actually nothing more than the time Elvis would be passing through their town. He encouraged the D.J.'s to tell their listeners and ask them to be on hand to wave to Elvis. As a result, cheering crowds greeted the train in every town. The Colonel had, once again, supplied publicity fodder for the newspapers.

With *King Creole* completed, Elvis's army induction took center stage. With four days to go, the Colonel met with Elvis at Graceland. Parker wanted to reassure Elvis that he would stay in the public eye. RCA would have some songs in the can for continued record releases. And the Colonel would keep up the steady stream of Elvis souvenirs, only now the singer would be in military garb.

The Colonel didn't see going into the army as necessarily a bad career move. "The whole world will be watching," he told Elvis. "And what they see, if we do it right, will make you a bigger star coming out of the army than you were when you were drafted."

On his last night of freedom, Elvis went to see *Sing Boy, Sing*, starring Tommy Sands, at a drive-in. The role had been offered to Elvis, but the Colonel turned it down. That night Elvis confided his despair at having to leave his career behind to childhood friend Barbara Pitman. He said, "Why me when I can stay here and make so much more money? My taxes would be more important than sticking me in the service."

March 24, 1958, was army induction day for Elvis. He reported to the Memphis draft board at 6:35 A.M. Accompanying him were Vernon, Gladys, his girlfriend Anita Wood, Lamar Fike, and a few other friends. The Colonel had gotten there one-and-a-half hours early to make sure that most of the people in the crowd were holding *King Creole* balloons and 8 x 10 pictures of Elvis when Presley arrived.

At 7:15 A.M., Elvis and his fellow inductees rode by bus to Kennedy Veterans Hospital for their medical exams. There were 200 reporters waiting for them. One from the *Memphis Commercial Appeal* asked if Elvis thought his popularity would slip while he was in the army. "That is the $64,000 question," he answered.

The Colonel guided Elvis to in front of the cameras to read some telegrams that had been sent by prominent well-wishers. Elvis read a couple and then wanted to stop. The Colonel urged him to continue. Elvis whispered an uncharacteristically defiant response to the Colonel. "It is me that is going in, and what happens will be to me, not you!"

At 4:00 P.M., Elvis returned to the draft board for the swearing-in ceremony. He had a new name other than "the Pelvis." He was now Private Elvis Presley, serial #53310761. Elvis and the other recruits boarded the bus bound for Fort Chaffee, Arkansas, at 5:00 P.M. Along the way, they stopped at a restaurant in West Memphis for sandwiches. When Elvis arrived at Fort Chaffee at 11:15 P.M., the Colonel and fifty reporters were waiting for him.

The next morning Elvis and the other soldiers were awakened at 5:30. Breakfast was served at 6:00 with the Colonel turning Elvis's first meal in the mess hall into another media event. More than two dozen photographers were present for Elvis's first army breakfast. Then it was time for a five-hour aptitude test.

That afternoon Elvis was given his army haircut by James D. Peterson. He had to pay sixty-five cents to have his famous locks shorn. The Colonel escorted fifty-five reporters and photographers to the event, where he directed the haircut as if he were a symphony conductor. Work slowly, he told the barber. Give the photographers plenty of time to snap pictures. He wanted everyone to get at least one closeup and at least one long shot. The Colonel escorted them up in small groups and instructed the barber to snip a clump of hair. Afterwards, when the hair clippings were swept up, the Colonel made a joke to the newsmen about the tremendous value of the artifacts that were about to be destroyed.

The next day March 28, Elvis was off for Fort Hood, Texas, for basic training. He wasn't scheduled to arrive at the fort until four, but the media were already converging there early that morning. The Colonel dropped by the office of the base information officer, Lt. Col. Marjorie Schulter, to offer assistance. Colonel Schulter promptly informed him that this would be the final day of his media circus. At last, Elvis was to be a solider and not a photo op, part of a tank battalion formerly under the command of Gen. George Patton. After twenty weeks of training at Fort Hood, his unit would ship off to Germany.

When basic training was completed on June 1, Elvis went on a two-week leave. The Colonel and Elvis's girlfriend, Anita Wood, were waiting at the front gate of the base to take him back to Memphis. While on leave, Elvis was asked by the *Memphis Press Scimitar* if he would be singing in the army. He answered, "I'd like to sing to entertain, but I'm not going to ask for it. I'm not going to ask for anything in the army."

Elvis was scheduled for a one-night Nashville recording session the following week. The Colonel had finally given in to Steve Sholes's begging. RCA had only four unreleased songs in their vaults, obviously not enough to last two years. Elvis could have easily spent a few days in the studio and recorded enough material for RCA to release regularly over his time in the service. For that matter, there was nothing in the army regulations prohibiting him from recording in Germany in his free time. The Colonel, however, had a different strategy.

The Colonel wanted RCA to run out of new material. He planned on renegotiating Elvis's contract at the end of his army stint and felt that their bargaining position would be stronger if RCA had no new songs to release when Elvis came marching triumphantly home. The company would be desperate for new product, and Colonel Parker could name his price.

A second part of the Colonel's strategy was to make Elvis desperate. If the continuity of record releases was broken, Elvis, in effect, would be starting his career all over again. He would need the Colonel to do that, or so the Colonel would have him believe.

On June 14, 1958, Elvis went back to Fort Hood. He began training as an armored crewman. A week later, Gladys and Vernon Presley arrived to live near the base for the remainder of Elvis's basic training. At first they lived in a trailer near the fort. After a few days, they rented a home in nearby Killeen, and Elvis was allowed to move in with them. His grandmother, Minnie Mae Presley, also moved in.

The Colonel visited Elvis several times to discuss business. He, Elvis, and Vernon held closed-door meetings in one of the bedrooms. Gladys Presley was never included.

While at Fort Hood with Elvis, the Colonel wrote one of his customarily strange letters to Hal Wallis. In it, he said he deserved an Academy Award for his skills as a negotiator. "Never have I seen so much snow fall in such a short time," he wrote. He concluded the letter by claiming he'd be forced to take a job with a friend as a laborer during Elvis's absence. When he got to the work site, he would be sure and send Wallis his new address.

In July, Gladys Presley began to have difficulty walking. During the first week of August 1958, she became ill, complaining of stomach discomfort. Gladys took diet pills because she didn't want Elvis to be embarrassed by her size. She also drank. Her drinking intensified when she was upset about something or when Elvis was away. Gladys was taken to a doctor in Temple, Texas. On the doctor's recommendation, Gladys and Vernon returned August 8 to Memphis, where Gladys checked into Baptist Hospital. She was diagnosed as having acute hepatitis.

On August 12, Elvis was granted an emergency leave and flew to Memphis. He visited Gladys that night for a few hours. Her condition got worse the next day, and Elvis remained at the hospital until midnight when he went home. At 3:15 A.M., August 14, 1958, Gladys Presley died.

The Colonel drove from his home in Madison as soon as he got the news of Gladys's death. He immediately took charge of planning the funeral. There was a disagreement, however, over where it should be held. Vernon and Elvis wanted to have the funeral at Graceland with a public viewing. The Colonel wanted it held at a funeral home. In the end, he prevailed, arguing that Graceland would be too big a security risk.

The Colonel orchestrated the funeral with the same precision that he used with Elvis's concerts. The Memphis police provided security. Press releases went out. The Colonel even planned the route the hearse carrying Gladys's body would take.

Gladys's funeral was held at one-o'clock on, August 15, at the Memphis Funeral Home, with 400 invited guests in attendance. Three thousand Elvis fans stood outside. Gladys was buried at Forest Hill Cemetery. Thousands of people lined the highway in front of the cemetery.

Elvis returned to Fort Hood August 25, 1958. On September 12, the Associated Press reported that he would soon be joining the Third Armored Division as a truck driver. He would be stationed in Germany. On September 19, Elvis left Fort Hood by train, heading for the military ocean terminal in Brooklyn, New York. The Colonel had requested that Elvis be allowed to fly to New York rather than riding the train with the other soldiers, but was informed that wouldn't be allowed. He had hoped to use Elvis's extra time in New York for press interviews.

Undaunted, the Colonel arranged for a media circus to greet Elvis. More than 125 reporters were on hand to document Presley's last day in the United States, and Elvis obligingly held an hour-long press conference.

Afterwards, he walked up the ship's gangplank eight times to make sure that all the photographers had a chance to get a good shot. Once on board, Elvis headed to the library for a final few words with the Colonel. Also on hand were Steve Sholes, Bill Bullock of RCA, Freddie Bienstock, and Gene and Julian Aberbach, all of whom stood by as Elvis recorded a short Christmas message that, with the press conference, would be released by RCA under the title "Elvis Sails."

As the ship pulled away from the dock, an army band played a melody of Elvis's hits. Elvis waved to the crowds and handed out to his shipmates picture postcards of himself that the Colonel had supplied. The Colonel stood smiling and waving until the ship left the dock. He would not see his boy again for eighteen months.

On October 1, Elvis's ship docked in Bremerhaven, West Germany. From there, Elvis boarded a train to Friedberg, Germany. A few days later, Vernon Presley, grandmother Minnie Mae, and friends Lamar Fike and Red West arrived in Germany to join Elvis. Anita Wood says that Elvis wanted her to come as well, and she even went as far as to get a passport. But the Colonel found out and put a stop to it. Again he argued it would make for bad publicity. The press would say that they were married or worse. Elvis would need all the positive press that he could get if he was to make a comeback when he got out of the army. After spending a few days in a hotel, the group settled into a house rented by Elvis in nearby Bad Nauheim.

In Germany, the military brass resumed pressure to transfer Elvis to special services. He was called to division headquarters in Frankfurt to discuss the subject with the commander, Maj. Gen. Thomas F. VanNattan. They agreed that there would be no special services, and Elvis went about the business of being a soldier.

Bob Hope approached Elvis directly about performing in his Christmas show for the troops after the Colonel turned him down.

The Colonel had him turn it down as well. It was against the Colonel's nature to allow Elvis to perform for free, but he tried to disguise his true motive by saying that he wanted Elvis to be treated like any other solider.

Even if there had been any altruism in the Colonel, he would have nixed the Hope show. It wasn't part of the grand scheme for Elvis's career and his own future. The Colonel had a reason for completely removing Elvis from entertaining during his army stint. There was the risk that Elvis's teenage fans would outgrow him. The Colonel was determined to make Elvis more palatable to older record buyers, thereby expanding his fan base. What better way for his boy to show he was no juvenile deliquent than by serving his time in the army like any other respectable, patriotic citizen?

With Elvis gone, the press had to settle for Colonel Parker, who, as part of his respectability plan, continually stressed Elvis's patriotism. For instance, he once reported that Elvis had turned down $500,000 in appearance money while in Germany so that he could "do his army duty like the other boys." But at the same time, the Colonel also wanted to emphasize that even though Elvis was away, his popularity remained strong. He revealed that in 1959 Elvis's income would be in excess of $1 million, of which $1,500 came from his army pay. The remainder was from record royalties, movie profit-sharing, and merchandise sales.

If the Colonel's plan worked, the public's demand for Elvis would only increase during his two-year absence. He would leave the entertainment world while he was on top, and the Colonel would keep the publicity campaign alive to make sure that no one forgot him. The Colonel was working on the fickle principle of knowing you can't have something, only makes you want it more. Elvis in the army was that unobtainable object of desire. If everything went as the Colonel planned, Elvis would still have his original kids screaming and yelling for him when he got out plus an entirely new fan base of more mature adults. The challenge was to make sure that the public did not completely forget about him while he was gone.

The Colonel's carefully mapped-out strategy was twofold. First was the nonstop publicity blitz. Second was the restriction of new Elvis product. Few records would be released. This would keep Elvis from becoming overexposed while at the same time putting RCA at the Colonel's mercy. When Elvis returned stateside, there would be no new material in the can. The Colonel would be in complete control of the flow of new songs.

The Colonel assigned Tom Diskin the duty of being his deputy of propaganda. Together they created Elvis "news," some real, some invented. The first news leak was that Elvis would give a concert to be televised in concert halls around the country via closed-circuit television once he got his discharge papers. Then Tom Diskin informed Nashville newspapers that the Colonel had signed Elvis to a series of annual ABC television specials. His salary for the first year would be $100,000 and would escalate annually. This story was picked up by the wire services and made it to newspapers all over the country.

While Diskin may have provided assistance, the Colonel, of course, retained the role of chief Elvis salesman. The day that Elvis arrived in Germany, the Colonel held a press conference in Nashville to talk about how much money he would be making while in the army. The message had to be continually emphasized that Elvis was away, but the juggernaut rolled on. "Despite the fact that Elvis hasn't released any recordings since July, his discs counted for eight million sales last year," Parker reported.

It was during this period that the Colonel developed a relationship with the fan magazines. He constantly fed them Cinderella stories of Elvis's humble background, complete with childhood photographs. The Colonel also reinforced Elvis's continuing popularity. He said, "Even with Elvis out of circulation, his last record

'One Night and I Got Stung' sold over two million. There were 800,000 advance orders on his new record coming out next week, 'A Fool Such As I' and 'I Need Your Love.'"

In 1959, the focus of the Colonel's promotional activity centered around Elvis's post-army career plans. In the March 5, 1959, issue of the *Memphis Press Scimitar*, the Colonel said that he had just wrapped up a deal with Hal Wallis for Elvis's first movie once he'd hung up his fatigues. He also said that a deal had been made with 20th Century-Fox for two other movies.

On August 3, 1959, *Billboard* magazine reported that "Big Hunk of Love" had just reached gold record status. It was Elvis's fifth gold record since entering the army. However, by the end of the year, the well had run dry. When the November 9 issue of *Billboard* magazine came out, there were no Elvis Presley records on any of the charts. This was the first time that had happened since Elvis began his recording career.

In the October 8, 1959, *Memphis Press Scimitar*, Elvis was interviewed on the occasion of his year anniversary in Germany. He denied that he planned to reenlist. "My manager would shoot me," he said. "I hope to come back to Europe as an entertainer."

The notion that Elvis might sign up for two more years sprung up from a joke the Colonel played on the press. Tired of being asked when Elvis would be released from the army, the Colonel finally said to a columnist, "Well, he'll be out sometime in March if he doesn't re-enlist." The columnist dutifully printed the quote, and it unleashed quite a commotion. The Colonel's phone rang almost off the hook with people wanting to know if it was true that he had said Elvis was re-enlisting. The Colonel replied that they were twisting his words around. All he had said was that Elvis would be out in March if he didn't re-enlist.

Just when he had denied everything, the Colonel threw out more bait. "How do I know whether he'll re-enlist? He's happy in the army, so he might. But, that's his personal business." He ended by suggesting that if they really wanted to know what Elvis was going to do, they should call the Pentagon. The Colonel must have laughed when the Pentagon phoned him, asking if it was true that Elvis was thinking about re-enlisting. The Colonel had a word for what he had done, "snowing."

He also poked fun at the controversy at Hal Wallis's expense. He sent Wallis a little something extra for Christmas in 1959, in addition to a picture postcard of him and Elvis. The Colonel had a fake newspaper created with the headline, "Elvis to Re-enlist." He mailed the paper to Wallis as a gag gift.

Occasionally the Colonel was faced with handling something more serious than Presley's re-enlistment plans. A death threat of sorts against Elvis was investigated by the FBI. The threat wasn't judged to be serious, and the matter was dropped. The Colonel managed to keep the incident private. The following memos from FBI files document the incident.

Memo: FBI file dated March 24, 1959
To: Director FBI
Subject: Elvis Presley

Enclosed herewith are the original and a photostat of the letter dated March 11, 1959, and the envelope postmarked March 12, 1959, addressed to RCA Victor Records, 155 East 24th Street, New York 10, New York, which contains information from an honest writer that plans have been made for a red army soldier to kill Elvis Presley, a well known entertainer, who is presently stationed in the US Army in West Germany. Legal department of RCA who made letter available on March 19, 1959, advised that it had been received March 15, 1959, and was handled by numerous people on the staff. They stated that Presley's manager, Colonel Thomas Parker, Box

417, Madison Tennessee, Phone number Nashville 8-2858 was informed of contents of the letter and he advised that the letter appeared identical to letters received in past from a woman in Ohio and that FBI had already looked into matter. Parker stated that the woman was "nuts." The letter contained no personal threats from writer.

Two photostats are being forwarded for assistance of Memphis office and is requested that Memphis instruct laboratories what action desired.

Memo dated April 22, 1959
To: Assistant chief of staff for Intelligence,
Department of the Army, J. Edgar Hoover,
Director, Federal Bureau of Investigations
Subject: Elvis Presley

Attached is a photostat of an anonymous letter dated March 11, 1959, postmarked Canton Ohio and addressed to RCA Victor Records, 155 East 24th Street, New York 10, New York, which contains information to the effect that a Red Army soldier in East Germany is trying to kill Elvis Presley, a well known entertainer presently attached to the U.S. Army. The legal department of RCA has advised that the contents of this letter have been made available to Presley's manager, Colonel Thomas Parker, Madison, Tennessee. For your information, during 1957 and 1958, an individual wrote several threatening letters to Presley and subsequently volunteered to enter an institution for mental patients. The assistant U.S. Attorney at Cleveland, Ohio, declined prosecution for the violations of the extortion statute in view of her mental condition. The handwriting on the enclosed letter was examined by the FBI laboratory and it was concluded that the handwriting was not identical with that of the known specimens by the same individual.

The above is being forwarded to you for your information and no further investigation will be conducted by this bureau.

The Colonel helped orchestrate RCA's Elvis releases while Elvis was in the army. First the *Love Me Tender* soundtrack was released, then "Loving You" and"King Creole." Old songs were repackaged into new releases. All sold extremely well. In February 1959, the album *For LP Fans Only* was released. RCA fleshed out what little material they had with songs from Elvis's Sun Record days. The album went to number nineteen on the charts.

In June 1959, the last original single in RCA's possession was released, "Big Hunk of Love." An album entitled *A Date with Elvis* was released, made up of strictly old material. It featured a picture of Elvis in his army uniform on the front. The back had a calendar with the date of his discharge circled. RCA continued begging the Colonel to allow Elvis to record while he was in the army. When they went directly to Elvis, he referred them back to the Colonel. The answer was still no.

During a press conference in New York City on November 19, 1959, an RCA records executive said that Elvis's singing style would probably change when he came home. The next day, Colonel Parker's office received a barrage of telegrams and telephone calls protesting any change in Elvis. The media immediately picked up the story.

An article appeared in the *Memphis Press Scimitar* on November 25, 1959, titled, "Music Circles in a Buzz. Will Elvis Change His Style?" The story read, "Will rock and roll Elvis Presley, whose heavily accented chant has sold $50 million worth of records for RCA Victor in five years and changed the music taste of the nation, change his singing style come spring? That is an issue being widely debated in some large metropolitan news-papers and music trade press these days."

Billboard magazine had this to say: "There is considerable dis-may that Victor execs did not parry questions which led to remarks relative to Elvis singing a different type of material or chanting in another matter. It is known that Presley's manager Colonel Tom Parker has been flooded with telephone calls from reporters, created late last week relative to published remarks about Presley changing his singing style, Parker remarked, 'I don't believe anyone connected with RCA Victor would make a state-ment such as that.'" But *Billboard* pointed out that RCA's Rod Lauren had told newsmen that the company was selecting a lot of nonrock material for Presley to record when he returned to civil-ian status. Parker, according to the story, appeared unexcited and had sent RCA a congratulatory telegram on discovering Lauren, a rock and roller.

In August 1959, Paramount made the announcement that Elvis's next movie would be called *G.I. Blues*. Later that month, Hal Wallis took a forty-man crew to West Germany for three weeks to film background scenes. Presley's own Third Armor Division with headquarters in Frankfurt furnished men and machines for action footage. The army also loaned Wallis tanks and other equip-ment, and soldiers were hired as extras. Elvis, however, did not par-ticipate in filming. One of his fellow soldiers acted as his stand-in for long-distance shots.

The Colonel remained in active control of Elvis's career dur-ing this period without ever having any face-to-face meetings with him. Gene Aberbach, Hal Wallis, and Freddie Bienstock all vis-ited Elvis in Germany, but not the Colonel. The official reason was that the Colonel had to remain in the U.S. to handle Elvis's business affairs, although it is hard to believe that this required his nonstop attention for the year and a half Elvis was in

Germany. The Colonel's illegal alien status was the real reason that he didn't want to travel abroad.

The Colonel's line to people at the time was that he could not get a passport because he was an orphan. Gene Aberbach said the the Colonel's explanation to him for not going was his inability to speak German. Ironically, the Colonel probably did know enough German to get by. Aberbach said that he always thought that Parker was from Wisconsin because of his accent. The Colonel wasn't big on going into his past history. In fact, except for saying he had once operated a pet cemetery, he never mentioned anything about his pre-show-business days to Aberbach.

With no in-person visits, the Colonel and Elvis relied upon written communication. Their letters demonstrate both the complete obedience of Elvis when it came to the Colonel's instructions about his career and the good-natured joking enjoyed by the two of them.

November 1, 1958

Dear Vernon and Elvis,

Enclosed are three separate night cables which I want you to send immediately from Germany as soon as you receive them in this letter.

I know that you and Vernon will be happy to know that, pending a few minor details which I will close out in the next few weeks, I have been able to negotiate and work out all our problems with Hal Wallis, Hazen and Paramount and also with 20th Century-Fox, solving all our problems and with a firm understanding. Now upon your discharge from the service I have you completely protected to make four more pictures for Mr. Wallis and two for Fox. All of them have options of course, with a very generous financial improvement from the old contracts.

As a matter of fact, I have been able to secure just about the type of contract I always wanted for you, but since you wanted to start a picture at that time I could not take a firm stand without disappointing you.

This should give you something to look forward to after you get out. That part of your future is protected where nothing could go wrong with this, other than any action on your account that would invoke the bad publicity clause which is in all the contracts and which I know you will never be a party of anyway.

On the cable I dictated for you to send me you can change it any way you want to as this is only the basic idea and I want to take it out to the studio for publicity purposes.

I will also give you all the other details later on when I get back to my office and I know that you will be amazed that we were able to come out on top without going to court and spending lots of money. You know of course without me telling you that I could never have done this without your complete confidence and your unusual talent.

Gene and Julian have helped me work the deal where we can protect all the songs and keep them in Elvis Presley Music, Inc., instead of having songs that sound good but where no money is coming in.

You will be happy to know that "I GOT STUNG" and "ONE NIGHT" has sold over 800,000 already and with the record business as it is this is fantastic. Let me know in the wire to me if you received the box of records I sent you of "I GOT STUNG."

You will be amused to know that Mrs. Sharp who owns the Beverly Wilshire Hotel moved into your room at the hotel.

She asked if any of Elvis's cousins were laying around in the closet and said that wouldn't be bad. However, she promised to move when you come back.

Your pal,
Admiral

P.S. Give my best wishes to your new girlfriend. I read about her in today's paper. It was a nice write-up.

To Buddy Adler

Manager
20th Century-Fox Studios
Los Angeles, California, U.S.A.

Dear Mr. Adler:

The Colonel told me that it looks like I will be back at the studio after I get out of the army. I wish to thank you for my father, the Colonel, and myself for having faith and confidence in me when I come out of the service.

Please thank all the folks at Fox and give my regards to the Colonel.

Respectfully yours,

Elvis Presley

To: Colonel Tom Parker
Beverly Wilshire Hotel
Beverly Hills, California

Dear Admiral:

Thanks for your letter. I have sent the cables as you requested.
I sure appreciate all you are doing and looking after our business while I am booked for Uncle Sam. This sure is a long
tour you sent me on. I am sorry the commissions are so small
on this engagement.

Thanks for fixing up the Paramount and Fox picture deals.
Daddy says hello, also Grandma, Lamar and Red West

Elvis

In December, the Colonel gave Elvis another career update.

December 8, 1958

Dear Vernon & Elvis,

Enclosed is some special mail that came in, also a package
from Hal Wallis and Mr. Hazen, it's a small medallion they
send for Xmas and ask me mail it on to Elvis, so we enclosed
it in This envelope.

We have gotten the Xmas cards they sure are nice, but how
come you printed so many—we will get a good many of them
to fans and other outlets, I guess you are handling most of
them from Memphis and Germany, enclosed are some of my
Xmas cards wich [sic] we have bombarded the fans and other
outlets which we have so far mailed out already over 25,000

with packages of them to the fanclubs all over the country.
Also to the studios, RCA Victor, Radio stations, TV actors
and many others. It will surely cause some comments, The
photo of Santa is a small picture of myself wich [sic] I had
from my Santa Days. We have already had a plug on the cards
on TV and some of the newspapers also have written about
the card.

I have not heard from Bob Hope since I told him the price
was $125,000 for the TV Guest shot from Germany. This
week's *Look* has a nice spread on Elvis from Germany, Tell
Elvis whenever they shoot pictures when he is on duty let
them shoot candid photos only while he is at work and not to
pose all the time when he is dressed up as they are all using
the glamor photos and it makes it rough to work with Victor
on trying to get them to use photos for special gimmicks
where he gets extra royalties. The "Elvis Sails" EP is doing
okay it is just like finding this and I made a special Deal on
royalties for this re-lease which will bring in over Ten
Thousand Dollars in January on this setup, I made a special
deal at 13 cents a copy royalties with One Hundred Thousand
for sure wich [sic] will give us in January around $9,000 for
Elvis flat royalties and since he does not sing on this record
and there are no writers it was a good gimmick wich [sic] I
sold them in September while Elvis did the interview from the
Boat.

We of course are running pretty tight on new re-leases for
1959 and will have to space them out so they hope to last till
we can come up with something new. By holding up the last
single re-lease we surely had a better run on sales as the way
record business is at present it does not take long to overload
the dealers so far we have been very lucky in handling this
without getting the dealers overloaded on any records to date.
Elvis should feel very good about the way we handled the

releasing of King creole merchandise as it surely has paid off the way we handled This, if we had let Sholes release the LP First we would have lost at least 50,000 in royalties from the EP releases wich went well over a Million copies together and are still no 1 and 2 in the Cashbox. Elvis was also voted the No 1 singer of 1958 by Cashbox. Well this is about all the news at present we are working several extra girls to get the fans mail out. Should you call for any reason at all ask for a cable call this way I can understand much better. The best from all of us.

Col.

Chapter 9

1960 to 1962

★   ★   ★   ★

*I*n an Associated Press release of February 25, 1960, entitled, "Presley Won't Change Style of Rock, Roller," Elvis said that there wouldn't be any change in his singing style. "I've no reason to change. The people will let you know when you should." Actually, the decision had already been made to change his style.

As Elvis's discharge date neared, the Colonel lead reporters to believe that a different Elvis would be coming out of the army than went in. "There is going to be a new Elvis, brand new," the Colonel declared. "I don't think he will go back to sideburns and ducktails. He is twenty-five now, and he has genuine adult appeal. I think he is going to surprise everyone and be more popular and more in demand than ever before."

According to longtime friend Marty Lacker, it was Elvis who decided that he wanted to be a crooner after the army. Mario Lanza and Dean Martin were two of his favorite singers.

He had preferred slow songs as far back as his early Sun days. It was Sam Phillips who pushed the rocking side of Elvis.

On March 3, 1960, Elvis left Frankfurt, Germany, on a military transport plane. *Life* magazine wanted to put his picture on its cover upon his discharge from the army. The Colonel asked for a twenty-five-thousand-dollar fee, but offered to refund the fee if the magazine's circulation did not increase by 35 percent for the Elvis issue. *Life* declined, and there was no cover shot.

The Associated Press reported that Elvis left behind a weeping, teenaged girlfriend. She was held back by MPs when she tried to get to Elvis to give him a final good-bye kiss. According to the AP, "In the crowd of several hundred newsmen, photographers and soldiers standing behind rope was Priscilla Beaulieu, daughter of a U.S. Air Force officer, who has been dating the teenage singing idol."

Air Force Capt. Joseph Beaulieu was assigned to the Weisbaden Air Force Base near Friedberg. His wife and two daughters had accompanied him overseas. The oldest daughter, age fourteen, was named Priscilla. Within two weeks of arriving in Friedberg, Priscilla had met Elvis at his home, where she visited every night thereafter until Elvis left Germany.

Priscilla was asked if she and Elvis had marriage plans. She answered, "I'm too young for marriage, but I think Elvis is a wonderful boy. So kind, so considerate, such a gentleman. He gives a girl everything she could possibly wish for."

At a Graceland press conference after his discharge, Elvis was to describe Priscilla as "very mature, very intelligent, and the most beautiful girl I have ever seen. But there is no romance, it is nothing serious."

Elvis's plane arrived at McGuire Air Force Base in New Jersey at 7:42 A.M., March 3, 1960. Lamar Fike and Colonel Parker were at the base to meet him, but relatively few reporters were part of the welcoming party due to a snowstorm. A press conference was held at nearby Fort Dix. In attendance were Tom Diskin, Steve Sholes,

Gene Aberbach, and Nancy Sinatra, who presented Elvis with two shirts, gifts from her father, Frank.

In the two-hour press conference that followed, Elvis told reporters, "My ambition now is to become a good actor." The Colonel was asked what had been Elvis's army salary. He replied that he didn't know since he didn't get a commission on that.

Colonel Parker got into Elvis's schedule for the upcoming year. "He will start work April 26 at Paramount on *G.I. Blues.* Seven pictures are lined up for Elvis including four at Paramount and two with 20th Century-Fox. For *G.I. Blues,* Elvis will get $165,000 plus a percentage of its gross. His second movie with Fox will earn him $250,000, plus 50 percent of the profits, and his third movie, also with Fox, will earn him $300,000 plus 50 percent of the profits," Parker said. "Elvis will get $125,000 for his appearance on the Sinatra show. That is the only TV appearance scheduled. We wouldn't have got these nice movie contracts is Elvis were on TV all the time."

Elvis's last day as a soldier was spent filling out piles of paper and hearing lectures of the rights and responsibilities of veterans. When Elvis was handed his final army paycheck of $145.24, the Colonel yelled, "Don't forget my commission." He was quick to remind the press that the government would get 91 percent of Elvis's check back in taxes. Elvis and the Colonel then hopped into a limousine and set off for New York.

That proved easier said than done, despite the Colonel's meticulous planning. The Colonel said that he had five different ways mapped out that Elvis could have left Fort Dix. "We left nine times from the base," the Colonel said. "To get away from the crowd, we used three station wagons, a bus, and two cars. We were halfway to a New York hotel when a crowd spotted us and started following. We turned around and went back to New Jersey. There were too many cars. I had a helicopter standing by if worse came to worse." In an attempt to throw reporters off the track, reservations were booked for Elvis on both planes and trains leaving New York, Philadelphia, Trenton, Baltimore, and Washington.

The Colonel and Elvis managed to board a train in New York bound for Memphis. It made stops along the way as if Elvis was campaigning for something. From the back platform of the train, Elvis would wave and the Colonel would toss pictures of Elvis in uniform to the crowd. This was the Colonel's way of reintroducing Presley to his fans and why they had taken the train as opposed to a plane, as Vernon and Grandma Presley had done.

In an interview given to the *Memphis Press Scimitar* during the train ride, Elvis blamed the extra sergeant's stripe on his uniform on his tailor. He said that he had given a rush job to a tailor in Germany, and the man had sewed on the wrong insignia. In fact, it was the Colonel who had a uniform made for him with an extra stripe, that of a master sergeant, because he thought it looked better for the cameras. Through some of his connections, the Colonel had also gotten Senator Estes Kefauver of Tennessee to read a speech into the Congressional Record praising Elvis. Elvis was being depicted as the war-hero-come-home.

On March 7, 1960, he finally did arrive home to Memphis. Waiting for him on the steps of Graceland was a commemorative television/stereo console from RCA that the Colonel made sure was presented with all due pomp and flourish. But it wasn't only a television Elvis found at Graceland. Vernon was living there with his girlfriend, Dee Stanley.

There was no way this sat well with the ever publicity-conscious Colonel. How would it look if it got out that Elvis's father was living in sin in Graceland? And it would get out. There were always reporters lurking about. The Colonel issued an order that either Vernon and Dee got married or they would have to leave. The ultimatum was fine with Elvis, who didn't like Dee and didn't want her around. But ever true to his weakness of character, Vernon caved in and married Dee.

Elvis's first order of business was to get into a recording studio. On March 7, *Billboard* magazine reported that "Colonel Tom Parker has taken on increased recording responsibilities to the point where Presley becomes much more isolated from direct Victor authority." On March 20, 1960, Elvis went to Nashville for his first post-army recording session. There was concern that the studio would be mobbed if it was known that Elvis was there. To throw the curious off the trail, the recording session was booked in the name "Silve Yelserp," Elvis Presley spelled backwards. Elvis recorded two songs for the release on a single. They were "Stuck on You" and "Fame and Fortune." RCA had orders for 1,275,077 of the single before it had been recorded.

But before he got into the studio, there were other details to be taken care of. At the top of the list was what should be done to properly welcome him home. The November 6, 1959, issue of the *Memphis Press Scimitar* had published a telegram Elvis sent to Colonel Tom Parker. In it he wrote, "Please convey my thanks to the various groups in Memphis who suggested a special home-coming for me when I returned to Memphis. However, I wish to return to Memphis the same way that any other serviceman returns to his hometown, without ceremony or fanfare. I served as they served and was proud to do it. Seeing the city of Memphis, my family and friends and fans will be the most welcome sight in the world to me. I appreciate their kind gesture and know they will understand and I'm glad that you are in agreement with me on this."

The Colonel was also quoted in the article. He told of a telephone conversation with Elvis on the subject. "Elvis said that there might be four or five guys from Memphis coming out of the army on the same day, and there wouldn't be any big party for them, and he hadn't done any more than they had."

This attitude went along nicely with the "I was just a regular GI doing my duty" line the Colonel had been hand-feeding the press. But there was no way the Colonel wasn't going to capitalize on

Presley's return to private live. A homecoming celebration in Memphis was local; a "party" on television was national.

Joe Esposito tells the story of the Colonel giving Jackie Gleason first crack at the "Welcome Home Elvis" television special. When the Colonel ran the idea past Gleason, he loved it. That is until the Colonel named his asking price, $125,000. "You gotta be out of your mind," Gleason said. This was far more than had ever been paid to an individual for a single television appearance. The Colonel had the perfect rebuttal to Gleason's indignation. "If I was your manager, I'd ask $125,000 for you." Though Gleason had no comeback, he still refused to pay the price.

The Colonel had a definite purpose in mind when he decided to pitch the show to Frank Sinatra. It was part of his effort to present Elvis as a mainstream artist, in both the music world and the movies. Who, at that time, was more mainstream than Sinatra?

Abe Lastfogel introduced the Colonel to Frank Sinatra. Sinatra had fairly regular television specials, but his ratings were dropping. Elvis could give those ratings a tremendous boost by attracting an entirely new audience. Sinatra agreed to pay the $125,000 and to bill the special as "Welcome Home Elvis."

In October 1957, Frank Sinatra was quoted as saying "Rock and roll smells phony and false. It is sung, played, and written for the most part by cretinous goons." When questioned about his decision to have a special center around Elvis in light of his previous criticism of rock and roll, Frank Sinatra said, "That doesn't mean I've changed my attitude toward it. I still don't like it, but after all, the kid's been away two years, and I get the feeling that he really believes in what he's doing. I don't think he needs the gyrations as much as he did. He's established now."

On March 22, Elvis departed Memphis by train, bound for Miami Beach, where the special would be taped. Again, the Colonel turned the trip into something resembling a whistle-stop presidential campaign tour. Elvis made an appearance on the train's rear platform in almost every town along the route. When the train reached Miami, Elvis managed to avoid the five thousand screaming fans waiting for him.

When the Colonel and Elvis arrived for rehearsals, Sinatra informed them of the show's dress code. Sinatra always performed in a tuxedo, and he required everyone on the show to wear one as well. The Colonel informed Sinatra that if he wanted Elvis to wear a tuxedo, he would have to buy one for him. Sinatra sent a tailor to Elvis's hotel suite.

Later that day, comedian Joey Bishop experienced the Colonel's no freebies policy. Bishop was scheduled to appear on the special. He wanted to get an autographed picture of Elvis as a souvenir for his niece. He sent an assistant to Elvis's dressing room to obtain the autograph. A short while later, the man returned mission unaccomplished. He said that when he got to Elvis's dressing room, the Colonel was standing guard at the door. The Colonel asked what he wanted, and he replied that he was there for Elvis's autograph. The Colonel responded that an autograph cost a dollar a picture. The man protested that the autograph was for Joey Bishop. "In that case, the charge for a picture is ten dollars," the Colonel said.

On Saturday, March 26, at a little after six in the evening, the Frank Sinatra special was videotaped from the Grand Ballroom of the Fountainebleu Hotel. There were 700 tickets available. The Colonel gave 400 of them to Elvis's fan club members to ensure the audience would be behind him. But to be extra sure, the ticket recipients had to agree to scream and yell when Elvis came on stage. The Colonel didn't want to leave anything to chance. Elvis didn't need the help. The crowd went wild on their own.

Sinatra and Elvis got along great despite the harsh words that Sinatra had for Elvis in the past. Elvis performed "Fame and Fortune" and "Stuck on You." He also performed a duet with Sinatra of "Witchcraft" and "Love Me Tender." The show got a whopping 41.5 percent rating.

Ed Sullivan made Elvis's Frank Sinatra appearance the subject of one of his columns in the New York *Daily News*. Sullivan observed that the younger singer's fans would probably criticize Ol' Blue Eyes for only letting Elvis sing two songs. Sullivan wrote that, in fact, Colonel Parker was responsible for this. Sullivan had asked the Colonel if he had insisted on Elvis's limited appearance. "I certainly did," the Colonel answered.

It was expected that the Colonel would take Elvis on a national concert tour after the television special. However, he had a completely different plan. The Colonel had more faith in the long-term potential of movies than he did in rock and roll. He felt that Elvis would have to be brought more in line with the mainstream if he were to have a long career in Hollywood. In the beginning, the Colonel had cultivated the controversy surrounding Elvis because he thought that it was good for business. Now the controversy surrounding rock music was getting too intense for him, having become the subject of congressional hearings. Brooklyn Congressman Emmanuel Cellar said, "The music of Elvis Presley and his animal gyrations are violative of all that I know to be in good taste." The Colonel would pull Elvis off the concert stage where most of his controversy was generated. Fans would see their idol on the silver screen. The movie sound stage was an environment the Colonel could control.

The Colonel's plan for Elvis's career when he got out of the army completely revolved around the movies. He mapped out a simple formula for Elvis. He would make three movies a year. Each movie would produce a soundtrack album. These albums would fulfill Elvis's commitment to RCA. The title song of each movie would be played enough in promotion for the movie to turn it into a hit. The one hit in turn would sell the album. After the surge of exposure for Elvis with the release of the movie and the album, the Colonel would withdraw him completely into seclusion. Elvis would remain hidden from the public for four months, building a frenzy of demand to see him again. The movie/album cycle would then start over again.

The Colonel had begun to renegotiate Elvis's movie contract even before he had shipped out for Germany. The first meeting was a surprise visit by the Colonel and Tom Diskin to Joe Hazen's office. It was then that the Colonel got Hazen to buy 500,000 pictures of Elvis in his army uniform, explaining that Elvis needed to supplement his income while he was away.

Of course, the Colonel pocketed the money.

The Colonel resumed his negotiations with Hazen in the late summer of 1958. He regaled Hazen with stories of the many film offers that he was receiving. He said that a German producer had offered $250,000 to shoot an Elvis movie on weekends. He also claimed that Loew's had a standing offer to pay Elvis $250,000 plus 50 percent of the profits to make a movie for them when he got out of the army. Then the Colonel got to his real point. He informed Hazen that when a man was inducted into the army and was unable to comply with an existing contract, the contract could not be extended. It was automatically void, and a man could walk away from it. Having made his point, the Colonel quickly reassured Hazen that he wouldn't press that issue.

That night, Abe Lastfogel called Joe Hazen to arrange a meeting the next day. When he and the Colonel arrived, he made it clear that the Colonel had changed his mind about voiding the contract. In the opinion of the William Morris Agency's attorney, the contract had indeed ended when Elvis entered the army.

Joe Hazen got an opinion from his own attorney and said that the contract was still valid. He contacted Hal Wallis and recommended that he pursue the matter in court, if necessary. For his part, Wallis had no desire to battle the Colonel. He preferred compromise. Colonel Parker signed the new contract "you know who."

While Elvis was busy driving a Jeep in Germany, the Colonel was in Hollywood playing with the future of his career. He, Hal

Wallis, and Lastfogel developed the master plan for the post-army Elvis. They envisioned him becoming a movie star/pop singer/comedian in the mold of Bing Crosby and Dean Martin. The Colonel felt that Elvis's audience was too narrow. He was afraid that the teenage girls who loved the wild rebellious Elvis might have grown up and lost interest in him. Elvis's discharge from the army provided the perfect opportunity to recast him as the ex-soldier, wholesome, boy next door.

The Colonel literally cast Elvis in the role of a soldier in his next movie. On April 18, 1960, Elvis left Memphis by train bound for Los Angeles and the filming of *G.I. Blues*. As was his habit, the Colonel notified all the towns along the way, and as was his habit, Elvis signed autographs on the rear platform at each stop while the Colonel passed out pictures and other promotional paraphernalia.

During the filming of *G.I. Blues*, Elvis complained about the excessive number of songs in the movie. He felt that the majority of them weren't any good and should be removed. He called Priscilla in Germany and expressed his displeasure. Priscilla recounted the conversation in her book, *Elvis and Me*. "'I just finished looping the God damned picture and I hate it. They had about twelve songs in it that aren't worth a cat's ass,' he said angrily. 'I feel like a damned idiot breaking into a song while I'm talking to some chick on a train. They seem to think it's wonderful. I'm damned miserable.'"

The Colonel's response was to say that they had already been paid for the movie, and there was nothing that he could do about it. In reality, the Colonel had been working on Hal Wallis behind the scenes to ensure that the movie was full of songs. He cared little about the quality: only their presence concerned him.

On the set of *G.I. Blues*, Colonel Parker was seen wearing a bright pink satin shirt with Elvis embroidered in giant letters on the back. The sign on his office door at the studio read, "Snow Division." By "snow," the Colonel meant con. Nothing gave the

Colonel more pleasure than coming up on top in a deal. It was twice the fun if he could con someone in the process. He so loved the art of the con that he started a club to celebrate it. There is an organization of circus executives called the International Showman's Association. It is a quality-control organization dedicated to maintaining a positive image for their industry. The Colonel parodied it by starting the Snowman's League of America. He appointed himself the "Chief Potentate." The Snowman's League was dedicated to the art of the con.

According to Elvis's cousin Billy Smith, the Colonel thought he could snow anyone. He called himself "The Snowman" or "Colonel Snow" and even kept a giant snowman in his office. In fact, his nom-de-plume in Las Vegas casinos was "Mr. Snow."

He had membership cards and rule booklets printed up. Some of the rules of the Snowman's League were, "Any of our members have to be good enough snowers so they can make up their own snow stories without calling on any of the top snowers." "There are no dues. There are no alms. There are no bylaws, only in-laws, and they don't belong to the snow club." The Colonel joked that the Snowman's League cost nothing to get into, but cost one thousand dollars to leave.

One Christmas, the Colonel mailed sheets of his Elvis and The Colonel Christmas postcards to reporters across the U.S. and enclosed a note requesting that they cut apart the cards on the sheets and mail them to their friends. Of course, the Colonel did not send stamps. They were to provide postage themselves. Some of the reporters went along with it. Many others criticized the tactic in print. The Colonel didn't care. He had snowed them into putting his and Elvis's name in the paper. As far as he was concerned, publicity was always good if it was free.

The Colonel drew satisfaction from being extraordinarily offensive. He would invite Abe Lastfogel, who was Jewish, to his house for dinner and then serve pork to see what he would do. He also

Elvis being discharged from the army.

Elvis with the Colonel én route to Memphis after leaving the army.

The Colonel presenting Elvis with a welcome home gift.

Elvis leaving the train in Miami. Destination: the Frank Sinatra "Welcome Home Elvis" television special.

Gladys and Vernon Presley sorting through their son's fan mail.

Elvis and the Colonel with an adoring fan.

Elvis, Colonel Parker, and director Philip Dunne, at the cast party for the film *Wild in the Country*.

On *The Ed Sullivan Show*.

After being pressured by sponsors, Steve Allen attempted to tone down Elvis's highly sexualized act by having him perform "Hound Dog" to an actual hound dog.

Elvis serenading Ann-Margret in the film *Viva Las Vegas*. Some speculate she was Elvis's only true love.

Despite appearing
here as happy newly-
weds, it is said that the
Colonel pressured
Elvis into his union
with Priscilla, believ-
ing that it would be
good for his image.

Lisa Marie Presley,
shown here just weeks
before her father's
death, completed the
image of the happy
family.

Upon accepting FDR's yacht as a charitable donation from Elvis on behalf of the St. Jude's Children's hospital, Danny Thomas was quoted as saying, "Why did you buy this piece of crap?"

Elvis was set to play at the White House until Colonel Parker's insistence on a $25,000 fee forced a Nixon staff member to retract the offer.

Despite Colonel Parker's insistence on charging a fee for all performances, Elvis himself paid all expenses at a benefit concert for the Elvis
Presley Youth Recreation Center so that all proceeds could go directly to
the charity.

An early Presley performance.

Elvis in full gold lamè regalia, circa 1957.

For Elvis's engagement at the Las Vegas Hilton, Colonel Parker had enormous signs constructed and strategically placed so they could be seen from every highway in Las Vegas.

Elvis arriving for his "Aloha from Hawaii" concert special.

The King's Graceland Estate.

The Colonel working on his tan.

Priscilla and Vernon Presley unveil an Elvis statue at a convention in September 1978.

loved practical jokes. During the filming of *G.I. Blues*, he attached a microphone to a pineapple. He walked around his hotel lobby telling people that he was with the Pineapple Network and asked to interview them.

In another snow job, the Colonel pretended that he had psychic powers. He talked some of the Memphis Mafia into playing along with him. They would act like he had hypnotized them and would engage in all manner of embarrassing acts. This included barking like a dog and quacking like a duck.

The Colonel was fond of telling stories, most of which undoubtedly swerved dramatically from the truth. "A guy asked me one time if I could get him an elephant," the Colonel said. "I asked him why only one? I could get him a better deal if he could use twelve. Then I found out that he did not have the money to buy even one. He told me how sorry he was for taking up my time and then wound up buying one of my Shetland ponies. I told him I would give him credit for what he paid for the pony if he ever wanted to buy an elephant. I never heard from him again, but I understand that the pony was doing pretty well."

Another Colonel Parker story went, "I had a guy call me in New York, and he sounded like he was going to crawl through the phone asking me if I would be interested in selling my life story. I told him that I was already writing a book on this and was presently selling advertising in my book. He asked me how much it would take if he bought a 50 percent interest in my book. I told him, $100,000. He waited a few seconds. I asked him if he was still on the phone. He said, yes, but I must be nuts. I told him that he could be right, but for $100,000, it did not matter.

"He said he would have to talk to me about it in person. I told him that I would have to charge him for my time at, at least, $2,500 per hour. He said, 'What about thirty minutes?' I said it would still be $2,500. He asked me something else, but I could not answer him as I did not know if he was good for the money. So I hung up.

I hope you agree with me that I did the right thing. After all, I do not want to cheat anyone."

At times Elvis found the Colonel's high jinks amusing. He loved to tell the story of the time when the Colonel played fortune-teller at a negotiation with movie executives. The Colonel was scheduled for a 9:00 A.M. appointment at the studio. He intentionally was fifteen minutes late to put everyone on edge.

He burst into the boardroom with his chief assistant, Tom Diskin, at his side. One of the studio executives began discussing the proposed contract. The Colonel cut him off in midsentence. "Diskin, let me have the ball!" he said. Diskin placed a bowling-ball bag on the table, unzipped it, and pulled out a fortune-teller's crystal ball. The Colonel gazed into it and began to rub it. "Let me see . . . that will be $1 million for Mr. Presley and $100,000 for the Colonel," he pronounced. "Mr. Diskin does the ball ever lie?" "No sir, Colonel!" Diskin answered. "Gentlemen, that's our deal," the Colonel said. With that, he left the room. Tom Diskin packed up the crystal ball and followed him out the door.

Elvis's original contract with the Hal Wallis was up upon the completion of *G.I. Blues*. The new contract that the Colonel signed with Wallis was for six years and six movies, and it outlined the fluff that the films were to be. They would "present the new mature Elvis in a series of pictures set in exotic locations."

The Colonel's commitment to Wallis for an extended period was not in line with his former strategy of rationing the Elvis product as a negotiating tactic. It would have been a smarter move to negotiate one picture at a time, and in that way, the Colonel could have used the box office success of one picture as a negotiating tool for the next. He could have shopped around Hollywood looking for the best deal. When the Colonel realized his mistake, he tried to renegotiate with Wallis to no avail.

Hal Wallis's desire to tie up Elvis with a long-term contract is easy to understand. Most of the movies earned four to five million dollars. Wallis received one million dollars a year or more in profits from the films. They were such certain moneymakers that Wallis would put their future profits up as collateral to borrow money to make other films. Wallis had no delusions that he was making art with Elvis's movies. "The Presley pictures were made, of course, for a strictly commercial reason," he said. However, the Colonel and Wallis lost sight of one important factor. Elvis's strength as a box office draw was based on his being the king of rock and roll. Over time, the "guaranteed" box office started to slip.

Fortunately, the Colonel had kept the clause in the new Wallis contract allowing Elvis to make movies for other producers. MGM became the other studio the Colonel favored. Parker liked MGM because the studio's Sam Katzman had the reputation of making very low budget movies. The Colonel negotiated a contract with MGM that gave Elvis a percentage of his movies' profits. The lower the cost, the Colonel reasoned, the greater the profits. The audience seemed to be proving the Colonel right by continuing to pay to see these movies, no matter how weak the plot.

Soon after the new contract was signed, the Colonel approached Wallis with two bizarre ideas for films. Both contained several elements of the Colonel's own life story. For example, both were set in Hawaii, the site of much of the Colonel's army service. The plot of the first centered around Elvis being a stowaway on a ship from an unknown country to Hawaii. Probably, this was similar to Parker's own travel by ship to the United States.

The second plot was obviously based on the Colonel's relationship with Elvis. The story begins with Elvis escaping from his fans by disappearing into the jungle, where he dons a disguise so he won't be recognized by the natives. His record company panics because they have no more songs to release. There are a group of promoters in the jungle who recognize Elvis, but don't let on to him who they are. They get him to perform for the natives and secretly record his singing. They then ship these tapes to the outside world to be sold under a different name.

Elvis finally comes out of seclusion to perform in Honolulu. Once there, he realizes that the jungle promoters had taken advantage of him. These stories aren't exactly the stuff from which Academy Awards spring. Hal Wallis politely thanked the Colonel for his input and tossed the outlines in the trash. He did like the idea of Hawaii as a location, and filed it away for a future Elvis project.

When Priscilla talked to Elvis after *G.I. Blues*, she learned that Elvis was still unhappy with his movie career. He believed that he was capable of performing more demanding roles than he was getting, and to prepare himself, he still studied certain actors whom he admired such as James Dean in *Giant* and Marlon Brando in *On The Waterfront* and *The Wild One*.

When the Colonel signed a deal with 20th Century-Fox, it seemed that Elvis would at last get the kind of opportunity that he craved. The agreement was for Elvis to make two movies for Fox, *Flaming Star* and *Wild in the Country*. Both were to be serious dramatic films with quality directors, good screenplays, and decent budgets.

When director David Weisbart first read the script for *Flaming Star*, he thought that it had the potential to gain acceptance for Elvis as a serious actor. When Weisbart touted the script to the Colonel, he was told that the Colonel was not interested in reading it. He never read Elvis's scripts. "If we start telling people what to do, they could blame us if the picture doesn't go. As it is, we both take bows if it hits, and if doesn't, they get more blame maybe than us. Anyway, what do I know about production?"

The only thing the Colonel wanted was plenty of songs. Weisbart protested that there were no logical places in the script for songs. Parker reminded him that songs would generate $100,000 in free publicity for the movie. Weisbart finally gave in and said that a song could be sung over the opening credits. A script was sent to the writers at Hill and Range to come up with a suitable tune.

But one song wasn't good enough for the Colonel. He wanted at least four included in *Flaming Star*, any less and there wouldn't be enough for an EP, much less a soundtrack album. Four songs were filmed to satisfy the Colonel's demand. However, the director was interested in a serious movie, not a musical, so he cut two of the songs at editing. This was fine with Elvis who wanted the focus to be on his acting. The Colonel didn't take it nearly as well, but there was nothing that he could do about it.

Flaming Star opened on December 22, 1960. In general, the movie and Elvis received good reviews. The *Hollywood Reporter* called *Flaming Star* "first rate entertainment." The *Los Angeles Examiner* said that the movie was "an extremely pleasant picture" and "should open up a whole new audience for Elvis."

While the reviews were good, the box office receipts were poor. The weak box office further emphasized to the Colonel the need to stick to the Elvis movie formula. Although it did not actually lose money, *Flaming Star* was a disaster by the standards of Elvis movies. If *Wild in the Country* did not prove successful, the "experiment" of Elvis the serious actor would be laid to rest. The Colonel wanted him in the movies to make money, not art.

Wild in the Country was initially to be a serious movie with a bare minimum of singing. As usual, the Colonel's concern revolved around the number of songs in the movie, or rather, the lack thereof. Director Philip Dunne did not like Colonel Parker and went out of his way to avoid him. This was made difficult by the Colonel's presence on the set every day. The Colonel's relationship with Dunne worsened as the filming went on. Dunne wanted the only song in the movie to be the one that played over the opening credits.

The Colonel went over Dunne's head to 20th Century-Fox President Spyros Skouras. He persuaded Skouras to overrule Dunne. More songs were inserted into the film. In Dunne's opinion, the romantic potential of the film had been ruined. *Wild in the Country* had become just another Elvis movie. Dunne later said, "What I had against Parker was that he was a tasteless man who had power and abused it."

The Colonel may have won the battle, but he had lost the war. The result was a miserable failure. On one hand, the movie was too serious for the fans of Elvis's cutsie musicals. On the other, the insertion of songs made the movie fail with the audience that might have been receptive to it as serious drama.

The battle with Dunne and the Colonel's complaints had left a bad taste in Spyros Skouras's mouth. Twentieth Century-Fox never hired Elvis for another movie. For his part, the Colonel was none to happy with the way things had gone at Fox. He turned down an invitation to attend the premiere of *Wild in the Country* on behalf of himself and Elvis. When asked why they did not attend, the Colonel said, "Unless we can do our own show, we don't go." The Colonel wasn't overly concerned over Fox's lack of interest in working with him anymore. He already had other studios beating down his door to get Elvis.

Reviews for *Wild in the Country* were generally bad. *Variety* said, "Dramatically there isn't a great deal of substance, novelty or spring to the somewhat wobbly and artificial tale." The *New York Times* said "Even with Mr. Presley in the cast, it should have been at least an honest drama if not a particularly brilliant one, it isn't. It is shamelessly dishonest. Indeed it is downright gross in its sacred distortion of human values and social relations."

Wild in the Country ended up making a profit, but the margin was slim in comparison to Elvis's other movies. The Colonel blamed the movie's failure completely on its serious dramatic nature. *Flaming Star*, another "serious movie attempt," had done poorly at the box office also. The Colonel used the disappointing receipts to persuade Elvis and the studios that they needed to stick with a singing formula if they wanted to make money.

As 1961 rolled around, the Colonel decided to return Elvis to the concert stage for his first two stage appearances since going into the army. Both would serve as publicity gimmicks rather than revenue generators.

At a press conference, the Colonel announced that Elvis would be performing in his hometown of Memphis at Ellis Auditorium on February 25, 1961. The concert was to be a benefit for Memphis charities. Originally only one performance was scheduled. However, ticket demand was so great that a matinee performance was added.

Unlike most charity concerts, Elvis paid all expenses so that every dollar taken in at the box office went to charity. The charities included the Elvis Presley Youth Center in Tupelo, Mississippi, the city where Elvis was born, as well as the *Memphis Press Scimitar*'s Cynthia Milk Fund, the Crippled Children's Hospital, Happy Acres, Goodwill Industries, the Jewish Community Center, the Junior League, Neighborhood House, Orange Mound Day Nursery for Negroes, St. Jude Hospital Foundation, the Salvation Army, Boys Town, the Memphis Mother's Service, and the Abe Charff branch of the YMCA for Negroes.

Before the benefit concert, RCA gave a luncheon in Elvis's honor. Attendees paid $100 per plate, with the proceeds going to charity. The governor of Tennessee, Buford Ellington, and the mayor of Memphis, Henry Locke, were in attendance. George Jessel was the celebrity speaker. RCA presented Elvis with a plaque in recognition of his selling seventy-five million records.

Later that day, Elvis gave the concerts at Ellis Auditorium. One at 3:00 P.M. and one at 8:30 P.M. Sharing the bill were country comedian Brother Dave Gardner, impressionist N. P. Nelson, Larry Owen and his orchestra, a troop of acrobats, and a tap dancer. Colonel Parker advertised that Elvis would sing twenty songs. He sang exactly twenty. In total, the day's events raised fifty-one thousand dollars for charity.

Elvis's next appearance was in Hawaii in March. The Colonel conceived of the concert when he read a story in the *Los Angeles Herald-Examiner* that asked for donations to build a memorial to the USS *Arizona*, a battleship sunk during the Japanese sneak attack on Pearl Harbor.

In 1949, the Pacific War Memorial Commission had been created. Among its various goals was to build a memorial structure in the water above the wreckage of the *Arizona*. On March 15, 1958, Congress finally authorized construction of the memorial, which was to be funded through donations. The projected cost of the project was $500,000. Three hundred thousand had already been raised when the appeal was made for additional funding.

Having been hit with the idea of Elvis performing a benefit concert in Hawaii for the memorial, Colonel Parker duly went there to negotiate with the chairman of the Arizona Memorial Committee, Tucker Grantz. The show was set for March 25, 1961.

The Colonel stipulated that all proceeds must go to the memorial, and further, there be no freebies. Tickets were priced at several levels, and everybody paid, even Elvis and the Colonel, who each bought ten top-priced, $100 tickets. When an aide to a navy admiral inquired about the admiral's seating arrangement, the Colonel replied, "What kind of tickets does he want to buy?" The aide said, "The admiral does not buy tickets." To which the Colonel replied, "Maybe somebody will buy him some because everybody pays. Elvis pays, I pay, everybody pays." The admiral decided to buy ten $100 tickets.

The Colonel seemed to particularly enjoy telling the officers that they could not have free tickets. A disc jockey, Ron Jacob, who was present at a meeting between the Colonel and military officers, related how he had spoken to them. "The Colonel started snowing on them about how important they were to the security of the world and how patriotic and so on, and if they would line up, he would give them a little something from Elvis. So, they lined up, all of these guys in charge of the security of the Pacific, and Colonel went over to the trunk and carefully, almost secretly, pulled some tiny Elvis pictures out and very stingily doled them out, one to each admiral and general."

In talking about the 1961 USS *Arizona* concert, the Colonel said "I have never worked as hard in my lifetime. If it was my own commercial show, I could not have worked harder." In promoting the concert, the Colonel returned to one of his favorite promotional stunts, midgets. During a radio interview, he announced that the first Hawaiian midget who came to the station would get free tickets to the show. He knew that there were few full-blooded Hawaiians anyway and even fewer midgets. No one came forward to claim their tickets.

The Colonel was able to get many companies to give plugs for the concert in their radio spots. Sears, Roebuck put them in all their ads without charge.

The Colonel was very loud about telling the press how much money he and Elvis were spending on the benefit. When everything was totaled, fifty-four thousand dollars had to be paid in expenses for travel, hotel, food, talent, etc. Out of their own pockets, Elvis paid half and the Colonel paid half so the benefit would be 100 percent for the Arizona memorial.

The morning of the concert, there were still some 100 seats left. Colonel Parker announced that he and Elvis would buy fifty of these tickets if H. Tucker Gregg, chairman of the Pacific War Memorial Commission, could sell fifty others by show time. The tickets purchased by the Colonel were donated to hospital patients. All six thousand seats were sold for the concert. More than $100,000 was raised for the memorial.

When Elvis arrived in Honolulu on March 25, 1961, more than three thousand fans were at the airport to see him. The concert was given that night at the Block Arena. Elvis wore his gold-lamé jacket for the occasion. He performed for forty-five minutes, singing fifteen songs, ending with a five-and-one-half minute version of "Hound Dog." It would be the last song he would sing in front of a live audience for a long time.

The Hawaii House of Representatives formally thanked Elvis and the Colonel. Colonel Parker sent a wire to Lyndon Johnson, then the vice president of the United States, advising, "Now, more than ever, we feel it proper to let you know that we are willing, able and available to serve in any way we can, our country and our president in any capacity. Whether it is to use our talents or help load trucks."

Elvis would not make another concert appearance for seven years. The Colonel saw Elvis's future as lying in the movies. On March 27, 1961, Elvis started filming *Blue Hawaii*.

The Colonel was fond of inserting all sorts of bizarre clauses into movie contracts. One called for Elvis to be paid an additional twenty-five thousand dollars if he wore any of his own clothes in the movie. This clause was invoked during the filming of *Blue Hawaii*. The Colonel ran right in front of the camera during the middle of shooting. He shouted to the director that Elvis was wearing his own watch. If they put any part of him wearing the watch in the movie, they would have to pay the twenty-five thousand. The director had Elvis take off his watch, and they refilmed the scene.

The Colonel was fond of Elvis's *Blue Hawaii* co-star Angela Lansbury. Every year for years after *Blue Hawaii* was made, Angela Lansbury would receive a Mother's Day card from Elvis. She never was sure if it came from him or the Colonel.

Instead of walking around the movie set in a suit and tie, as most managers did, the Colonel was just as likely to be wearing a giant robe with "Elvis, Elvis, Elvis" printed all over it. If someone questioned the professionalism of the Colonel's attire, he would tell them that they must not be reading the name he had printed on his outfit close enough. It said Elvis Presley. He was Elvis Presley's manager. He did not need to wear a suit to signify that he was a professional. His client's name said it all.

Anyone could make an Elvis movie as long as they came up with enough money to satisfy the Colonel. Brothers Harold and Walter Mirisch found that it took a considerable sum to make the Colonel happy. The Mirisch brothers owned an independent production company. Their films were distributed by United Artists and included *West Side Story* and *The Magnificent Seven.*

When the Colonel and Abe Lastfogel met with the Mirisch brothers to discuss a contract, the Colonel made it clear that they could make any kind of movie they wanted. He was only concerned with being in control of the music used in the film. If they met these conditions, he would be happy to sign a two-movie deal for $1 million per movie. At first, the Mirisch brothers were taken aback by this figure. However, meetings with United Artists convinced them that it was worth taking a chance. Elvis's first movie for them was *Follow That Dream.* The movie was successful at the box office and set a pattern for future Elvis movies.

When dealing with movie executives, the Colonel would often use fits of rage as a diversionary tactic to get what he wanted. When Elvis arrived on a location shoot in Florida for *Follow That Dream,* his trailer was the same size as the other actors. In the Colonel's eyes, Elvis, as the star, deserved a bigger trailer. He ordered one that was several feet longer than the others and billed it to the studio. The day the trailer was delivered, the Colonel threw a tirade at the director for not being informed of the time that Elvis would be breaking for lunch. Not wanting to anger the Colonel further, no one questioned him about the trailer. It had gone just as the Colonel had planned.

While Elvis was filming *Follow That Dream* in 1961, a group of people in Crystal River, Florida, asked the Colonel if Elvis would attend a party and sign autographs. The Colonel didn't particularly want to get his star involved in such an unstarlike undertaking, but he hated to say no to anyone who wanted to hire Elvis. As always, his policy was to ask for so much money that they would say no to him. Occasionally someone would accept one of the Colonel's ridiculous demands, and he would be forced to go through with the bargain. The Colonel said that Elvis would be happy to appear at the party for ten thousand dollars. He was stunned when they agreed to meet his price. Elvis attended the party and signed autographs for two hours.

Chapter 10

1963 to 1967

★ ★ ★ ★

*I*n 1963, the Colonel negotiated a five-year contract for Elvis with Metro-Goldwyn-Mayer. The contract made Elvis the highest paid actor in Hollywood. As with other studios, the quality of the Presley pictures were of no concern to MGM. The movies would be very cheaply made and very short on plot. An MGM studio executive said of their Elvis movies, "They could be numbered instead of titled, and they would still sell."

As expected, the Colonel put MGM officials through an ordeal before he signed the contract. He loved to turn every negotiation into a game. One of his bargaining ploys was to give tentative approval to a deal for which the studio would create a document. When the contract was presented for signature, he would make changes that would necessitate the contract being completely rewritten. He would repeat this process several times before finally signing the deal. The final contract, even though it had been rewritten several times, ended up being almost identical to the original draft. The Colonel had been playing his game of control.

His final jab came when the contract was delivered to him. Normally the papers were delivered to the Colonel by a courier. The Colonel would send the courier back to the studio with the contract and instructions that if they wanted him to sign, they better have the president of the studio deliver it himself.

On July 13, 1963, Elvis began filming *Viva Las Vegas*. During its production, the Colonel met an unfamiliar obstacle to his customary side deals. He offered to provide the security force for the film. The producer, Jack Cummings, turned him down. Next, the Colonel offered to secure the Sahara Hotel, which was run by his friend, Milton Prell, as a site for much of the location shooting. Of course, Prell was going to hand some money the Colonel's way. Cummings again turned down the Colonel, saying that the Sahara was not suitable. He had already made an arrangement with the Flamingo.

Now enraged, the Colonel began to nitpick. He demanded that an entire production number be reshot because the cameras had failed to capture Elvis's feet. Cummings refused, and the Colonel tried to go over his head. Unfortunately for the Colonel, Cummings was even better connected than he. His father-in-law had been Louis B. Mayer. The Colonel lost, and the scene was not reshot.

Next the Colonel complained that Ann-Margret was getting too much camera time. It seemed that the director was just as infatuated with her as Elvis was. To make matters worse, he wanted Elvis and Ann-Margret to sing together. The Colonel informed the producer that he would have to pay Elvis extra money to sing a duet. Again, the Colonel was rebuffed. Parker became so angry that he tried to sell Elvis's 50 percent share in the movie's profits. Fortunately for Elvis, he was unsuccessful. *Viva Las Vegas* was one of Elvis's higher grossing movies.

It was convenient for the Colonel to conduct business while he kept on eye on the filming of *Viva Las Vegas* thanks to the suite of offices MGM had provided for him on the lot. In the Colonel's personal office, elephant knickknacks were almost as prevalent as images of Elvis. Instead of chairs for guests, he had stools that resembled elephants' feet.

The Colonel often told of how he fell in love with elephants. According to his story, he found himself stranded in a faraway town with no money to eat on or to pay his hotel bill. He managed to find an elephant and used it as a promotion for a local grocery store. The grocery store paid him enough to cover several days of food and his hotel room. From that time on, he had a special place in his heart for the pachyderms.

The Colonel would begin every day with a meeting of his staff. Present at most were Tom Diskin, George Parkhill, and Jim O'Brien. Diskin had joined the Colonel before Elvis did. The Colonel paid him well, but doled out considerable abuse in return. The Colonel believed that money was the best way to create loyalty. George Parkhill was hired away from RCA. He was a very sharp dresser and had a sort of regal air. He was less tolerant than anyone else of the Colonel's harassing. Jim O'Brien was the Colonel's secretary. The Colonel found him working for Hill and Range.

The Colonel ran his outfit like it was the military. Even though he had known Tom Diskin for years, he never referred to him by his first name. When he wanted him, he would bark out, "Diskin!" The Colonel would often say, "Isn't that right, Diskin?" Diskin would answer like a private responding to his commanding officer. "That's right, Colonel!"

Even the Colonel's brother-in-law, Bitsy Mott, was not immune from the Colonel's military style of command. "You are on twenty-four hours a day when you are under his wing. It is an awful strain. Of course, he put a strain on himself by trying to be on top of everybody including his star performer. He did it because it was his way.

The Colonel could operate on almost no sleep. He could sleep two hours and be as fresh as I would be after eight hours. He is the most active person I have been around. He just never gets tired. He has an abundance of energy. He can just go and go. Sometimes he would wear me out," Mott said.

The Colonel always wanted it to appear that he had a hundred projects going on at once whenever an outsider came to visit him at his office. When the Colonel had an appointment, or even if he heard someone walking down the hall, he would bark out the command for everyone to "get busy." This meant that everyone had to immediately start doing something whether it be making an imaginary phone call or typing a letter to no one.

As a part of his look-busy operation, the Colonel had a ticker tape installed. He had a button that he could push under his desk to make it start printing tape. When a visitor entered, the Colonel would be pouring over the blank tape as if it contained information of a life-and-death nature.

The Colonel would conduct evacuation drills that he referred to as fire drills. He practiced his staff to a point where they could have his entire office packed and moved out in fifteen minutes. The message that the Colonel wanted to send to the studio was that if they upset him, that's how long it would take for him and Elvis to be gone.

After the meeting every morning, the Colonel would telephone his wife, Marie. Marie Parker rarely traveled with her husband. She did not like being on the road. Her passion was cats. Her favorite was named Midnight. The Colonel did not like Marie's cats. Lamar Fike was at Colonel Parker's house in Palm Springs one day when Marie Parker came in hysterical. Midnight had climbed up on the roof. The Colonel said he would come down on his own sooner or later. Marie went outside, but returned in a few minutes. Midnight was still on the roof, and the Colonel needed to do something to get him down. Parker walked outside, turned on a hose as big as one used by the fire department, and blew the cat off the roof.

By the time that the Colonel was finished talking with Marie, it would be time for lunch. One of the Colonel's favorite pastimes was eating. Some of the "trainees" provided by William Morris would serve as waiters. The Colonel would order ten times as much as he could possibly eat just because someone else was paying for it. All of the activity in the office would stop, and the entire entourage would gather for the feast. The Colonel would often have Abe Lastfogel, by now the chairman of the William Morris Agency, join him for lunch when he was in Hollywood. He had a director's chair made for Lastfogel with the Colonel's nickname for him, "The Admiral," printed on the back.

The Colonel turned the conference room of his MGM office into a replica of the mess hall from his carnival days. MGM had furnished the Colonel with a giant mahogany table. He turned this beautiful table into the dining table for the mess hall. A crony was dispatched to find an old oilcloth that was large enough to cover it. He pressured his business associates into donating the remainder of the items for his mess hall. RCA got the word that the Colonel would be appreciative if they would supply him with appliances. RCA came through with a complete kitchen, including freezer and stove.

With a movie ready for release, the Colonel cranked up his Elvis publicity machine. He often returned to one of his favorite gimmicks for getting Elvis in the newspapers, a charitable contribution. Elvis freely gave to various charities. On some occasions though, Colonel Parker helped Elvis decide where to make his donations in the interest of publicity. For example, in late 1963, the Colonel heard that Franklin Roosevelt's presidential yacht, the *Potomac*, was for sale. If a buyer could not be found, the yacht was scheduled to be destroyed. The Colonel thought that it would be a good publicity stunt for Elvis to save the famous boat from destruction. At the his suggestion, Elvis bought the yacht for fifty-five thousand dollars on January 20, 1964.

The *Potomac* was in complete disrepair. It needed to be painted so that it would look good when it was photographed for the newspapers. When he was told that it would take eighteen thousand dollars to paint the entire boat, the Colonel instructed that only one side be painted. He had the boat roped off so that no one could get close enough to see the unpainted rear.

Colonel Parker then decided that the *Potomac* should be given to charity to create yet another media event. But, giving the boat away was not easy. It was in such bad condition that the cost of restoring it would exceed its value. Even the March of Dimes, FDR's pet charity, refused to accept it.

Finally, actor/entertainer Danny Thomas agreed to accept the *Potomac* on behalf of St. Jude's Children's Hospital in Memphis. In news reports about the yacht, Tom Diskin claimed that several groups had asked for it, but Elvis chose St. Jude's. At the donation ceremony, while they were both smiling for the cameras, Thomas reportedly whispered to Elvis, "Why did you buy this piece of crap?"

In 1964, Elvis's first real competition for the title of king of rock and roll emerged. Oddly enough, the contender hailed from England. Four young men calling themselves the Beatles generated hysteria and record sales like no one had except Elvis.

The Colonel went on the offensive. He wanted to make it clear that he and Elvis did not fear the Beatles. He sent a telegram to them on the occasion of their first appearance on *The Ed Sullivan Show*. Sullivan read it on the air. It was a good luck message and was signed Elvis and the Colonel. Elvis, in fact, had no idea that the Colonel had sent the telegram. The Colonel wanted to use the public reading as a way of saying that he and Elvis were not threatened by the Beatles.

When the Fab Four arrived in America, they gave a press conference in which they said that the thing they most wanted to do while they were here was meet Elvis. As it turned out, they didn't get the chance on that tour, but they did get a present from the

Colonel. Instead of providing Elvis, he sent the Beatles four cowboy suits complete with guns and holsters.

Chris Hutchinson, a reporter for the British magazine *New Musical Express*, revived the idea of the Beatles meeting Elvis during their 1965 visit to America. He knew that the meeting would create a fantastic story. Hutchinson approached the Beatles's manager, Brian Epstein, with the idea. Epstein was agreeable under the condition that Hutchinson keep the meeting a secret until after it had happened. Of course, Hutchinson was willing to comply because he wanted the story to be his exclusive. Hutchinson would be allowed to come along for the visit, but had to leave his camera and tape recorder at home.

Brian Epstein was charged with calling the Colonel and making the arrangements. Epstein was ashamed to admit that he didn't have the Colonel's telephone number. Fortunately, someone came to the rescue, and Epstein put the call through.

Of course, the Colonel had a demand to which Epstein acquiesced. The Beatles would have to come to Elvis rather than Elvis going to them. It was agreed that the meeting would take place August 26, in Los Angeles. The Beatles would be town to perform at the Hollywood Bowl.

According to his associates, when the Colonel first proposed that Elvis meet the Beatles, his response was "Hell no. I don't want to meet them sons-of-bitches!" Elvis finally relented. Joe Esposito told of the maneuverings that went over arrangements.

Elvis was in the middle of filming *Paradise Hawaiian Style* for Paramount when the Colonel asked Esposito to come to his office on the lot.

When Esposito arrived, he was introduced to Malcolm Evans, the Beatles's road manager. The Colonel asked Esposito to take Evans to the set and introduce him to Elvis.

On the way to the sound stage, Evans informed Esposito that the Colonel and Brian Epstein, the Beatles' manager, were arranging for Elvis and the Beatles to get together. When they reached Elvis, he confirmed a meeting would take place at his house the following week. Esposito says that Elvis acted very excited over the prospect when Evans was around, but actually, he had no interest in meeting the Beatles.

A few days later, the Colonel called Esposito back to his office. He said that Elvis had asked him cancel the meeting, but he had refused. The meeting would go on as scheduled. He didn't want to give the impression that Elvis was afraid of the Beatles.

The Colonel arranged to personally pick up the Beatles and bring them to Elvis's house. He arrived at the place the Beatles were renting in Coldwater Canyon at 7:30 P.M. on August 26. The Colonel was introduced to the Beatles by Brian Epstein. According to those present, they seemed a little nervous at meeting the Colonel. He tried to put them at ease by offering them cigars. After a few minutes of small talk, they left for Elvis's house.

The Colonel, Brian Epstein, John Lennon, and Paul McCartney rode in the lead limo. Joe Esposito, Malcolm Evans, George Harrison, and Ringo Starr followed behind in a second one. On arriving, the Beatles were ushered into the den to meet Elvis. John Lennon was the first to speak. He offered his hand saying, "Oh, you must be Elvis." Everybody laughed. Elvis shot back, "Oh, you guys must be friends of Malcolm's." More laughter.

During the visit, the Colonel and Brian Epstein spent some time alone talking. Reportedly, Epstein needled the Colonel about the Beatles being as big as Elvis. The Colonel responded that he was willing to put that theory to a test. Epstein could book the Beatles in the arena of his choice. The Colonel would put Elvis in a tent next door to that arena. Whoever drew the biggest crowd would take the proceeds from both shows.

While Epstein declined this bet, he did take up the Colonel's offer to make another wager. One of Elvis's guys turned over a table top to reveal a roulette wheel. Brian Epstein, Ringo, and the Colonel played. Joe Esposito acted as the bank. The Colonel bragged later that he had taken three thousand dollars from Epstein.

Before they left, the Colonel presented the Beatles with little covered wagons that lit up. The covered wagon was part of the logo that the Colonel used on all his printed matter. He also gave each of them collections of Elvis's albums.

During the visit, John Lennon asked Elvis when he was going to tour again. Elvis responded that he had too many movie commitments. Maybe he would tour when they were finished. In fact, the Colonel did have something of an Elvis tour in mind. Luckily it was not mentioned to the sarcastic Lennon. One can only imagine what he would have said about the Colonel's bizarre alternative to having Elvis go on a concert tour. He was sending Elvis's gold Cadillac instead.

In Parker's defense, this was no straight-from-the-assembly-line car. It had been customized to the hilt. Its paint contained gold flakes and diamond dust. It was equipped with an electric razor, a record player, a television, a gold-plated telephone, and a shoe buffer. Elvis couldn't actually drive it because it drew too much attention. It was parked in the garage at Graceland until the Colonel took it on tour.

The tour was conducted in conjunction with the release of the movie *Frankie and Johnny*. The Colonel got RCA to pay expenses, arguing it would promote the soundtrack album. The Colonel was not about to give anyone free advertising. He billed the vehicle as "Elvis Presley's Gold Car," never mentioning the word Cadillac. Amazingly, crowds lined up to see it. Hundreds of thousands of people paid to see the car. As many as forty thousand people paraded past it in one day. There were more than a million souvenir picture postcards sold. One would have thought that the huge crowds might have given the Colonel the idea of sending Elvis himself on tour.

By 1964, when the movies really started to get bad and the

songs became jokes, Elvis began to question the Colonel about continuing to do them. The Colonel settled him down by reminding him how much money he was making. Elvis craved a challenge, but the Colonel was fixated on the quick buck. Vernon cautioned Elvis against upsetting the Colonel. He was constantly reminding Elvis about how much the Colonel had done for him.

When the sales of Elvis's soundtrack albums started to slip, the Colonel devised a trick to disguise it. He had RCA put pressure on its dealers to preorder Elvis albums in massive quantities. The orders would be held until one million dollars in advance sales had been reached. RCA would then tout that the album had shipped gold. Later hundreds of thousands of the albums would be returned unsold. Of course, RCA did not create a press release to announce this.

The Colonel also had an answer when the box office receipts started to slip. They would just have to make them cheaper. One way he reduced the cost was to get chambers of commerce and hotels to pick up the cost of location shooting. He also hired television directors because they were accustomed to fast filming schedules. A faster production was a cheaper production. The Colonel's favorite director was Sam Katzman. Katzman was able to complete a movie from start to finish in seventeen days.

In 1964, the Colonel decided that Elvis should only record soundtrack albums. Other albums would only water down the product and cause them to compete with each other, the Colonel reasoned. Elvis hated the soundtracks, but went along with the idea anyway. He gave up on trying to create quality music. For the next five years, Elvis would come into the studio to lay down a vocal over pre-recorded backing tracks. He stopped functioning as a producer of his sessions. He simply wanted to get in and out of the studio as quickly as possibly.

Since it had been repeatedly shown that the quality of an Elvis movie had little to do with the profit it made, the Colonel and the movie studios lowered the budget of successive films. This meant that the profits got bigger. By the time Elvis filmed *Kissin' Cousins*, the budget was down to $800,000. Still the crowds kept coming. Songs would be sprinkled throughout the film, every ten minutes. This was what the audience wanted, not an elaborate production. Eventually this shoestring budget approach caught up with the box office, and profitability went down. The Colonel rode the horse until it died.

According to his associates, Elvis completely lost interest in movies in 1966. He resigned himself to the fact that he wasn't going to be doing serious roles. It was at this time that he began to focus on religion and philosophy. His drug intake also increased. This increased drug use culminated in his slipping and falling. This caused a delay in the filming of Elvis's movie *Clambake*.

Elvis had been very vocally upset at the script for *Clambake*. When he arrived in Hollywood for its filming, he had ballooned from his usual 170 pounds to 200 pounds. The wardrobe was redesigned to hide his weight. To curb his appetite, Elvis took to popping diet pills, lots of diet pills.

Priscilla traveled with Elvis to the *Clambake* shoot. She said that he was groggy when he woke up the morning that the movie was scheduled to begin filming. He was in the bathroom when Priscilla heard a loud crash. Jumping out of bed to see what happened, she found Elvis lying on the floor rubbing his head. Elvis said that he had tripped over the telephone cord and hit his head on the bathtub. He was so dizzy, Priscilla had to help him back to bed. She then telephoned Joe Esposito. Esposito in turn telephoned the Colonel and a doctor.

When Elvis finally came out of his bedroom, he was walking unsteadily. He fell into a chair holding his head, saying the large lump on his head had been caused by a fall in his bathroom. He complained that his head hurt and his vision was blurry. Shortly thereafter, the Colonel walked through the front door.

When the Colonel got to Elvis's suite, he was furious. He said to Larry Geller, "You get rid of those books right now, and he's not to read any more books whatsoever." Geller was both Elvis's hairstylist and spiritual guru.

In 1959, Larry Geller went to work in Jay Sebring's hairstyling salon in Hollywood. Sebring had a celebrity clientele that included Frank Sinatra, Peter Sellers, Milton Berle, and Henry Fonda. In April 1964, Geller was in the middle of doing singer Johnny Rivers's hair when he got a call from a member of Elvis's entourage, Allan Fortis. Fortis told Geller that Elvis's hairstylist, Sal Orifice, was unable to continue working for him and had recommended Geller as his replacement.

That afternoon Geller drove to Elvis's Bel-Air home to style his hair. In addition to working on Elvis's hair, Geller discussed his religious philosophy and his search for his purpose for living. Geller was raised in the Jewish religion. However, he because interested in eastern religions when he had a vision driving his car thorough the Arizona desert in August 1960.

The search for one's purpose in life struck a chord with Elvis. He wondered why he had been "chosen" to become king of rock and roll. Why would a kid from the lower classes of a tiny Mississippi town be selected to become one of the most famous and revered man in history? By the time Larry Geller left, Elvis had persuaded him to work full-time as his hairstylist. Geller would bring a stack of new books each time he came to do Elvis's hair.

In his book, *If I Can Dream*, Geller told the story of the first time that the Colonel tried to put an end to Elvis's spiritual studies with him. In the summer of 1964, Geller was at Elvis's home when the Colonel telephoned. After only a couple of minutes, Elvis hung up and announced that he had to go to meet with the Colonel. Geller said that he found this unusual because during the time he had been with Elvis, the Colonel rarely telephoned, much less requested a meeting. Geller accompanied Elvis to the Colonel's office at MGM Studios. (The sign on the Colonel's door read, "Elvis Exploitations.")

Elvis had Geller wait in the car. Ten minutes passed before he emerged, visibly angry. As soon as he got in the car, he let out a tirade against the Colonel. "How dare that son of a bitch," he said. "He doesn't know the first thing about my life. He doesn't know anything about me. He says that I'm on a kick, a religious kick. It's not a kick. It's my life, and my life is not a kick."

At first Larry Geller thought that the Colonel suspected he and Elvis were having a homosexual relationship. The Colonel had an associate invite Geller to dinner and proposition him. The man made remarks to Geller throughout dinner about how nice his body looked. He ended by inviting Geller back to his house to go swimming. Geller, a happily married heterosexual, turned him down. He managed to survive the Colonel's attack and was still with Elvis in late 1966 when the bathroom accident occurred.

After admonishing Larry Geller, Colonel Parker went in with Elvis. "Do you know how much money the studio will lose? Do you know how much a day costs? What about your daddy? What about Priscilla? What about your aunt and your grandmother and your fans? They're going to find out that you're blacklisted from Hollywood," he said.

The Colonel gave Elvis an ultimatum. He told him that from now on, he was going to do exactly what the Colonel said. If not, the Colonel would leave, and Elvis would be finished. The Colonel also said that from now on the Memphis Mafia was going to do as he said. He wanted a meeting set up with them, and Elvis was to tell them that the Colonel's word was now law.

The Colonel attributed the fall to pills, and he told Elvis that he was going to have him constantly watched to make sure that accidents did not happen again. In return for the extra work, Parker demanded 50 percent of his earnings. If Elvis refused, Parker said he would resign and Elvis's career would be ruined.

Elvis grudgingly agreed to the increase as the Colonel knew he would.

On January 2, 1967, Colonel Parker amended his contract with Elvis. It would run until January 22, 1976. The Colonel wrote a letter of agreement to Elvis which said "As of this date, all existing contracts change. The renewals will be 50 percent to Elvis Presley and 50 percent to All-Star Shows [Colonel Parker's company]." The 50-percent commission stayed in place for the rest of Elvis's life.

Ironically, in the movie *Fun in Acapulco*, Elvis plays a singer who objects when a manager who wants to represent him asks for half of his earnings. Elvis's character says, "That is pretty much for a commission." What with the Colonel being paid to act as "technical advisor" on most of Elvis's movies (though he did little more than deliver his client), the commissions, and side fees, Parker made more from an Elvis movie than Elvis did.

Soon after the Colonel arrived, a doctor arrived and headed straight for Elvis's bedroom. Next, two movie studio executives came and were ushered into the bedroom. When the doctor had finished his examination, he announced that Elvis had suffered a concussion. The filming of *Clambake* would be delayed until he recovered.

Elvis stayed in his room for the next week. No visitors were permitted except for the Colonel and Priscilla. When Elvis was pronounced by the Colonel to be fit for visitors, he called a meeting of everyone at Elvis's house.

When the Colonel arrived, he took Joe Esposito and Marty Lacker off to speak with Elvis in private. The Colonel did all the talking. He said that Esposito would have complete control of the Memphis Mafia. If they had any problem, they were to go to Esposito, not Elvis. The Colonel told Lacker that he would be in charge of special projects for Elvis. He gave him the title of "Special Chief Aide to Elvis." He also said that no one was to be talking to

Elvis about religion. It was clear that this was in reference to Larry Geller. He ordered that all the books that Geller had given Elvis be burned.

They then went into the living room to address the rest of the group. Elvis started off by saying that the Colonel wanted to have a few words with them. He said that everything the Colonel was going to say, he agreed with. Elvis then lowered his head and ducked off into the corner. The Colonel told them that they were not to go to Elvis any longer with their personal problems. He said that they were causing problems for Elvis and that they did not take care of him like they should.

He also announced that Elvis would be cutting back on his payroll. After filming *Clambake*, some of them would probably be let go. The ones who remained would have to start working. "Some of you," the Colonel said looking directly at Larry Geller, "think maybe he's Jesus Christ who should wear robes and walk down the street helping people. But that's not who he is. I don't want Elvis reading any more books to clutter up his mind."

Afterwards, the Colonel told Elvis privately that he should get Larry out of his life. He said that Larry was using some kind of hypnotic manipulation to control his thinking and was causing the quality of his acting and recording to suffer by "jamming up your mind with a lot of garbage."

At first Elvis protested the Colonel's criticism of Geller, although mildly so. After a few weeks, he started coming around to the Colonel's way of thinking. He promised not to spend any time alone with Geller. A few weeks later, Elvis and Priscilla put a large stack of the spiritual books into a box and threw them into an empty well in the backyard of Graceland. They then doused the box with gasoline and set it on fire.

When it became obvious that Geller was no longer Elvis's darling, the Memphis Mafia became openly hostile toward him. They regularly made insulting remarks when they were sure that he could hear. Geller soon saw that the time had come for him to leave. He resigned as Elvis's hairstylist in April 1967.

Shortly after Elvis's fall in the bathroom, the Colonel met with Joe Esposito and Marty Lacker. He had one of the "special projects" that he had talked about. Elvis and Priscilla were going to be married. The bathroom fall was the final straw that made the marriage happen.

Within days after the accident, the Colonel told Elvis that it was time for him to settle down. This meant marrying Priscilla. Priscilla's father had been applying pressure. She had been allowed to move to Graceland only after Elvis had promised to marry her one day. In the fall of 1966, her father called to remind Elvis of that promise. He would no longer accept the excuse that marriage would be a bad career move for Elvis. It had been four years, and it was time for Elvis to live up to his word. The Colonel said he was afraid of a lawsuit from Priscilla's family if Elvis failed to do so.

There is little question that the Colonel desperately wanted Elvis to marry Priscilla. There are three theories of why. One is that he hoped it would settle down Elvis and help his drug problem.

The second theory is that the Colonel thought a marriage would give a boost to Elvis's career. The Colonel looked for any way to build Elvis's box office other than improving the quality of the product. Before the wedding idea, the Colonel had toyed with the idea of staging Elvis's retirement. He envisioned a giant party being held in Hollywood. At its conclusion, he and Elvis would announce that they were retiring from show business. The next day, billboards all over Los Angeles would read "Elvis and the Colonel, bid you a fond farewell." After a suitable time had passed, Elvis would come out of retirement with huge fanfare. It was the army scheme all over again. Somehow, the Colonel could not bring himself to carry out the plan. He could not stand another break in the action.

Frank Sinatra had married Mia Farrow in 1967. The Colonel noticed a sudden surge in Sinatra's popularity as a result. In the teen idol days, the Colonel had been adamantly opposed to Elvis marrying. He viewed it as professional suicide. Now that he was presenting Elvis as the respectable all-American boy, marriage would enhance his image.

The third reason proposed for the Colonel's push for the marriage was his fear that the press might someday publicize that Priscilla had been living with Elvis since 1963. Colonel Parker was enraged when he learned that she had been spotted roaming the grounds of Graceland. He immediately telephoned Vernon Presley. "This is a very dangerous situation. It is bad enough that Elvis has the girl there at all. We certainly don't want anyone ever thinking that she's living in Graceland," the Colonel said. Of course, Priscilla had already moved in. The idea that she was going to live with Vernon and Dee lasted only a few days. "This could not only ruin his career, but could land him in prison," the Colonel warned. This certainly was not the family image that the Colonel was trying to project.

In the Colonel's version of the Elvis wedding story, Elvis telephoned him in Palm Springs and said that he and Priscilla wanted to get married in Las Vegas. He asked the Colonel to make the arrangements.

According to Marty Lacker, Elvis confided to him before the wedding that he wasn't ready for marriage. Lacker asked Elvis why he didn't back out. Elvis replied, "I can't. Priscilla's father has contacted the Colonel demanding that I make good on my word to marry Cilla now that she's twenty-one."

Lacker said that Elvis wanted a child, but not anything that went along with being married. If he was to marry Priscilla, it was only because of the pressure being applied by her parents and the Colonel. Both Lacker and Lamar Fike claim that the woman that Elvis cared about the most was his sometime co-star Ann-Margret.

Priscilla said that Elvis proposed to her shortly before Christmas 1966 and that she knew the Colonel encouraged him to ask her. "I know that Colonel Parker asked him to take a long look at our relationship and decide where he wanted it to go. Curiously enough, after his talk with Colonel, it didn't take him long to decide the time was right."

Colonel Parker wanted to keep the details of the wedding completely secret until he felt the time was right. He didn't even want anyone to know that it was taking place, much less the day and time. Even the bride-to-be was in on the espionage act. She had flown up to San Francisco to shop for her wedding gown and bought it there under an assumed name. Later she altered it herself.

The Colonel called his friend Milton Prell, who now owned the Aladdin Hotel in Las Vegas, and arranged to use his suite in the hotel for the ceremony. The Colonel had become friends with Milton Prell when they were neighbors in Palm Springs. Prell asked Judge David Zenoff of the Supreme Court of Nevada to perform a wedding in Las Vegas. He told the judge that he couldn't tell him who it was, only that it would take place at his hotel on May 1, 1967.

The invited wedding guests were not notified until Sunday afternoon, the day before the wedding. Even then they didn't know whose wedding they would be attending. They were booked in several different hotels. Late Sunday night, they received messages telling them to be in the Aladdin lobby at five-thirty Monday morning. They were then rounded up and taken to a room and told about the wedding. They had to stay in the room until the ceremony.

The Colonel even kept in the dark such people as Abe Lastfogel, Stan Borssette, MGM's head of publicity, Henry Brand, who held the same position at 20th Century-Fox, and RCA executive Harry Jenkins. He sent them each a cryptic telegram the day before the wedding. It instructed them to proceed to Los Angeles International Airport and pick up their tickets for a trip he had arranged for them. When they arrived at the airport, they learned that their destination was Las Vegas.

In Vegas, they were met by a driver who took them to their hotel for the night. The next morning at seven, a pair of limousines picked them up and drove them to the Aladdin Hotel. They were brought in through the rear entrance and each taken to separate rooms. A couple of hours later, they were telephoned by the Colonel and informed that Elvis had been married. He told them where to go in the hotel to attend the reception.

The Colonel even extended the security web to the bridal shower Nancy Sinatra gave for Priscilla. The Colonel told Priscilla to make sure that all the pictures taken at the shower were given to her. That way none of them would end up in a magazine. Even the wedding cake was done covertly. The Aladdin's chef baked one, but left the names blank. As the guests arrived, he hastily iced in "Elvis and Priscilla."

The arrangements for the wedding photography were equally clandestine. Colonel Parker called MGM and requested two photographers to shoot an upcoming event in Las Vegas. The photographers did not know that the event that they were to record was Elvis's wedding until they were in Milton Prell's suite.

Despite the Colonel's attempts at keeping the wedding a secret, rumors started. Somehow news that Elvis was going to be married leaked out to reporters. The game, as far as the Colonel was concerned, was to hide the exact date and place from them until he thought the time was right. To confuse reporters, the Colonel had Elvis and Priscilla, Joe Esposito and his wife, and Elvis's friend from high school, George Klein, fly to Palm Springs on April 29. Vernon and Dee Presley traveled by train from Memphis to San Bernadino, California. Marty Lacker picked them up and drove them to Palm Springs.

Reporters were tipped off as to Elvis's whereabouts and a crowd of them converged on the Palm Springs house. Colonel Parker went outside and told them they were wasting their time there. Neither he nor Elvis had any comment on what was going on inside. However, he told them a press conference would be held at the Aladdin Hotel at one, May 1, for a special announcement. With that, the reporters ended the stakeout and headed for Las Vegas.

On the night of April 30, Elvis, Priscilla, Joe Esposito, and his wife flew to Las Vegas. The rest of the group followed a few hours later. The Colonel had made reservations under different names at different hotels. When Elvis got into town, a limousine met him at the airport and whisked him to one hotel where he went out the back door into another car that took him to the Aladdin. At four in the morning, Elvis, Priscilla, and Joe went to the Las Vegas courthouse to obtain a fifteen-dollar marriage license. It would have only cost five dollars if they bought it between 8:00 A.M. and 5:00 P.M.

At around 9:30 in the morning, Elvis and Priscilla and the rest of the wedding party gathered in Milton Prell's penthouse. There were only seventeen people present for the ceremony. Many of those attending were the Colonel's friends and business associates while several of Elvis's close friends were left out. The Colonel purposely excluded people from the ceremony that he did not like, such as Red West and his brother Sonny.

Red West told in his book, *Elvis, What Happened?*, of not being allowed to attend the wedding. He says that he was told by Joe Esposito that Elvis was getting married in Las Vegas at the Aladdin Hotel. He was instructed to fly to Vegas to attend the wedding. Red brought his wife along with him. Joe Esposito was Red's line of communication to the Colonel. Red kept waiting for a call from Esposito to tell him when the wedding would start. Finally Red grew impatient and went to Esposito's room. When Joe answered the door, he was wearing a tuxedo. Red asked Joe why he hadn't called him with the details about the wedding time. Esposito informed him that he wouldn't be attending the wedding. Only Esposito and Marty Lacker would be there. Red and the rest of the guys would be at the reception. Red blamed the Colonel and Joe

Esposito for the slight. He skipped the reception and headed back to Los Angeles.

Some years later, Elvis confided his true feelings about marrying Priscilla in telephone conversations with Red West. "Elvis said, 'That wedding thing [his marriage to Priscilla], I had nothing to do with that. That was railroaded through. I didn't even know who was there in that little ole room the size of a bathroom with the Supreme Court justice. It was over and done so quick I didn't realize I was married. I could see it back then, but that wasn't my doing. I had nothing to do with it, you know. All of a sudden I was getting married.'"

Red West was not the only member of Elvis' entourage to be surprised by the guest list. After helping Elvis get dressed, Marty Lacker told Joe Esposito that he was going to tell the rest of the guys that it was time to get ready. Esposito informed him that none of the other guys would be attending. The excuse given was that the room in which the ceremony was to be held was too small. This was completely untrue.

Judge Zenoff asked to speak with the bride and groom separately before the ceremony. Colonel Parker brought Elvis in, and he chatted with the judge for a few minutes. Elvis was nervous. The judge told him that all he had to do was answer his question. Elvis would know that it was over when the judge said, "You may kiss your bride." Then the judge went to talk to Priscilla. The wedding vows were nothing special, just standard for the state of Nevada. She was so nervous that she couldn't do anything but nod.

After the wedding ceremony was over, the Colonel had Elvis give the press conference that he had promised the reporters in Palm Springs. Next there was a small reception. Elvis and Priscilla had a six-tier wedding cake that was five feet high. At the reception, there were as many business associates of the Colonel as there were friends of Elvis.

The Colonel even interfered with Elvis and Priscilla's honey-

moon plans. They wanted to travel through Europe. According to
Marty Lacker, Colonel Parker told Elvis that it would be a mistake
for them to go to Europe. The Colonel had turned down European
promoters wanting Elvis to preform there by saying that he had
commitments in the United States that didn't leave him enough
time. He persuaded Elvis that these promoters and his fans would
hound him about performing the entire time that he was there.
Elvis and Priscilla ended up in the Bahamas.

After his marriage, Elvis began to reexamine his career. He came
to the conclusion that it was time to do something about the horrible movies that now were his entire creative output. He was tired of
them, the reviewers were tired of them, and slipping box office
receipts indicated that the public was tired of them. Elvis
approached the Colonel about his desire to get back in front of a
live audience. Finally the Colonel agreed. It was time to move Elvis
on to a new game. When his current contracts ran out, there would
be no more movies.

Elvis's last movie for Hal Wallis was *Easy Come, Easy Go*. Elvis
and the movie's director, John Rich, did not get along at all. At one
point, Rich admonished Elvis for laughing in the middle of a take.
Elvis shot back, "We're doing these movies because it's supposed
to be fun, nothing more. When they cease to be fun, then we'll
cease to do them."

While Elvis was grateful to Hal Wallis for the breaks that he had
given him, Wallis sensed some resentment from Elvis at the type of
roles he was given. The money that Wallis earned from Presley
movies allowed him to finance more serious pictures. It couldn't
have escaped Elvis that he was financing the type of films that he
desperately wanted to appear in.

Hal Wallis said that his biggest regret as far as his Elvis pictures
were concerned was that he had been unable to pair John Wayne
and Elvis in a movie. He envisioned Wayne as an aging gunfighter
and Elvis as his protégée.

When asked why he had stopped making movies, Elvis said, "It was getting harder and harder singing to the camera all day long. Let's face it, when you have ten different songs for each movie, well, they can't all be good. Eventually I got tired of singing to turtles and guys I had just beaten up."

Elvis would soon be in front of a live audience where he belonged.

Chapter 11

The 1968 Comeback Special

★ ★ ★ ★

Colonel Parker had been selling an edited tape of Elvis's Christmas songs, with a few spoken words in between from Elvis, for several years. He called it the *Elvis Presley Christmas Show*. Then he got the idea of taking it to television. The Colonel liked a Christmas format for the special because he thought that it could be become an annual event. He contacted NBC and offered the network a program to be called *Elvis and the Wonderful World of Christmas*.

The Colonel negotiated with Tom Sarnoff, NBC's vice president of operations for the West Coast. The Colonel outlined terms under which he would sign for Elvis to appear. NBC would be allowed to broadcast the show twice. After that, control would revert to Elvis and Colonel Parker. The soundtrack album would be owned by Elvis and the Colonel and would be released through

RCA. He also proposed that NBC agree to finance Elvis's next movie as a part of the deal.

NBC accepted the Colonel's proposal by telegram on January 12, 1968. "Confirming our phone conversation. We have a deal for production of one Elvis feature and one TV special according to the terms discussed between us during last couple of days. Congratulations to both of us. We are all extremely pleased to have Elvis as another branch of our RCA family. Looking forward to long and successful association. Will discuss details with you next week. Best Personal Regards, Tom Sarnoff, NBC, Burbank, California"

The Singer Sewing Machine Company signed on as the special's sponsor for $400,000. They were interested in Elvis doing a commercial for them to be broadcast during the program. The Colonel, as usual, had no interest in Elvis being a shill. True to form, he didn't turn them down. He simply set the astronomical fee of $500,000. Singer wasn't prepared to pay more than $50,000 and dropped the idea.

Elvis and the Colonel held a press conference at the NBC studios to announce the upcoming show. It would be the first television appearance for Elvis since the Frank Sinatra special in 1960. When asked why he was finally returning Elvis to TV, the Colonel said, "As you know, we have another mouth to feed next month, and we need the extra income." The Colonel was referring to the impending birth of Lisa Marie Presley, who was born on February 1.

For his part, Elvis said, "We figured it was about time. Besides, I thought I had better do it before I get too old." Colonel Parker added, "We also got a very good deal." Elvis was asked if he would be acting or singing in the special. "I'm going to sing almost exclusively in it, and I'm going to sing the songs that I'm known for," he said. The Colonel added, "If he sings the songs he's known for, that would take a couple of weeks."

Tom Sarnoff put Bob Finkel in charge of the Elvis special.

Finkel spent most of his time trying to pacify Colonel Parker. The Colonel demanded an office at NBC's Burbank studios. When he got one, he constantly complained about how small it was. The Colonel and Finkel finally warmed too each other and began exchanging practical jokes. One morning Finkel found his office blocked by two of the Colonel's William Morris trainees dressed as Buckingham Palace guards. Finkel went to the studio wardrobe and the next day pulled the same trick on the Colonel.

Colonel Parker got the last laugh. He sent a case of what Finkel believed was expensive champagne to Finkel's house. Finkel gave a dinner party and told his guests that he was going break out some excellent champagne given to him by Colonel Tom Parker. Finkel's guests one by one took a sip of the champagne and quickly shot looks his way. It seems that the Colonel's expensive champagne was in reality tonic water.

Bob Finkel hired an independent producer, Steve Binder, to produce and direct the show. Binder was a widely known producer of television music programs and variety shows. He had been a teenager in 1956 when Elvis came on the scene and wanted to present the same Elvis that had excited him as a youngster.

Binder first met Elvis when he was on the crew of *Viva Las Vegas* and had witnessed firsthand the Colonel's constant complaints to director George Sidney about seemingly minor things. Binder, therefore, was not surprised when, almost immediately, he had difficulties with the Colonel.

For one thing, they had different visions of the special. The Colonel told Binder at their first meeting that the special should be looked at as a gift to the American public. He then proceeded to outline how he envisioned the structure of the show. It should be a Christmas special. Elvis would sing a mixture of Christmas carols, some fast, some slow, some traditional, and some of Elvis's rocking Christmas songs. Colonel Parker suggested Milton Berle and Ray Bolger as guests. He even had the ending mapped out. Elvis would sing a traditional song like "Silent Night." He would then say, "Merry Christmas everyone," smile, and the show fades to black.

Although he hated this idea, Steve Binder tried to hide it from the Colonel. He decided on focusing on winning Elvis over to his way of thinking. He talked with Elvis about some of the popular artists of the day and which of the current hits he liked. At the end of the meeting, it was agreed that Elvis would go to Hawaii to rest, lose weight, and get ready for the special. In the meantime, Binder would develop an outline for the show.

After Elvis returned from his R and R, Binder sat down with him to go over ideas for the program's content. He told Elvis that he had two choices. He could do the Christmas carol show that the Colonel proposed and fade off into history as a viable artist, becoming the Bing Crosby of the rock era. Or he could take some chances and prove that he still had a place at the top of the music business. Elvis agreed completely with Binder.

After considerable consultation with Elvis and NBC, the Colonel was also finally convinced to go along with Binder's format. The Colonel may have lost the battle, but he was determined not to be a gracious loser. He was going to do everything possible to harass Binder throughout the entire production. He argued over everything that Binder wanted to do. Any change that Binder wanted to make necessitated a meeting with the Colonel. To cause further irritation, the Colonel intentionally mispronounced Binder's name as "Bindel." Throughout rehearsals, the Colonel kept saying, "Bindel, where is my Christmas music?" With the Colonel out of sight, Elvis would tell Binder not to pay any attention to him.

Colonel and Binder argued about the closing number right up to the very end of production. The Colonel wanted to close with his original idea of a traditional Christmas carol and Elvis wishing everyone a Merry Christmas. Artificial snow would begin to fall as the credits rolled.

Binder argued against this. The Colonel finally relented on the Christmas carol and instead suggested that Elvis finish with the gospel song "I Believe."

Binder had ideas of his own. He wanted the show to end with a bang, not a whimper. He wanted a song that had a hint of social awareness without being so radical as to incur the Colonel's veto. He gave songwriters Billy Goldberg and Earl Brown an outline of what he wanted. The next day, they came back with a new song, "If I Can Dream." Binder had them perform the song for Elvis in private. Elvis agreed that the tune was perfect for closing the show. The only remaining obstacle was the Colonel.

Elvis had stayed away from the social commentary that was so prevalent in the 1960s. The Colonel instructed him never to discuss religion or politics in public. He persuaded Elvis that he would lose the 50 percent of his fans who would not share his viewpoint. Elvis followed the Colonel's instructions so closely that he never even voted. The Colonel objected to "If I Can Dream" because he felt that its peace and unity message was controversial.

The Colonel finally took the matter of the closing song to Tom Sarnoff. Sarnoff called a meeting of himself, the Colonel, and Steve Binder to resolve the issue. The Colonel resorted to a variation of his Binder name game. Whenever the Colonel made his argument, he correctly said "Binder." When he responded to one of Binder's arguments, he would say "Bindel."

The Colonel also attempted to stare down Binder, but found him a difficult opponent. Binder wasn't afraid of him, or if he was, he was smart enough to know that it would be suicide to show it. If he let the Colonel smell blood in the water, he would move in for the kill. Instead Binder kept his cool and argued the Colonel to a draw. A decision on the final number was postponed.

Binder came up with a way of painting the Colonel into a corner where it would be impossible for him to argue against the song. He summoned Colonel Parker and executives from RCA and NBC to the studio. "We have a new closing song," he announced. "Elvis is going to sing it for you." The Colonel's face turned red with rage. Elvis performed the song accompanied by piano. When he was finished, everyone congratulated him on a sure hit. Everyone that is except the Colonel. He did not say anything. With all the praise being heaped on the song, he wasn't in the position of speaking out against it, but he was not about to say he liked it.

Steve Binder expected to receive a producer's royalty on the soundtrack album and "If I Can Dream." But here, the Colonel was able to extract some revenge on Binder for defying him with the closing number. "Read the contract, Bindel," he said. "You are not getting anything."

Colonel Parker promised NBC that he would fill the audience for the taping of the special with fans who would go wild for Elvis. These were the people that NBC needed for the broadcast. However, in return for the Colonel delivering the perfect audience, he demanded he be given all the tickets to the show.

On June 11, 1968, Binder sent a letter to the Colonel confirming that he would be responsible for distributing the tickets.

Dear Colonel Parker,

It is my understanding that you will lend your help in the selection of the audience for the Elvis Presley special. With this in mind, the following are our audience requirements. #1) 328 young people for taping for arena segment in their seats at 6:00 P.M. on Saturday, June 29th. #2) 328 young people for second taping of arena segment in their seats at 8:00 p.m. on Saturday, June 29th.

I will be in touch with NBC and see that they deliver to you
656 tickets for the above audience as soon as possible.

Best Regards,

Steve Binder

On the day of the broadcast, a parking lot attendant at NBC studios approached Steve Binder as he got out of his car. He handed
Binder a stack of tickets to the broadcast that Colonel Parker had
given him. Almost all the tickets were being returned. Binder was
hours away from taping, and he didn't have an audience.

Why did the Colonel intentionally fail to distribute the tickets?
Did he want an empty house? Binder felt the Colonel was trying to
sabotage the broadcast. Binder had battled the Colonel all the way
and was the winner on virtually every issue. The Colonel was
determined to see him fail. He wanted to prove that the Colonel
knew best about how the special should have been done. The segment where Elvis performed sitting down surrounded by an audience, in particular, was targeted by the Colonel for failure. Binder
had stressed to Elvis that it would be the highlight of the show. By
ruining it, the Colonel would receive his ultimate revenge on
Binder. He would also erase the idea from Elvis's mind that people
like Steve Binder knew more about what was good for his career
than the Colonel did.

Binder sent his staff out frantically distributing the tickets for the
two scheduled sit-down shows. Unfortunately, for the Colonel, the
undistributed tickets were an easy bomb to defuse. Finding enough
enthusiastic people to watch Elvis perform was a simple matter.
The Colonel's trick had merely resulted in inconvenience for
Binder.

Videotaping of the special began on June 27. Before Elvis went out to the stage for the first time, the Colonel ordered everyone from his dressing room. No one knew exactly what went on or what was said. The Colonel probably gave Elvis a pregame pep talk.

Originally Binder planned to film Elvis jamming in his dressing room. He got the idea when he walked in on him and the guys fooling around singing one day before rehearsals. The Colonel was confused about why Binder wanted to do this. Why present Elvis in an informal setting? What they needed was a lavish production. Binder and the Colonel met several times to discuss the issue and finally reached a compromise. Elvis and some of his old bandmates would give an informal in-the-round sit-down performance for an audience. In between songs, Elvis would work in anecdotes about his career.

Elvis performed two one-hour sit-down concerts in front of live audiences. Accompanying him were Scotty Moore and Charlie Hodge on guitar, D. J. Fontana playing a drum pad, and Allen Fortis playing a tambourine. The next night's portion of production numbers were taped. The following night, Elvis was again in front of a live audience for two half-hour concerts on a small stage. Elvis completed taping the special on June 30, 1968. More production numbers were taped that day, as well as the closing song, "If I Can Dream."

The NBC special aired on December 3, 1968. It won its time slot with a 33.2 percent rating. The single release of "If I Can Dream" eventually made it to number twelve on the *Billboard* Hot 100 chart. It was Elvis's highest charting song since "Crying in the Chapel" in 1965.

The media was unanimous in praising the special as the return of the King. Music critic John Landau, who later became Bruce Springsteen's manager, said of Elvis's performance, "There is something magical about watching a man who has lost himself find his way home. He sang with a kind of power that people no longer expect from rock and roll performers."

When the special was over, the Colonel congratulated Steve Binder and told him that he would direct Elvis's next movie. It never happened. Binder tried several times to telephone Elvis, but could never get by the Memphis Mafia. Binder's next Elvis project was in 1980 when he produced a tour of Graceland for television, hosted by Priscilla Presley.

Filled with excitement from the NBC special and the thought of performing in front of a live audience again, Elvis decided to record some real music. On January 13, 1969, he began a recording session at American Studios in Memphis. This was the first time that he had recorded in Memphis since leaving Sun Records.

It had been four years since an Elvis single had reached the Top 5, much less number one. Elvis was convinced that he needed better material. For this session, Elvis tried something new. He decided to use some non-Hill-and-Range songs. One of them was "Kentucky Rain." Another was "In the Ghetto." The Colonel cautioned against "In the Ghetto," saying that it was too political.

The producer of the session, Chips Moman, had another non-Hill-and-Range song that he thought would be perfect for Elvis. Moman owned his own publishing company. Mark James, one of his writers, had a song that Moman wanted Elvis to hear called "Suspicious Minds." After hearing it, Elvis decided to record it. Tom Diskin, who was at the recording session as Colonel Parker's representative, demanded that Moman give them a share of the publishing of the song. Moman refused and said they could just call off the recording session.

Diskin decided to discuss the situation with Elvis. Elvis told Diskin to leave the session to him. Diskin was not accustomed to independent thinking from Elvis. He phoned the Colonel to say that Elvis was out of control. The Colonel told Diskin to come back to California and let Elvis attempt to fend for himself. Now they would see how well Elvis did on his own. This was the first and last time that either Colonel Parker or one of his people was absent from an Elvis Presley recording session.

The American Records studio session would result in three million-selling singles and two gold albums. On May 31, 1969, "In the Ghetto" reached number nine on *Billboard*'s Hot 100 chart. It was Elvis's first top-ten single since "If I Can Dream." The Colonel extracted a little revenge by calling *Billboard* magazine and telling them that they had made a mistake by listing Chips Moman as the producer of "In the Ghetto" on its Top 40 chart. The next week, *Billboard* had removed Moman's name in favor of "no producer." "Suspicious Minds" hit number one on *Billboard*'s Hot 100 chart on November 1, 1969. It was Elvis's first number one record since "Good Luck Charm" in April 1962.

After the special aired, Elvis and the guys flew to Las Vegas to celebrate. The Colonel met them at the airport. In the car on their way to their hotel, the Colonel suggested to Elvis that they could do a special live from Las Vegas. The Colonel had received an offer for Elvis to perform at a new Las Vegas hotel, the International, which was to be the largest hotel in the world when it was completed. The International wanted to find the biggest name possible to open its new show room.

Elvis was hesitant to return to Vegas. He remembered Las Vegas as the site of one of the only failures in his career. The Colonel said that a lot of things had changed in the thirteen years since he had performed there last. His audience now was older; they were the kind of people who went to Las Vegas. Elvis gave in. Elvis said that when he was finished in Vegas, he would go on a national tour. That tour would last, with an occasional break, for the rest of his life.

Chapter 12

Las Vegas

★　★　★　★

ow that Elvis was back on the charts, the time was right for
the Colonel to return him to the concert stage, and the
International would be the venue for his return.

In 1968, Kirk Kerkorian, owner of the Flamingo Hotel,
announced plans to build what would be the largest hotel in Las
Vegas. It would have fifteen hundred rooms, more than twice the
number of the largest existing hotel. The Colonel first met Kirk
Kerkorian when Kerkorian was working at MGM. The general
manager of the International Hotel, Alex Shoofey, had become
acquainted with the Colonel when he was working for the
Colonel's friend Milton Prell at the Sahara Hotel. With the familiar
faces, the International was where the Colonel thought he would be
most comfortable.

Alex Shoofey was responsible for lining up big name acts to
draw a crowd for the hotel's grand opening. Shoofey, with the

reputation of being one of the smartest businessmen in Las Vegas, got in the casino business literally by accident. On a drive through town, his car broke down in front of a casino named the Club Bingo. He went inside and, by chance, met the owner Milton Prell. The two began to talk, and by the time the conversation was finished, Shoofey had a job. Later Prell moved Shoofey to his Sahara Hotel. Kerkorian hired Shoofey as a part of a raid on Sahara employees and put him in charge of the Flamingo. When the International was opened, Shoofey was named its general manger.

He approached the Colonel about Elvis christening the International's show room. The Colonel told him that he would rather let someone else work out the bugs. "Let someone else get stuck with failing lights and the sound cutting in and out," the Colonel said. Barbra Streisand was Shoofey's second choice, and she accepted. Elvis would follow her. The Colonel signed a contract with the International Hotel for Elvis to appear beginning July 31, 1969. The agreement was for four weeks at $125,000 per week.

Immediately after Barbra Streisand's last performance, the Colonel turned his crew loose blanketing the hotel with Elvis's name and image. There was even an Elvis souvenir stand set up near the hotel's entrance.

The International had a giant marquee at the entrance that was used to advertise the acts that were appearing at the hotel. The Colonel instructed the hotel that Elvis's first name only would be listed on the marquee. The last name was not necessary. And he made sure huge letters were used that could be seen from a great distance.

On July 5, 1969, Elvis traveled to Los Angeles to begin rehearsals for his International Hotel engagement on the MGM lot, which was the Colonel's home base. On July 9, *Variety* reported that Elvis's Las Vegas show was already 80 percent sold out. This was the most advanced reservations in Las Vegas history.

Colonel Parker completely took over the International publicity

department. He had a much more intensive campaign in mind than
the hotel originally planned. The International was going to run a
very low-key radio spot with Elvis issuing an invitation at the end.
The Colonel had something in mind that was closer to an advertisement for a demolition derby. Screams of "Elvis, Elvis, Elvis,
Now, Now, Now, at the International Hotel" came blasting out of
the radio.

Elvis's picture was plastered on billboards all over Las Vegas
and on the highways leading to it. The Colonel-placed newspaper
advertisements were four-page pullouts. He told Elvis, "I'm the
manager. All that I can do is let everyone know you are here. If you
don't do any business, don't ever blame me because the gophers in
the desert know you're here. Believe me, everybody in town will
know Elvis Presley is coming, but you're the only one who can
bring them in."

In an interview that ran in mid-August 1969 in the *Memphis
Press Scimitar*, Elvis discussed his return to Las Vegas.

"We didn't decide to come back here for the money, I'll tell you
that," Elvis laughed. "I've always wanted to perform on stage again
for the last nine years, and it's been building up inside of me since
1965, until the strain became intolerable. I get all het up about it,
and I don't think I could have left it much longer. The time is just
right. The money, I have no idea at all about that. I just don't want
to know. You can stuff it."

"I wouldn't be honest with you," he said later in the interview,
"if I said I wasn't ashamed of some of the movies and songs I've
had to sing in them. I would like to say that they were good, but I
can't. I have been extremely unhappy with that side of my career for
some time. But how can you find twelve good songs for every film
when you're making three films a year? I knew a lot of them were
bad songs, and they used to bother the heck out of me, but I had to
do them. They fit in the situation."

While the Colonel was happy to have Elvis performing in Vegas, he was not happy with the size of the show that Elvis had in mind. Elvis became enamored with lavish productions while working on the comeback special. For Vegas, in addition to his band, he added a thirty-five-piece orchestra and seven backup singers. The Colonel looked at this as a costly extravagance that would send profits down the drain.

Elvis insisted on a big show saying that the Las Vegas audience expected it. He was not about to have a repeat of his 1956 flop. The Colonel did manage to put his hokey touch on the show. He installed comedian Sammy Shore as Elvis's opening act.

The Las Vegas opening on July 31, 1969, was like a carnival. Two shows were given for VIPs. The Colonel had Kirk Kerkorian's private plane flown to New York to bring the press to opening night. RCA brought radio and press people in from all over the world.

Elvis's bodyguard, Sonny West, relates an emotional exchange between the Colonel and Elvis backstage after the opening. "The Colonel came down after the show into the dressing room. He just said, 'Where is he?' The Colonel, that old man, had tears in his eyes. His face was twisted in emotion. I have never seen him like that before. I was with Joe Esposito, and he pointed inside. Elvis came out. The Colonel took one step forward, and so did Elvis. There were no words, they just put their arms around each other in a big hug. The Colonel had his back to me, and I knew it was a private thing where we shouldn't hang around. We excused ourselves, but the Colonel's body was shaking with emotion."

The morning after opening night, the Colonel met with Alex Shoofey at Shoofey's request. Tom Diskin and Bitsy Mott accompanied the Colonel to the meeting in the International Hotel's dining room. After some initial small talk, Shoofey got to the point. He wanted to offer the Colonel a five-year contract for Elvis to play two months a year, February and August, at the International Hotel. He would be paid $125,000-a-week.

The Colonel agreed to Shoofey's offer. He wrote the terms out on a tablecloth and had Shoofey sign it. One provision that the Colonel added said that the contract would be void should Alex Shoofey leave the International. The Colonel had made the deal with Shoofey and said that was with whom he wanted to work. He didn't want to be stuck with a contract that would obligate him to work with a new manager, even if they didn't get along. When lunch was over, the Colonel took the tablecloth with him.

Shoofey had also offered the Colonel the opportunity to buy stock options in the International for Elvis as a way of building loyalty. He was willing to give Elvis an option on twenty thousand shares at $5 per share. The Colonel told Shoofey that he did not believe in stocks. He wanted a bonus plan instead. Shoofey agreed to a bonus that in the long run never netted Elvis more than $50,000 per year. If the Colonel had accepted the stock options, their value would have climbed to $1.4 million in a few years as the stock rose to $70 per share.

On August 28, 1969, Elvis closed his first four-week International stint. He set records for Las Vegas for both total attendance, 101,509 and total gross receipts, $1,522,635. This was in addition to the amount that the casino raked in. During the five years of Elvis's appearances, the hotel grossed $10 million. Subtracting Elvis's salary, the International netted $5 million. This is even more amazing when you realize that most acts in Vegas operated as a lost leader to draw gamblers to the hotel's casino.

In 1971, Kirk Kerkorian sold the International Hotel to the Hilton chain. Colonel Parker had also inserted a clause that enabled him to void Elvis's contract if Kerkorian sold the hotel. The Colonel met with Hilton vice president Henri Lewin and agreed to continue with the Hilton under the same terms as the International deal. The Colonel turned down a golden opportunity to increase Elvis's fee. Elvis had shattered attendance records for Las Vegas. The new ownership most certainly would not have been willing to let him slip away. Perhaps the Colonel was counting on his generosity to result in the Hilton being generous to him with perks.

In the spring of 1973, Elvis's contract with the Hilton ran out. Several other hotels tried to persuade the Colonel to sign with them. A Las Vegas newspaper reported a rumor that Elvis would be leaving the Hilton for a new hotel that was opening, the MGM Grand. The MGM was owned by Kirk Kerkorian.

It was also rumored that the Colonel and Elvis would be putting up six million dollars for an ownership interest with Kerkorian in the hotel. The Colonel was quick to deny the rumor. "The MGM show room will seat 600 fewer people than the Hilton. Besides, what hotel could match the Hilton's generous offer?" Unfortunately for his boy, it was the Colonel who was receiving the generous offer, not Elvis.

The Colonel met with Hilton vice president Henri Lewin and told him that he had a strong offer from MGM. However, he was going to give Lewin the opportunity to keep Elvis. If the Hilton did not agree to the Colonel's requirements, Elvis would be in the MGM show room on opening night. The deal the Colonel outlined called for Elvis to make two two-week appearances a year at the Hilton. This was down from the two four-week engagements called for under the old contract. Elvis was to be paid $150,000 per week plus expenses. This was more than any other performer in Las Vegas was making. However, Lewin knew a bargain when he saw it. Elvis drew larger crowds than any other performer in Las Vegas by a substantial margin. He agreed to the Colonel's terms. Elvis was signed for two more years at the Las Vegas Hilton.

With a Vegas contract signed and the shows sold out every night, there wasn't much left for the Colonel to do. Increasingly the focus of his attention in Las Vegas became gambling. Perhaps this was part of the attraction of Vegas as a concert site for the Colonel. He had started gambling seriously while Elvis was in the army.

The Colonel neither drank nor took drugs. He had only two dangerous habits. One was an addiction to food. At his heaviest, he weighed more than 300 pounds. His other vice was gambling. By most accounts, his fondness for gambling was an addiction by 1970. He no longer was playing to win, he was playing to feed his addiction. The Colonel couldn't leave a game, no matter how far he was ahead or behind.

Abe Lastfogel had introduced Parker to the show business elite of Hollywood. The Colonel's new Hollywood friends took frequent trips to Las Vegas. The Colonel started going with them. Gambling would prove to be the one game the Colonel couldn't win.

He developed a reputation as one of the highest rollers in Las Vegas. He spent at least ten months a year there and was at the tables every day. He gambled in the public portion of the casino rather than the private area reserved for high rollers. After his morning phone call to his wife, the Colonel would head to the casino. He put money into the slots as he made his way through the room, not stopping to see if he won or lost. His entourage would follow him collecting any winnings. At times, the Colonel had his assistants trailing him with buckets full of silver dollars. They would carry out the physical act of feeding the slot machines for him. He would point at a machine with a cane and instruct them to start playing it.

While the Colonel played the slots for fun, he was deadly serious about his favorite games, craps and roulette. When engaging in these "games," the Colonel always played for high stakes and usually lost. Inexplicably, it almost seemed that the Colonel used methods that assured he would lose. Perhaps his techniques were driven by the knowledge that the casino would forgive his gambling losses in return for his continuing to deliver Elvis to the show room.

According to Joe Esposito, the Colonel was a compulsive loser when it came to gambling. At the craps table, he would occasionally cover every bet. This meant he would win something on every throw of the dice. However, on that same throw, he would, of course, have several losing bets. This system guarantees a net loss. It got so bad that people accompanying the Colonel would slip some of his chips in his pocket just so he wouldn't throw it all away.

The Colonel's final destination in the casino would normally be the roulette table where he would request a huge stack of chips. When playing roulette, he would usually bet the maximum of $10,000 per spin. With the speed of the wheel, wagers of this size made it possible to lose $300,000 in one hour. There are even rumors that when the Colonel was forced to be away from Vegas on one of Elvis's concert tours, he would send a representative to the casino and gamble by telephone.

In *If I Can Dream*, Larry Geller tells of watching the Colonel rack up huge gambling losses the night of December 13, 1976, in Las Vegas. Geller was walking through the casino at around nine. The casino was nearly empty except for a crowd around one table. Geller went to see what was going on. There was Colonel Parker sitting by himself. A rope had been erected to fence him off from the crowd. He was playing a game called the Wheel of Fortune, the object of which is to guess the number the wheel stops on. The odds of winning are horrible.

The Colonel spotted Geller and asked him to sit with him for luck. Geller's presence did nothing to improve the Colonel's success. For the next two hours, he lost one huge bag of chips after another. Geller left the table and went to his hotel room. Unable to sleep, he returned to the casino at 2:00 A.M. The Colonel was still at the table, still losing. Geller heard whispers in the crowd that he had dropped more than one million dollars.

The date was December 13th 1976.

Chapter 13

1970 to 1973

★
★
★
★

With Las Vegas conquered, the Colonel was ready to take Elvis across America. Houston was chosen as the site of Elvis's first appearance outside of Las Vegas since his return to performing. Elvis's appearances were in conjunction with the Texas Livestock Show and Rodeo. The Colonel had been reluctant to put Elvis in a huge venue like the Astrodome for fear that there would be a lot of empty seats. A million-dollar check helped the Colonel overcome his apprehension.

On February 25, 1970, the Colonel flew to Houston to make final preparations for Elvis's three days of concerts at the Astrodome. Elvis followed the Colonel to Houston on February 26, flying on Kirk Kerkorian's private jet.

When only 16,708 people showed up for the first performance, a 2:00 P.M. Friday show, it looked as though the Colonel's fears were coming true. However, the small attendance was due to the concert being performed in the middle of a weekday rather than Elvis's inability to draw a large audience. The audience more than doubled for the next show, and the crowds poured in for the remainder of the engagement. In total, 207,494 people saw Elvis's six concerts at the Astrodome. After the final performance on March 1, a banquet was held in Elvis's honor. The Colonel and Elvis both received gold watches as tokens of appreciation from the Texas Livestock Show and Rodeo officials.

Elvis and the Colonel's next move was the subject of considerable speculation. On March 19, 1970, the *Los Angeles Times* reported that one of Elvis's August Las Vegas concerts would be broadcast via closed circuit television to 275 cities. Reportedly Elvis would be paid one million dollars for the broadcast. The rumors were just that. The Colonel had a documentary movie next in line for his boy. On May 22, 1970, he reached an agreement with MGM for a documentary centered around Elvis's summer concerts at the International Hotel in Las Vegas.

On July 5, Elvis flew to Los Angeles to begin rehearsals for his International show. The rehearsals were filmed for inclusion in the documentary known at the time as *Standing Room Only*. It would be later changed to *Elvis, That's the Way It Is*. Elvis opened at the International on August 10. MGM filmed the dinner show the first week.

A Las Vegas waitress named Pat Parker gave the Colonel something to do during lulls in his gambling by filing a paternity suit against Elvis. Her only proof that she ever even met Elvis was a picture of them taken backstage in Las Vegas. Colonel Parker turned the matter over to attorney Ed Hookstratten. Hookstratten, in turn, hired a private investigator named John O'Grady. O'Grady eventually proved that Elvis was not the father of Ms. Parker's child.

Production of *Elvis, That's the Way It Is* was being rushed so that it would hit the theaters at the same time as Elvis's national tour. An album of the film's soundtrack would be released at the same time. The Colonel was the ringmaster of the entire package. Every day he was on the phone several times with the director of the documentary, Denise Sanders. There were several meetings with RCA to make certain that the soundtrack would be in stores by the time the film was released and Elvis's concerts began. The Colonel retained final say over everything from the album cover to the movie poster.

After three successful engagements in Las Vegas and success at the Astrodome, the Colonel had finally decided that Elvis was ready to tour the country. Actually, he had begun laying the groundwork for Elvis's return to national touring before the first Las Vegas concert in 1969. He started by looking for someone to book Elvis's shows.

Booking a concert tour in 1970 was a much bigger job than it had been when Elvis stopped touring in the late 1950s. The shows were larger productions requiring a mobile army of men and equipment. The Colonel decided to hire some help. After researching several of the big players in the business, he put Tom Hulett and Jerry Weintraub at the top of his list of candidates.

Hulett and Weintraub rose to prominence by promoting rock acts in the 1960s. Hulett booked tours for Jimi Hendrix. Weintraub had booked Cream and then Eric Clapton after he left the group. In the late 1960s, they joined forces and started Concerts West. Concerts West soon established a relationship with most of the arena managers across the country.

On September 9, 1970, Jerry Weintraub received a telephone call from Colonel Parker. The Colonel said, "Jerry, this may be the happiest day of your life. We should take a meeting. I want to talk to you about doing some dates with Elvis."

The Colonel met with Hulett and Weintraub at his office on the MGM studio lot. He told them that if they wanted to book Elvis's tours, they would have to pay an advance of one million dollars against the gate receipts. Without hesitation, Hulett told him that he had a deal and extended his hand for the Colonel to shake. The Colonel's hand remained motionless. He told Hulett that they didn't have a deal until he had a cashier's check in his hand. He wanted it by noon the next day.

The following day, Hulett presented the Colonel with a check for one million dollars. Still, the Colonel was not satisfied. The million dollars would only buy them the right to promote a ten-concert, six-city tour. If the Colonel was happy with the way they handled the short tour, he would engage them on a more permanent basis.

The Colonel did not make the test easy. He chose cities that were widely geographically dispersed. The tour would begin in Phoenix and then travel to St. Louis, Detroit, Miami, Tampa, and Miami. It was a challenge due to the massive amount of equipment that had to be moved from city to city. In the 1950s, Elvis had used the public address system that was available in the site he was playing. By 1970, giant sound systems were the standard for concerts. The artists carried their own systems with them.

The Colonel was alarmed when Elvis told him that he wanted his Las Vegas conductor, Joe Guercio, and an orchestra to accompany him. All these extra bodies would add considerably to the expense of the tour. The Colonel came up with a solution that would accommodate Elvis in a significantly less expensive manner than a traveling orchestra. Joe Guercio traveled as Elvis's conductor accompanied by only two horn players. The remainder of the musicians would be hastily assembled from local orchestras in each city.

The Colonel only got away with this for a year. By 1971, Elvis was insisting that he wanted the same musicians in the orchestra every night. Soon, instead of two horn players, a twelve-piece orchestra was added to the traveling crew.

While the Colonel would occasionally let Elvis have his way, he would not tolerate anyone else challenging him. Joe Miscule, a member of Elvis's male backup group, the Imperials, decided to demand a raise for the group and a solo spot in the show in the middle of a Las Vegas engagement. Miscule searched out Colonel Parker and found him at one of his favorite spots, the roulette table. Miscule first went up to Tom Diskin who was standing behind the Colonel. Rather than speaking directly to the Colonel, Miscule told Diskin that he needed to speak to the Colonel. Diskin relayed the message to the Colonel who was in easy earshot of Miscule. The Colonel told Diskin that he was busy. Miscule proceeded to tell Diskin that the Imperials needed more money. Before Diskin could relay the message, the Colonel told him to tell Miscule that he was wasting his time, there wouldn't be any raises. Miscule gave up. The next day, he told Elvis that the Imperials would be leaving him at the end of the Las Vegas engagement.

Hulett and Weintraub's test tour began in Phoenix two days after Elvis's Labor Day closing show at the International. Tickets, in general, sold out within hours of being released. The average gross receipts per show was $100,000. Hulett and Weintraub had passed the Colonel's test.

From then on, Tom Hulett and the Colonel would meet at the Colonel's office to plan Elvis's tours. They sat at a table with the map of the United States in front of them. They would plan a general route the tour would take, and then Hulett would call the arenas to check availability on certain dates. Hulett was successful at playing nearby cities against each other to get any date he wanted at the best price possible. He would call Houston to inquire about the availability of a certain date and throw in a "Don't worry if you're booked, we can just go to Dallas." Often, events would be canceled for the chance to get Elvis.

Usually the Colonel would be listening in on another phone when Hulett called an arena manager. The manager wouldn't know that the Colonel was listening. The Colonel would coach Hulett with hand signals during the conversations. Hulett acted the part of being the manager's friend. The Colonel was the heavy who Hulett could blame for the tough demands that he made in order to secure an appearance by Elvis.

One of these demands was that every venue had to make two nights available. If the first concert sold out, that allowed for the possibility of adding a second concert the next night. The venue manager was also required to hold a press conference announcing that Elvis was coming to town. The Colonel would instruct Hulett on the day that the press conference should take place. He would then pass this on to the arena manager. This generated publicity that the Colonel didn't have to pay for. The Colonel, through Hulett, even dictated when tickets would go on sale.

San Diego promoter Gerald Pagni told of receiving a telephone call from Jerry Weintraub. Weintraub said that he had been hired by Colonel Parker to book an eight-city western tour for Elvis. San Diego was one of the cities that had been selected for the tour. Weintraub and Pagni discussed some preliminary details over the phone. Two weeks later, the Colonel flew to San Diego along with Weintraub to meet with Pagni.

The Colonel detailed the requirements that Pagni would have to meet if he wanted Elvis to appear. He wanted all the arena's 14,500 seats to be sold in one week. Equal amounts of advertising were to be run on each of eleven San Diego radio stations. There were to be no tickets given away. The first five rows of seats could not be reserved for special purchasers. None of the tickets could be traded for advertising. No interviews would be allowed with Elvis or any member of the show. There would be no biography or pictures of Elvis supplied by the Colonel to use in publicity.

The Colonel also made accommodation and transportation demands of Pagni. Two floors of a hotel were to be reserved. For the twenty-four hours surrounding the concert, Pagni was to have available three limousines with drivers, a thirty-passenger bus, and a twenty-foot truck.

The Colonel promised Pagni that if he handled everything exactly according to these instructions, he could have Elvis the next time he came to San Diego. If anything at all was out of order, he would never see Elvis again.

The Colonel slashed the fee that the arena normally received. The standard for the time was for the arena to retain 10 percent of the gate receipts. Hulett, under the direction of the Colonel, demanded that the arena's fee be capped at four thousand dollars. The arenas were willing to go along with this because they knew that an Elvis Presley concert was a sure sellout. Plenty of money could be made selling popcorn and Cokes. This cut rate netted five thousand dollars or more per show for Elvis and the Colonel.

With Hulett and Weintraub handling most of the legwork on tours, the Colonel was free to devote his time to promoting the concerts. The Colonel related a story to Jerry Hopkins for his book *Elvis, The Final Years* about how he managed to sell two thousand remaining seats for a 1971 Salt Lake City concert.

"The rest of the auditorium was sold out, and we couldn't sell the last two thousand seats for anything. Then, on the Sunday before the show, Elder Stevens [the head of the Mormon church] died. The show was set for Wednesday. I called the radio stations and canceled all of the ads. We were not selling tickets anyway and I thought I would save $1,900. What we did was that instead of taking out ads, we made an announcement that we were dropping the ads until after Elder Stevens's funeral on Tuesday. Of course, the radio stations gave us all of the announcements free. Then, on Wednesday, the ads started again, and we sold out all two thousand seats in two hours between 10:00 A.M. and 12:00 noon. It had to be the Mormons who bought the tickets, right."

The Colonel traveled as the advance man on every one of Elvis's tours from the time that he started managing him until Elvis died. The Colonel couldn't resist pulling one of his gags now and then. Sometimes before a concert, he would walk out into the crowd and claim he could predict the attendance figure for that night. He would hold his hand to his head as if getting a psychic message. Every few seconds, he would announce, "The attendance tonight is 10,897." Later when the attendance was announced at 10,897, those who had witnessed the display were amazed. However, the Colonel wasn't psychic. He had already been given the number from the box office before he went down in the crowd to make his prediction.

The Colonel's entourage, in conjunction with some of Elvis's guys, handled arranging the hotel rooms, security, and other logistics of a traveling show. Elvis took nine to ten cases of wardrobe with him. The Colonel's main priority was to make sure that he had received their share of the concert gate prior to the show taking place.

The Colonel would arrive the day before Elvis's scheduled appearance. Accompanying him would be members of his staff and at least one of Elvis's. The first step when they arrived was to go to the hotel in which Elvis would be staying. Everything from which entrance to the building Elvis would use to room arrangements for the members of the show and the crew were planned to the tiniest detail. After the hotel was prepared, the Colonel would go to the airport to meet Elvis.

The next morning the Colonel would turn his attention to the concert site itself. He would ride to the arena in Elvis's limousine. The driver was always instructed to have alternate routes in mind in case there was a problem. It was imperative that Elvis was not late arriving for the show. After making sure that all the equipment and the Elvis souvenirs were at the arena, the Colonel would make stops at local radio stations to check that they were hyping the show.

That night, the Colonel would pick up a cashier's check for Elvis's share of the gate receipts, say a few words to Elvis, and leave for the airport to head for the next stop on the tour. When Elvis was on tour, he and the Colonel talked every day, though usually only for a few minutes. Between tours, they almost never talked. If they needed to communicate, they would relay messages through associates. Tom Diskin would usually call Joe Esposito to deliver messages from the Colonel to Elvis and vice versa.

At the Colonel's suggestion, everyone who went on tour with Elvis received a bonus at its end. Vernon Presley complained that Elvis should be keeping the money rather than paying it out in bonuses. The Colonel decided to pay Vernon a bigger bonus than anyone else was receiving. This ended Vernon's complaints.

In *Good Rockin' Tonight*, Joe Esposito told the story of the time that George Parkhill and Pat Kelleher were driving with the Colonel and Tom Hulett to the building in Cleveland where Elvis was to perform that night. About a block away from the arena, they spotted a bootlegger on a street corner selling Elvis albums for five dollars a piece. "Colonel, he's selling records!" Hulett yelled, ready to jump out of the limo and collar the guy. "Keep going," the Colonel told the driver. "You don't see no one out there selling Paul Anka tapes and records, do you? If you're not hot, you got no bootleggers. Just be happy we got 'em. It means we're hot."

Back in the limelight, Elvis began to receive various awards and honors. In 1971, the National Academy of Recording Artists informed Colonel Parker they wanted to give Elvis a Lifetime Achievement Award. The academy, which gives out the Grammys, hadn't been particularly generous to Elvis over the years. They had only recognized him previously for his gospel songs. They wanted to make up for this by giving him the Lifetime Achievement Award.

The Colonel was all for Elvis receiving awards. Everything was fine until he was asked how many songs Elvis would want to perform when he accepted the award on the television broadcast. The Colonel responded that the number of songs that Elvis performed would depend on how much money they were paying him. The gentlemen from the academy said that they didn't pay for performances on the show. In that case, the Colonel said, Elvis wouldn't be singing any songs. Elvis ended up receiving his award in the dressing room before a concert, rather than at the telecast.

On another occasion, the individual responsible for arranging performers for the White House called the Colonel and issued an invitation for Elvis to play for President Richard Nixon. The Colonel said that he was certain that Elvis would accept. His fee would be twenty-five thousand dollars, which included an orchestra. The Colonel caught the gentleman completely off guard. Once he recovered from his shock, he told the Colonel that no one got paid to play at the White House. Fine, then Elvis would not be performing. Elvis never played unless he was paid.

In 1972, Elvis began work on what would be his last movie. It was a documentary for MGM called *Elvis On Tour*. Bob Abel and Pierre Adidge were chosen by the studio to make the movie, although the Colonel retained veto power over the choice. Several days of filming took place in the studio, and one concert was filmed. Yet, the Colonel had not given his official sanction to the pair, who had just completed a documentary of a Joe Cocker tour.

On March 27, Elvis began an RCA recording session at their Hollywood studios. MGM also filmed several of Elvis's concerts during his early April tour. In an interview before Elvis's April 9 Hampton Roads, Virginia, concert, the Colonel said that Elvis was filming a new movie called *Remnants of the Old West*.

Abel sent the film of Elvis's Hampton Roads concert to Hollywood for a rush development. As soon as the developed film was sent back, he had a private screening for the Colonel. The Colonel liked what he saw and told Abel that he and Adidge had his blessing to make the movie. However, he warned Abel that he had spent years building and preserving Elvis's image. If they filmed anything that detracted from that image, they were through.

Adidge spent quite a bit of time alone with Elvis during the making of *Elvis on Tour*. Away from the Colonel's ear, Elvis told him how happy he was to be making a quality film and that making those old movies made him physically ill and that "It was just that Hollywood's image of me was wrong, and I knew it and couldn't do anything about it."

Elvis on Tour cost $1.6 million. One million of that was Elvis's salary. The documentary opened in theaters on November 1, 1972, and recovered its costs in the first three days of release. It went on to win a Golden Globe award for best documentary.

Once the making of *Elvis on Tour* was completed in April of 1972, the Colonel turned his attention to the next big event, bringing Elvis to New York's Madison Square Garden. Colonel Parker had never booked Elvis into New York in the 1950s or put him into big stadiums for that matter. The Beatles were selling out ballparks in 1965. Elvis's drawing power in 1956 had to have been equal to that of the Beatles nine years later. It remains a mystery why the Colonel passed up the opportunity to put Elvis in front of huge crowds.

Before his Garden appearance, Elvis held a press conference. After a few minutes of questions in which Elvis revealed very little of himself, the Colonel walked onto the platform and said, "I like to live up to my reputation of being a nice guy. This is it, folks."

On June 9, 1972, Elvis made his first-ever concert appearance in New York City, playing four sold-out shows in three days. Several celebrities were in attendance including John Lennon, George Harrison, and Bob Dylan.

Two Madison Square Garden performances were recorded by RCA. Elvis was not told that they were being recorded to make his performance as natural as possible. The June 10 evening performance was released by RCA nine days later.

The New York concerts were extremely profitable for Elvis and the Colonel. The gross was more than $730,000. Elvis's share of the concert gate came to about $250,000. He made another million dollars from the album. Of course, the Colonel got his 50 percent.

When it was all over, Elvis and the Colonel each took home $650,000.

With America conquered, the next logical move was for Elvis to tour the world. He had expressed the desire to appear in Europe as early as 1958. Scotty Moore had dinner at Elvis's house during the 1968 comeback special project. Elvis told him then that he had plans to tour England. He asked Scotty if he would be willing to play in his band on the tour. At a press conference at his 1969 Las Vegas opening, Elvis again alluded to a European tour.

On January 6, 1971, the Elvis Presley Fan Club of Great Britain reported in its newsletter that Tom Diskin had officially denied that Elvis would appear in Europe in 1972. Despite Diskin's statement, rumors continued to circulate that Elvis would be appearing in Europe. The most likely site was thought to be Paris or England. Tom Diskin, speaking for Colonel Parker, again flatly denied the rumors.

In a visit with Colonel Parker in Las Vegas, in August 1972, Todd Slaughter, president of the Official Elvis Presley Fan Club of Great Britain, asked the Colonel if Elvis would be performing in England. He said that the Colonel told him there weren't enough big arenas there. Elvis does not want to appear in an open-air stadium, the Colonel said.

On February 20, 1973, *Variety* reported that the Colonel had been offered $500,000 for Elvis to make six appearances at Earl's Court Stadium in London. One of the concerts would be broadcast throughout England on closed-circuit television.

While many of these reports were false, the Colonel did receive several legitimate offers, two of which were for Elvis to appear in London. The first would have paid one million pounds and the second two million, or four million dollars, to appear at Wembley Stadium. The Colonel turned down the first offer because he said the ticket prices were too high. He was afraid that the show might not sell out. He turned down the Wembley shows saying that Elvis didn't like to play ballparks. This seems a strange excuse given that Elvis played several "ballparks" in the United States, including the Houston Astrodome.

The Commonwealth was also eager for an appearance by Elvis. In June 1972, the Colonel had been offered $900,000 by an Australian promoter for Elvis to make two appearances in Sydney and one in Melbourne. He was also offered the use of a private jet, a pilot, and a house for Elvis to stay in while he was in Australia. In September 1974, the Sydney newspaper, the *Daily Telegraph*, reported that Elvis turned down a two-million-dollar offer for two shows made by Australian promoter, Bob Pritchard. Pritchard said that Presley's management had said, "Thank you, but if we ever need a million bucks that badly, we'll give you a ring."

The Middle East wanted Elvis as well. Saudi billionaire Adnan Khashoggi tried to hire Elvis to perform in front of the great pyramids. The Colonel asked a price that he thought Khashoggi would never pay, five million dollars. He was shocked when he accepted. The Colonel told Khashoggi that he would have to talk with Elvis and get back with him. After a few days, the Colonel came back with a line that Elvis had insisted on ten million dollars. To his astonishment, Khashoggi again accepted. Elvis was excited at the prospect of the concert and the money, but the Colonel eventually brought up familiar logistics and security excuses, and the deal was dropped.

Led by Japan, the noncommunist countries of the Far East were also clamoring loudly for appearances by Elvis. With their new industrial influence, they had the money to pay for them. Having no reasonable excuse as to why Elvis should not have a blockbuster Japanese tour, all the Colonel could do was duck the issue.

In addition to his work booking Elvis's tours, Tom Hulett was involved with several other artists including the Moody Blues. In 1973, Hulett booked the group on a tour of Japan. Elvis had Lamar Fike call Hulett when he returned from Japan to say that he wanted to talk with him. Hulett knew that what Elvis wanted to talk about was touring Japan. He also knew that it would be the end of his working with Elvis if he talked to him without the Colonel's knowledge. Hulett telephoned the Colonel to inform him of Elvis's call. The Colonel told Hulett that he could talk to Elvis about Japan all he wanted. However, there was no way that Elvis would be touring there.

Publicly the Colonel said that it didn't make any sense for Elvis to be touring Japan. The largest arena there had only twelve thousand seats. This meant that Elvis would have to give at least thirty performances to meet the public's demand. The Colonel also said that security would be a problem. The police wouldn't be as cooperative as they were in the United States. He even cited Elvis's inability to speak Japanese as a reason why he shouldn't perform there. How would Elvis conduct a press conference?

What was the real reason the Colonel never booked Elvis outside of the United States? The first answer to spring to mind was that the Colonel had no passport. But why didn't he book the tour and stay home? Jerry Weintraub and Tom Hulett could have handled it. The Colonel's need for control over everything would not allow him to do this. Also, he did not want Elvis to get the idea that he did not really need the Colonel.

According to Elvis's cousin Billy Smith, the Colonel said about the possibility of a foreign tour, "Security just won't be good, and we don't want something to happen over there. Besides, I can make you just as much money here. Let's just increase the tours in the States." The security argument was an attempt to play upon the kidnapping and death threats that Elvis had been receiving. The argument about making as much money in the United States by doing more shows does not make any sense. Why would a manager advise his client to perform ten shows to make one million dollars when he could make the same in one night in London? He wouldn't unless he was in this country illegally.

Joe Esposito tried to refute the claims that the Colonel did not book Elvis outside the U.S. because of his own illegal alien status. He cited the fact that the Colonel accompanied Elvis on his brief 1957 Canadian tour as an example of the Colonel's ability to travel outside the U.S. However, entering Canada is a much simpler affair than traveling to London, Sydney, or Tokyo. It didn't require a passport.

Joe Esposito gives another version of why the Colonel turned town the European tour offers. He was afraid that Elvis would carry his usual assortment of guns and drugs with him and get arrested. He also feared that the European media would trash Elvis in print. About half of Elvis's fan base resided outside the U.S. The bad publicity Elvis might generate in his current condition would then destroy his fan base. Marty Lacker said that he never heard that. He was told that security problems and the lack of Colonel Parker's connections in Europe were the reasons.

Esposito also claimed that Elvis lost interest in going outside the United States when he found out that he wouldn't be able to take his guns with him. According to Esposito, Elvis told the Colonel this after he heard the Osmond Brothers had been searched for drugs and guns when they went on their European tour.

If it is to be believed that everything that happened with Elvis Presley's career was part of the master plan, there is a bizarre logic to the Colonel passing on multimillion dollar deals. If he kept Elvis needing money, he would need to work. If he needed to work, he would always need the Colonel. The Colonel was purposely rationing the amount of money Elvis earned to keep him under control. It was the same strategy that he used with RCA, making sure that they were always in need of more songs. Need created power. This also explains the Colonel's recommendation that Elvis seek no expert financial advice. He wanted to make sure that Elvis always needed money. The Colonel knew that no matter how rebellious Elvis might get, whenever he needed money, he would return to the fold.

The answer to the Colonel's problems came from an unlikely source, heavyweight boxing. Demand for tickets to Muhammad Ali fights was much greater than the number of seats in any single arena. In addition, the demand for Ali tickets came from all over the world. The solution was to televise the fights via satellite on closed-circuit television. This same idea could be applied to Elvis to allow him to go on a world tour without leaving the United States.

There are two versions of who conceived the idea of a satellite concert performance by Elvis. The president of RCA, Rocco Laginestra, said that the Colonel had never even heard of the communication satellite. He said that RCA was under tremendous pressure from its foreign affiliates for Elvis to perform in their country in support of his record releases. With the Colonel refusing to make such a tour, RCA conceived the television broadcast as an alternative.

With the exception of Laginestra, most people credit the Colonel with the satellite broadcast concept. Joe Esposito told of the Colonel's first discussion of an Elvis concert to be televised around the world via satellite. The Colonel called a meeting with RCA's representatives at his Las Vegas Hilton suite. "I had a dream last night. I dreamed that an Elvis performance was beamed around the world by satellite. Would you be interested?" he said. The Colonel envisioned the concert taking place in Hawaii. He chose Hawaii as the location because its time zone would allow the concert to air in prime time in much of the world. He also knew that Elvis liked being in Hawaii, and that couldn't hurt his performance. The RCA representatives agreed that it was a great idea.

After he had approached RCA with the idea, the Colonel went to Elvis. After the meeting, according to Joe Esposito, Elvis was very excited. The Colonel had told him that he was going to make history by being the first entertainer to have a live satellite performance.

NBC agreed to finance the program to support its subsidiary RCA. As a bargaining chip when NBC asked to be able to broadcast the concert twice, the Colonel agreed, as long as they would pick up all the expenses involved with the concert. The Colonel continued his tradition of getting someone else to pick up the tab.

The day after Elvis closed at the Las Vegas Hilton, in September 1972, the Colonel held a press conference. "Folks, get a seat and sit down, or you'll have to pay five dollars for standing up," the Colonel said before announcing that the concert, named "Aloha from Hawaii," would be televised via satellite around the world on January 14, 1973.

Appearing with Elvis and the Colonel was Rocco Laginestra who said that among countries negotiating for transmission were China and the USSR. Already set to receive the broadcast live were Japan, Australia, and parts of Southeast Asia. The next night, it would be seen throughout Europe. Broadcast in the United States would follow at a later date. RCA would be simultaneously releasing an album of the concert around the world. The Colonel predicted that advance orders for the album would be more than one million units. Elvis also was present at the press conference. He humbly said that he hoped that he wouldn't let down the fans.

In November 1972, Elvis flew to Honolulu for two days of concerts. On November 20, a press conference was held announcing that the upcoming January concert would be a benefit for the Kui Lee Cancer Fund. Lee, who had died of the disease, was the most famous singer/songwriter in Hawaii's history. The Colonel started the donations by presenting a one-thousand-dollar check on behalf of himself and Elvis. The concert eventually raised seventy-five thousand dollars for the fund.

On January 7, 1973, tickets went on sale for the "Aloha from Hawaii" concert. By early evening, only 100 tickets remained. After the January 14 show sold out, tickets were sold for a January 12 dress rehearsal.

Elvis arrived in Honolulu on January 9. He was on a 600-calorie-a-day diet to get ready for the concert. By the day of the show, he was down to 170 pounds. He rehearsed for the show on the tenth, eleventh, and twelfth. The twelfth was a full show in front of an audience. It was filmed as a backup to the January 14 concert.

The Aloha concert began at 12:30 A.M. on January 14, 1972. The ratings for the show set records around the world. In the Philippines, 91.8 percent of the television audience watched the concert. In North Korea, 80 percent of the audience tuned in.

The concert was shown on tape delay in thirty European countries. On April 4, the "Aloha From Hawaii" concert was broadcast in the United States and was watched by 51 percent of the U.S. television audience.

The day after the concert, the Colonel arrived at Elvis's suite carrying a stack of newspapers. Each one had a story about the broadcast. They estimated that the total worldwide audience for the show was in excess of one billion people. This was the largest single audience for any television broadcast to date.

While RCA was ecstatic over the success of the Aloha special and the soundtrack album, they were still frustrated with the difficulty of getting studio recordings from Elvis and the Colonel. Elvis's perpetual tour left little time for him to record. The Colonel had a solution for this problem. Elvis would begin cutting a long series of live albums, and RCA's quota could be met without his setting foot in the studio. The Colonel was creating a 1970's live-touring rut that was as deep and as damaging as the sixties movie rut had been.

RCA was too afraid of the Colonel to complain very loudly. RCA's Joan Deary was not about to get in a battle with the master of her company's crown prince. Deary had started her career at RCA as Steve Sholes's secretary. She was in that position when Sholes got RCA to buy Elvis's contract. Later she became the assistant to RCA vice president, Harry Jenkins, who was in charge of RCA's Elvis operation. By the 1970s, Deary was in charge of the Presley catalog and in the unenviable position of dealing with the

Colonel. Deary was clearly afraid of him, as is evidenced by this memo in which she discussed who was going to ask the Colonel for a copy of his fan club list.

RCA Internal Memo

October 12, 1973
To: R. Laginestra
From: J. Deary
Subj: Elvis Presley Legendary Performer Package

Attached is a brief rundown I prepared on the above album along with a list of the repertoire and pertinent recording information. As we have previously discussed, I think it is very important that we have some sort of press release on this newly discovered tape from the old Sun days. And, also that we get the word out that there are un-released collector's items in this package. Most of the feedback I have gotten indicates that the general opinion is that this is just another re-issue of the same songs.

I would like to offer a suggestion that if possible we obtain a list of all of Elvis's fan clubs and send them a note regarding our approach to this series and requesting input on what they would like to see in future volumes.

If you agree with this approach, and if so, would *you* like to ask the Colonel for the fan club list.

Thanks,

Joan

The Colonel never gave up complete control over all facets of Elvis's record releases. He required RCA to send him the final mixes on the records for his approval. Without fail, the Colonel would tell RCA that they needed to turn up Elvis's voice in relation to the band. It was Elvis who was responsible for the original mix, but RCA took their orders from the Colonel. Elvis's voice was brought up.

The Colonel also was in charge of Elvis's record jacket design. They were all very simple. Each was required to have a picture of Elvis. After his first album, the word "Presley" never appeared on a cover, only "Elvis." The Colonel also insisted that no other name were to appear anywhere on the cover. No producers or company musicians were allowed to be listed.

He required RCA to buy the pictures of Elvis from him to use for album jackets and for 45-rpm record sleeves. Most record companies have their artist sit for photo sessions. The Colonel simply refused. Anytime that Elvis did sit for photographers, whether it was for movie publicity or a magazine, the Colonel demanded that all negatives be turned over to him. He would then sell pictures to RCA, one at a time, and tell them what they were going to pay him for them. It is doubtful that he shared any of this money with Elvis.

It is puzzling that RCA did not try to capitalize on Elvis and add other rock musicians to their roster. One theory is that the company was highbrow at its roots and only tolerated Elvis as a rock singer on its roster because they had to financially. The other competing reason that has circulated over the years is that the Colonel threatened to take Elvis to another record company if they brought anyone else in.

The Colonel had RCA at his mercy. The company was in decline when Elvis came along. Elvis revived it and accounted for more than 25 percent of its total sales. Between 1956 and 1962, RCA released thirty-nine singles that became gold records. Thirty-one of them belonged to Elvis. This gave the Colonel carte blanche to treat RCA as he pleased and to dictate the kind of recording that Elvis would make.

In 1973, RCA did manage to achieve a measure of revenge against the Colonel, although it would take a few years to become apparent. On March 1, 1973, Elvis signed a new seven-year contract with RCA that the Colonel had negotiated. This was despite Elvis's current contract not expiring until December 31, 1974. The contract specified that Elvis must make two albums and four singles per year. Elvis's royalty would be ten cents per single sold and fifty cents per album. The contract also called for a lump sum of $100,000 to be paid to both Elvis and Colonel Parker's All Star Shows at the end of the contract.

Colonel Parker made plenty of special deals that benefited him as part of the new contract. Elvis agreed to pay the Colonel's company, All Star Tours $675,000 over seven years. RCA's division that promoted concert tours for its artists, RCA Record Tours, also agreed to pay All Star Tours $675,000 plus 10 percent of its tours' profits. In return, the Colonel was to assist in "planning, promotion, and merchandising." In a separate agreement, RCA agreed to pay All Star Tours $350,000 for assisting RCA Record Tours. RCA also hired Colonel Parker as a consultant for a sum of $50,000.

The most amazing agreement signed that day sold all of Elvis's royalty rights to any song recorded prior to March 1973 back to RCA for a lump sum of $5.5 million. This meant that RCA would never have to pay Elvis any royalty on future sales of the hundreds of songs he had recorded prior to this date.

Joan Deary said that the Colonel thought all the value was gone from Elvis's songs when he sold the royalty rights in March 1973. He questioned how many times they could reissue the songs. The average person probably would have thought the same thing. However, Deary knew that RCA was sitting on a gold mine of unreleased outtakes and live performances. She got the idea to do the legendary performers series. She would combine unreleased alternate takes with a souvenir booklet. The first record in the series earned RCA more than one million dollars. They had already earned 20 percent of their purchase price for all the masters.

Joe Esposito said that the royalty sale to RCA was Elvis's idea. He needed the money. He said that RCA originally approached the Colonel with an offer of $2.5 million. He took the deal to Elvis, but recommended against it. When Elvis insisted on selling, the Colonel was able to negotiate his way into another $3 million.

Record industry executive Mac Wiseman said that the consensus in the music business was that the Colonel had thrown Elvis to the wolves with the terrible movies and cheap Las Vegas deals. There was also a feeling that he started believing his own publicity about his greatness. He started thinking *he* was the star.

Chapter 14

1974 to 1976

$\mathcal{I}$n 1974, the relationship between Elvis and the Colonel
rapidly deteriorated. Ironically, the start of the downhill slide
had nothing to do with the Colonel. Elvis was in the middle of an
engagement at the Las Vegas Hilton when a chef that he was close
to was fired. Elvis berated the management of the Hilton to the
audience during his performance that night. Colonel Parker stood
backstage listening, at first stunned and then angry. He was friends
with Baron Hilton, and they had substantial economic ties.

Henri Lewin, now president of the Las Vegas Hilton, met with
Colonel Parker after the show to complain about Elvis's disparaging remarks and asked the Colonel to discuss the matter with him.
The Colonel telephoned Elvis in his suite to let him know that he
was coming up.

A couple of minutes later, the Colonel arrived at the suite. He
told Elvis that he needed to talk to him in private. Elvis got off the

couch and walked into his bedroom with the Colonel following. The door remained open so the Memphis Mafia heard the conversation. The Colonel said, "Elvis, you made a big mistake tonight. The management is paying you good money to perform here, not to tell them how to run their hotel. If you have a problem pertaining to the hotel, you should come to me."

Uncharacteristically, Elvis lashed back at the Colonel. He brought up the Colonel's gambling as a hindrance to his ability to get a better deal from another hotel. He said that the only reason the Colonel was worried about Baron Hilton was because he owed him so much money. The Colonel threatened to call a press conference in the morning to announce his resignation as Elvis's manager. Elvis shot back that he was calling a press conference that night to say that he had fired the Colonel. When Elvis came out of the bedroom, he told those present that he had just fired the Colonel.

The next afternoon, the Colonel had delivered to Elvis's suite the legal documents necessary to end their relationship. He would dissolve the contract and leave without making a fuss. But first, Elvis would have to come up with a little cash, two million dollars and unpaid expenses. Elvis passed this on to Vernon, completed his Las Vegas engagement, and left for Memphis without speaking to the Colonel.

On getting home, Elvis talked to Jerry Weintraub about becoming his manager. Weintraub told him that he was getting out of the artist management end of the business to become strictly a concert promoter. Elvis next went to Tom Hulett. Hulett said no one could do a better job for him than the Colonel.

Elvis turned to his father for support, but Vernon maintained that it would be a disastrous and costly mistake to fire the Colonel. For one thing, there was no way that they could come up with the money that the Colonel said they owed him. Elvis reluctantly agreed to make up with him. Why Elvis did not realize that he could have gotten any number of people to put up the two million dollars to buy his contract from Colonel Parker is anyone's guess.

According to a close associate, Elvis respected Colonel Parker for his ability to manipulate those with whom he negotiated. However, personally Elvis felt very uncomfortable around the Colonel. Another friend said he never once saw Elvis and Parker together for a social occasion in the twenty-one years he knew them. Elvis kept his business and private lives separate. When he and the Colonel met, it was always to conduct business. After the Baron Hilton incident, their relationship became even more distant.

Elvis began his summer 1974 stint at the Las Vegas Hilton on August 19, 1974. The Colonel had a new souvenir for sale, an album with Elvis talking during performances called *Having Fun with Elvis on Stage*.

The Colonel had formed a record label in partnership with Elvis called Boxcar Records. Originally, Elvis had wanted Boxcar to be a working label that would release records by new artists. Ultimately, Boxcar Records' only release was *Having Fun with Elvis on Stage*.

During the summer engagement, Barbra Streisand and her boyfriend, Jon Peters, came backstage at the Hilton to talk to Elvis about their remake of *A Star Is Born*. They wanted Elvis to take the male lead. Streisand spent two hours talking to Elvis about the project. Elvis was excited over the opportunity and said he would have the Colonel discuss the details with her.

According to Joe Esposito, Elvis's enthusiasm was dampened when he learned that Peters, a hairdresser, was going to direct the movie. Esposito said that Elvis let the Colonel know that he had changed his mind about doing the movie. The Colonel told Elvis not to worry. He had sent Streisand a proposal that called for Elvis to get star billing. He was confident she would turn him down.

The Colonel tried dealing with Streisand as he had Hal Wallis. Besides demanding top billing for Elvis, he asked for one million dollars plus 50 percent of the profits. Not surprisingly, Streisand turned this down. She insisted that she and Elvis receive equal billing. No matter how Elvis felt, this would have been a deal breaker for the Colonel. Streisand moved on to Kris Kristofferson with a less-than-successful outcome. Some people took to calling the finished film *A Bore Is Starred*.

Without a challenge like *A Star Is Born* to keep him motivated, Elvis sank deeper into his drug habit to the point where it was seriously endangering his life. The quality of his concert performances began to suffer. One night he would be fine. The next night he would stumble his way through the show, forgetting lyrics to songs he had sung hundreds of times. Incredibly, the Colonel did nothing to encourage Elvis to seek help. One would have thought that the Colonel would have wanted Elvis to kick his habit for selfish reasons. Since he and Elvis were equal partners, the Colonel stood to lose millions if Elvis overdosed. Yet he did nothing. In fact, he was still denying detailed knowledge of Elvis' drug problems two years after Elvis died.

After Elvis's death, the state of Tennessee began looking into charges against Dr. George Nichopoulos for overprescribing medication to Elvis and others. Colonel Parker was interviewed as a part of the investigation. He denied any longstanding awareness of Elvis's drug problem. He said that the first hint he got was in the mid-1970s when Elvis visited him at his Palm Springs home. Elvis appeared ill. The Colonel had asked him if he needed a break. According to the Colonel's statement, Elvis responded that he was taking drugs that made him look sick. The Colonel offered to help, but Elvis refused and told him to mind his own business. The Colonel claimed that this was the first he knew of Elvis's drug problems.

The Colonel went on to say that later he became concerned with Elvis's radical weight gain. "I said, 'You have gained so much weight.' He said, 'I know what I'm doing, Colonel. Please don't interfere.'" "You never did interfere into his personal life," Larry Hutchinson, chief criminal investigator for the state's attorney general, said. "I never have from the start," the Colonel replied.

Elvis insiders say that contrary to what the Colonel claimed, he was well aware of Elvis's drug problems for a number of years before he died. John O'Grady, the former Los Angeles Police Department narcotics officer, turned private investigator, who looked into the paternity suit filed against Elvis, was hired to investigate sources of Elvis's drugs. According to O'Grady, Colonel Parker was well aware of the extent of Elvis's addiction. "Parker knew about the drugs and didn't care a bit as long as it didn't affect his pocketbook," he said.

Elvis's primary physician and drug prescriber, Dr. George Nichopoulos said that it was hard to persuade the Colonel that it was best for Elvis if he toured for ten to twelve days and then rested. The Colonel would have him booked twenty or thirty days in a row. Elvis loved to preform, but too much, too soon was a source of stress. When Elvis became stressed, he increased his drug intake. Dr. Nick said that when he tried to get the Colonel to cut back on the concert schedule, the Colonel responded by saying, "No! Absolutely not. We have to keep him current. Keep him before the public."

Red West also claimed the Colonel was aware of Elvis's drug problems. It got to the point where the Colonel would routinely call West the day of a show and ask if he thought Elvis would be able to perform that night. Occasionally, Red's answer was no.

In Houston, on August 28, 1976, Elvis's concert started one-and-a-half hours late. When he finally made it to the stage, the audience was shocked by his appearance. His eyes were glazed, his skin yellow, and he completely messed up the words to his opening song, "C. C. Rider." The same thing happened with the next song. The crowd started to get up and leave. They thought that Elvis was on drugs or drunk. Halfway through the show, Elvis had the house lights turned up, and he apologized for his performance. He said that he was sick. Elvis then stood on stage, shaking hands with everyone who came up to it. The next day, newspapers said that the audience had witnessed the death of rock and roll.

Dr. Nick has said that this behavior was a side effect of Elvis taking drugs. After the Houston show, the Colonel called Dr. Nick and asked him to come back on tour with Elvis. Dr. Nick had had a falling out with Elvis a couple of months before. They couldn't have Elvis canceling shows and giving performances like he had. The Colonel said that he would have to pull Elvis off the tour if Dr. Nick didn't come back. After receiving a half-hearted apology from Elvis, Dr. Nick agreed to return.

When the Colonel should have been giving Elvis challenges, giving him a reason to stay in shape and off drugs, he was doing exactly the opposite in favor of maintaining the status quo. It is not clear why the Colonel did not also demand that Elvis stop his self-destructive behavior. Rather than trying to persuade him to get help, the Colonel seemed to use Elvis's drug abuse to feather his own nest, such as by upping his commission to 50 percent.

In the last few years of his life, Elvis's favorite pastime was practicing karate. He was so enamored with the marital art, he wanted to produce and narrate a documentary on it. He asked the Colonel to arrange the distribution for the completed film. The Colonel was very unenthusiastic. In his opinion, it was too far removed from Elvis's image. Vernon was against the movie because of the money it would cost. Between them, they talked Elvis into dropping the project. This only furthered Elvis's disenchantment with the Colonel.

According to Joe Esposito, in the early days, the Colonel came by Graceland on a regular basis to have dinner with Elvis and talk business. He said that the Colonel frequently reminded the Memphis Mafia that everyone there, including himself, owed everything to Elvis. "Just remember, boys," the Colonel would say, "if we didn't have Elvis, I couldn't make these deals, and we wouldn't be having dinner in this beautiful home."

Esposito said that after the early 1960s, the Colonel and Elvis saw each other less and less often. Eventually, Esposito delivered messages back and forth when the Colonel wanted to convey something to Elvis. In the last few years of his life, Elvis usually refused to talk directly to the Colonel, even if Parker requested that through Esposito. Esposito would often make up excuses to the Colonel as to why Elvis couldn't come to the phone. Sometimes the Colonel would go along with the excuse and sometimes he would yell at Esposito to have Elvis call him when he wasn't busy.

Elvis's health deteriorated in 1975. On January 8, 1975, Elvis celebrated his fortieth birthday. The "Elvis is fat and forty" story appeared in many newspapers and magazines. The *Memphis Press Scimitar* reported that Elvis had canceled his upcoming Las Vegas concerts. The Hilton was quick to deny the story. It was not so much a cancellation as a postponement, the official line went. By putting off the appearance date, Elvis would be the first performer to appear at the grand opening of the hotel's twenty-million-dollar million addition.

On January 29, 1975, Elvis was admitted to Baptist Hospital in Memphis. He was said to have a "liver problem." During his stay, Elvis decided that he wanted to hire one of the nurses to accompany him on tour. When the Colonel found out, he immediately gave the message to Joe Esposito that traveling with a nurse would be bad for Elvis's image. The public would speculate over why it was necessary for Elvis to have a nurse with him wherever he went. Esposito relayed the message to Elvis, who agreed and gave up on the nurse idea.

On August 16, 1975, Elvis took off from Memphis for a Las Vegas engagement. He developed difficulty breathing during the flight, so the plane made an emergency landing in Dallas. Elvis waited there for five hours before continuing on to Vegas.

According to Sonny West, Elvis had wanted to cancel the rest of the two-week engagement just before the second show was scheduled to begin. The show room was already packed with people when Elvis went to the Colonel and told him that he wanted to call off the remaining performances because he was sick. The Colonel, however, was not about to walk out on stage and tell an eager full house there would be no Elvis. If Elvis wanted that night's show canceled, Vernon would have to do it. Elvis went ahead and performed. Immediately afterwards, he was on a jet bound for Memphis.

Signs were posted in the hotel saying, "The remainder of the Elvis Presley engagement has been canceled due to illness." Back home, Elvis was admitted to Baptist Hospital for "fatigue." He was released from the hospital on September 5.

Variety reported the events in its August 27, 1975, issue. It said, "Presley may be suffering from a continuing physical disability. His overweight condition and lack of stamina, poor vocal projection may spring from such a malady. It is difficult for him to maintain any credible vocal lines."

Four months later, Elvis was briefly back in something approaching top form. The Colonel scheduled Elvis in Las Vegas in December 1975, to make up the shows that he had canceled in August. November and December are the two slowest months of the year in Las Vegas. Normally the show rooms are 75 to 80 percent empty. Elvis proved the exception to this rule. He sold out every show. According to Henri Lewin, the casino slot-machine revenue doubled when Elvis was there.

Lewin tried to get the Colonel to extend Elvis's engagement to New Year's Eve. The Colonel, however, had already booked him in the eighty-thousand- seat Pontiac Silverdome. Elvis played stadiums only twice in the 1970s. The Colonel was obsessed with every show selling out and was afraid that it might not happen in a giant venue. The Silverdome carried a bigger risk than just its size. A snowstorm in Michigan was not only a possibility, it was a probability. However, neither the weather nor the size of the arena proved to be unfriendly. The total attendance for the Silverdome show was 62,500, a record at the time. Total receipts were in excess of $800,000. Elvis and the Colonel split their half of this, each receiving $200,000.

While all was well with the Colonel and Elvis's professional ventures, their personal relationship continued to be cold. On August 11, 1976, the *Memphis Press Scimitar* said, "*London Daily Express* on page one of its Monday edition this week states flatly that Elvis Presley and Colonel Tom Parker have come to a parting of the ways. That Elvis's new business manager will be a well-known Memphian."

Elvis and the Colonel were having fairly regular disagreements. The Colonel wanted Elvis to do a ninety-minute gospel television special which Elvis was against. Elvis wanted to appear in larger cities instead of the small ones that the Colonel was booking him in. Elvis hated the *Having Fun with Elvis on Stage* album. Elvis and the Colonel even fought over the amount of karate moves Elvis was using in his act. Despite the mounting antagonism, Elvis still had some carryover feelings of gratitude to Colonel Parker from the early days. And besides, when it came down to it, Elvis's main interest was having enough money to do whatever he wanted, and the Colonel kept the money flowing.

Elvis's longtime friend George Klein said that Elvis listened to the Colonel's advise completely up until the last few years that they were together. Toward the end, he became more assertive with the Colonel and several times wanted to fire him. However, the Colonel knew Elvis, and he knew Vernon. He knew that he could con Vernon and that Vernon, in turn, would influence Elvis.

Dr. Nick also asserted that toward the end, Elvis avoided talking to the Colonel. While he respected what the Colonel had done for him in the early days, he had no respect for what he had been doing over the last few years.

Larry Geller said that Elvis lost respect for the Colonel when he realized Parker was using him. Elvis felt that the Colonel mishandled his career in the latter years. Geller, too, maintained that at the end, Elvis was going to fire Colonel Parker. He wanted to have Tom Hulett as his manager and planned to let the Colonel go after his next tour. Elvis died before he could do that.

The Colonel was as frustrated with Elvis as Elvis was with him. According to Steve Binder, the Colonel tried to sell Elvis's contract in late 1976. He spoke to several people in Hollywood, but couldn't find any takers. This sounds more like a rumor than the truth. It is hard to believe that the Colonel would be unsuccessful in finding anyone interested in managing Elvis. It is far more likely that he quoted an asking price so outrageously high that no one wanted to meet it.

Despite their differences, the Colonel and Elvis pressed on. On August 21, 1976, RCA announced that Elvis's record sales had passed the 400-million mark. Elvis was on tour in the Midwest. The Colonel knew that the news that Elvis was coming to places like Bloomington, Indiana, would be a major news event. Part of his promotional plans had arena managers holding press conferences to announce that Elvis would be coming to town. Almost always, every local media outlet would be there. Free publicity helped sell out most shows within forty-eight hours of tickets going on sale.

Elvis appeared at the Hilton for the last time in December 1976. The Colonel agreed to let him play ten days in exchange for the box office receipts. The Colonel charged thirty dollars a ticket and still sold out. Elvis's performance was not a good one. He relied on his backup group, the Stamps Quartet, to perform several numbers. He also spent much of the show sitting on a stool.

After the show several people asked for their money back.

Chapter 15

1977, The King Is Dead, Long Live the King

★ ★ ★ ★

*R*CA was not happy with Elvis at the beginning of 1977. In the previous year and a half, his recording output had only allowed them to release one album of new material. On January 22, 1977, Elvis flew to Nashville for a recording session. However, rather than attending the session, he remained at the hotel listening to demonstration tapes with his producer, Felton Jarvis. Elvis kept his band waiting for him at the studio for three days.

Finally, the session was called off. Elvis left Nashville complaining of a cold. He promised to return in a couple of days, but did not. The Colonel exploded, warning Elvis that if he "didn't get off his tail and make some records, there would be no more concert tours."

News of Elvis failing to show up made its way into the media. On February 2, the *Memphis Press Scimitar* ran an article headlined "Elvis Presley No-Shows Recording Session." The *Press*

Scimitar reported that when they questioned RCA officials about what had kept Elvis from the studio, RCA referred all questions to the Colonel. The article speculated that Elvis was afraid to record because of disappointing sales. When asked how Elvis's latest album, *From Elvis Presley Blvd., Memphis Tennessee*, was selling RCA again referred the question to Colonel Parker. However, Presley insiders say that he failed to keep the recording appointment because he was fighting with his new girlfriend, Ginger Alden. (He and Priscilla had divorced in 1973.)

In early February, following the Colonel's suggestion, RCA set up a makeshift recording studio at Graceland. Elvis kept the musicians and singers waiting again for three days before finally sending them home. He complained of a sore throat. On February 12, 1977, the Colonel had Elvis back on tour. Reviews of his first show in Hollywood, Florida, mentioned that he had lost weight since the year before.

Another tour began in March 1977. On March 31, 1977, Elvis was scheduled to appear in Alexandria, Virginia. Elvis never made it. Instead, he flew back to Memphis and checked into Baptist Hospital with Dr. Nick accompanying him. The official reason for his stay was exhaustion.

On April 21, 1977, Elvis was back on the road. It was a thirteen-day, thirteen-city tour. On April 30, the *Nashville Banner* ran a story saying the Colonel had put Elvis's contract up for sale because Parker was in bad health and needed the money due to gambling losses. According to the report, the Colonel had lost another million dollars in December of 1976 alone. The story claimed that Elvis and the Colonel had not spoken for two years, and that a West Coast group was interested in the contract.

The Colonel denied the *Nashville Banner* story from Elvis's tour stop in St. Paul, Minnesota. "I'm working with Elvis. I'm in good health, and I don't have any debts, at least, none that I can't pay," Parker said. Joe Esposito, supposedly representing Elvis, also called the *Banner* and denied the report.

On May 20, Elvis began a fourteen-day, fourteen-city tour. On May 29, at the Baltimore Civic Center, he stopped in the middle of the show and left the stage. Thirty minutes later, he returned to finish the show. Some reviews said that it appeared that Elvis was high on drugs. Still the Colonel kept booking him for concerts. He had blinders on.

Larry Geller told of Colonel Parker's push to keep Elvis on stage at all costs. Geller was sitting in Elvis's suite the afternoon before a May 1977 Louisville, Kentucky, concert. Dr. Nick was with Elvis in his bedroom. The Colonel came through the door of Elvis's suite clenching his cane. Geller stood up to greet him, but the Colonel refused his handshake. He looked around the room and barked, "Where is he?" Geller said that he would let Elvis know that the Colonel was there, and started to head for Elvis's bedroom. The Colonel pushed past Geller, saying he would talk to Elvis himself.

When the Colonel opened the door, he saw Dr. Nick kneeling over Elvis, holding up his head. Elvis appeared to be unconscious. Dr. Nick began putting water from an ice bucket on Elvis's forehead. The Colonel slammed the door shut behind him.

A couple of minutes later, the Colonel came out of the bedroom. He stared at Geller, his cane pointing up in the air. "The only thing that's important is that he's on that stage tonight. Nothing else matters!" With that he left the suite as abruptly as he had come. Somehow Elvis made it to the concert that night.

It was a couple of nights later that Elvis let Larry Geller in on the secret that he was planning to fire the Colonel. "I'm going to get rid of the old Colonel. I need a change, new blood. I've always been loyal to the Colonel, and I appreciate what he's done, but nothing can last forever. The times are changing, and I don't think the Colonel is up to date with what's going on like Tom Hulett. I've had it with him."

The Colonel made two big deals for Elvis in the spring of 1977.

One was for an engagement at the Las Vegas Hilton in October of that year to open its new seven-thousand-seat arena, for which Colonel Parker's staff helped to put together the sound system. A Muhammed Ali-Leon Spinks fight was the opening event there after Elvis's death precluded him from christening it.

The other project was a CBS television special to be called "Elvis in Concert." When the Colonel conceived of this special, he purposefully did not offer it to NBC. NBC had televised both the "1968 Comeback Special" and "Aloha from Hawaii." After NBC aired the rerun of "Aloha From Hawaii," the ratings fell dramatically. When the Colonel approached NBC with another special, the response was lukewarm. This lack of enthusiasm was not forgotten by the Colonel. He held a grudge. He had William Morris contact CBS, and they bought the idea.

William Morris arranged for two of its clients, Bill Harbach and Gary Smith, to produce the broadcast. The pair were veteran television producers. Harbach and Smith flew to Las Vegas to meet the Colonel and discuss the special. The Colonel made it clear that Elvis was not interested in spending any extra time on the show. They would have to rely on filming him in concert and create the program around that.

According to Larry Geller, the most nervous he had ever seen Elvis was in the days leading up to the CBS television special. When the Elvis's plane, the *Lisa Marie*, named for his daughter, landed in Omaha, the Colonel made his way on to the plane before anyone had a chance to get off. He went straight into Elvis's compartment where Elvis was being made up. After talking to Elvis for a couple of minutes, the Colonel cornered Larry Geller. Putting his arm around Geller, he said, "Larry, you got an important job tonight. I'm countin' on ya." The Colonel began whispering. "Tonight CBS is selling a very important television special, and I need you to help us. You gotta get Elvis up for the show. Now remember, Larry, make sure his attitude is just right. Talk to him.

Talk to him. He listens to you. You know how to do it. I know you do. Just make sure he's in good shape psychologically."

Twenty cameramen were sent on the June tour to shoot footage for the special. Three cities were chosen for the filming, in Nebraska, Omaha and Lincoln and Rapid City, South Dakota. According to Gary Smith, Rapid City was chosen because Elvis had never performed there before. It was felt that fans who had never seen him in person might be more forgiving of his weight. Between the Lincoln and Rapid City show, Elvis went on a crash diet and lost ten pounds. The Rapid City show accounted for all but one song when the editing of the special was completed.

The final concert of the June tour was held in Indianapolis's Market Square Arena. Elvis's announcer Al Devonian closed the show with the words he always used, "Ladies and gentlemen, Elvis has left the building. Thank you and good night." These words would never be heard at the conclusion of another Elvis Presley concert. There was a slight pause, and the voice continued. "We'd like to remind you that following this evening's concert, the Elvis Super Souvenir Concert Concession stands will be open for a short while. If you didn't get your souvenirs of your evening with Elvis, be sure to do it before you leave. Thank you for coming. Be careful when driving home. Good night."

The Colonel booked another tour for Elvis in the summer which was to start on August 17 in Portland, Maine. He had been choosing smaller cities like Portland as venues in an effort to hide Elvis's increasingly shocking appearance from the media.

The Colonel had Portland ready for Elvis's arrival. He had made certain that RCA had plenty of records in local stores. Programs, pennants, and photos were on hand to meet the crowd's souvenir needs. The morning of the sixteenth, the Colonel was at the arena meeting with the building manager. He also watched Elvis's sound equipment being put into place.

By the afternoon, Colonel Parker was back in his suite at the

Sheraton Hotel. It was there that he received the telephone call telling him that Elvis had died. "Nothing has changed. This doesn't change a thing," he said. The Colonel made this statement because he honestly believed that nothing would change. Elvis had long since ceased to exist as a person as far as the Colonel was concerned. He had been selling the image. The Colonel could sell the image of a dead man just as well as he could a live one. In fact, it was easier because he could totally control the image. There were no more worries about Elvis's weight or drugs.

After hanging up with Esposito, the Colonel placed a call to RCA Records to confirm that the company would still be paying all the expenses he had incurred in Portland. RCA assured the Colonel that the record company would take care of everything. They knew that there would be an explosion in demand for Elvis's records. They still needed to keep the Colonel happy.

When Elvis died, the Colonel must have viewed it as him having gone into the army all over again. The Colonel had kept things going with Elvis gone then, and he could do it now. He also had the opportunity to reshape Elvis's image just as he had then.

"Nothing has changed" was indeed a cold phrase. However, it was a prophetic statement. When the Colonel spoke of Elvis, he always was speaking from the state of the business position. He was correct that the Elvis business went on. Elvis's death didn't stop it, in fact, it intensified the public's demand. The sale of Elvis Presley records and memorabilia skyrocketed.

The Colonel wasn't about to let happen to him what happened to Oscar Davis when Hank Williams died. Davis was nearly broke in a matter of months and forced to work for the Colonel. The Colonel was determined to stay on top as the king of the managers. As he saw it, in many ways, he now had the perfect client to promote. A dead client couldn't talk back, threaten to fire you, or generate unfavorable publicity that threatened the image you wanted him to portray. Elvis's death did nothing to lessen the public's fascination with him. In fact, it did just the opposite. There was an excitement and opportunity in the air that the Colonel had not sensed since the 1950s.

Colonel Parker didn't book the first flight out to Memphis. Instead he turned his attention to gaining complete control of the burgeoning world of Elvis merchandise. Parker wanted an exclusive licensor, a company that would manage and protect the merchandising of the name and likeness of Elvis Presley and all associated products, except records. The Colonel had already sold all pre-1993 rights to Elvis's music to RCA.

When Abe Lastfogel retired, Roger Davis became the Colonel's go-to man at William Morris. Davis, an entertainment attorney, had taken notes at most of the meetings between the Colonel and Lastfogel since joining William Morris in 1962. The Colonel instructed Davis to set up a meeting the next day between with Harry Geissler to discuss an Elvis merchandising contract.

Harry Geissler owned Factors Etc., a merchandising company that was to become known for its handling of such such blockbuster movies as *Rocky*, *Star Wars*, *Grease*, and *Superman* and big-name clients as Farrah Fawcett-Majors. Geissler, a third-grade dropout was a steelworker before he went into merchandising. Factor's Etc. was, by August 16, 1977, a multimillion dollar company.

Harry Geissler's childhood, in many ways, was similar to the Colonel's. He dropped out of school when he was sixteen. At first he floated from job to job. For awhile, he sold Christmas trees. When the season was over, he took a job selling supplies to carnivals. On the side, he sold bowling shirts on which his wife embroidered names.

One of Geissler's biggest successes was with the Farrah Fawcett-Majors t-shirt. Geissler paid $300,000 for the right to create the t-shirt. It was so successful that in the first year, Geissler made an additional royalty payment of $400,000 to Fawcett-Majors. Before achieving its first big success with the Farrah Fawcett swimsuit poster, Geissler's company was probably best known for its legal difficulties. Unfortunately, Geissler did not pay much attention to copyrights on the images he was using and ended up paying $100,000 in fines.

Factors Etc. also had a reputation for aggressively pursuing violators of its own exclusive licensing agreements. Bootleg products had plagued the Elvis market for years, and the Colonel was eager to let Factors foot the bill for chasing down the new crop of post-mortem opportunists.

The Colonel, Roger Davis, and Harry Geissler met in New York the day after Elvis died. By Thursday, they had reached a twelve-page agreement that conveyed to Factors the exclusive rights to merchandise the name and likeness of Elvis Presley for eighteen months. Factors would pay a $150,000 advance against royalties. Strangely, it was Tom Diskin whose signature ended up on the contract and not the Colonel's.

The merchandising agreement with Factors was unusually complex. Rather than contracting directly with the Elvis Presley estate, Parker set up the agreement between Factors and another company Boxcar Enterprises. Parker had formed Boxcar in 1974 to licence and merchandise Elvis Presley products. At the time, it was a relatively small gear in the Elvis money machine. Typically rock-star merchandise is only in demand when the fan base for the artist is teenagers. When Elvis died, a licence to merchandise suddenly became an extremely lucrative property.

The ownership distribution of Boxcar was puzzling. The Colonel owned 40 percent with Elvis, Tom Diskin, RCA's George Parkhill, and Hill and Range Music's Freddie Bienstock each getting 15 percent. It is not clear why payments for Elvis Presley merchandising should have gone to Diskin, Parkhill, and Bienstock. When Parkhill's and Bienstock's shares in Boxcar were later bought back by the company, Colonel Parker owned 56 percent and Elvis and Tom Diskin each owned 22 percent.

It is quite possible that Colonel Parker formed Boxcar with
Elvis's death in mind. Even in 1974, it was obvious that his client
was having serious health problems. Most of Elvis's inner circle
believed that he could go at anytime. When he did, there would be
no more concert income and no more new records, but there might
be a heck of a souvenir business.

Factors agreement with Boxcar called for a seemingly arbitrary
distribution. Twenty-five percent of all royalties would be paid to
Parker, 25 percent to the Presley estate, of which the Colonel also
collected half, and 50 percent to Boxcar. At the end of this convo-
luted road, Parker ended up with 53 percent of all royalties on
Elvis's merchandising. Only thirty-nine cents out of every dollar
went to the Presley estate. Adding insult to injury, the ever-present
William Morris Agency collected a commission on the deal for
"introducing" Harry Geissler to Parker.

With the merchandising agreement wrapped up, the Colonel
headed for Graceland where he found Vernon hiding from the
crowd of people in the home in a back bedroom. At this time of
Vernon's greatest grief, the Colonel pulled out the Factor's agreement for him to sign, which he did without question. Those present were amazed at the Colonel's lack of tact. But it wasn't by
accident that he picked then to present the contract to Vernon. He
caught Vernon when he couldn't think clearly. The Colonel was not
interested in questions, only signatures.

During the days following the death of Elvis, the Colonel was
often quoted as saying, "I owned 50 percent of Elvis when he was
alive, and I own 50 percent of him now that he is dead." He came
to Memphis prepared to formalize his 50 percent cut. The Colonel
had come with a contract in hand ready for Vernon's signature.
That piece of paper would keep him on as manager despite his
client's death. There was never really any doubt that the contract
would be signed. Vernon had always been a pushover as far as the
Colonel was concerned. An associate of the Colonel's from the

1950s recalls Parker commenting that all he ever had to do with Vernon was mention money.

With Elvis dead and the financial future of the Presley estate unexpectedly resting entirely on his shoulders, Vernon knew that he needed help. So it is not surprising that he turned to Colonel Parker, the man he believed responsible for so much of his son's success.

Vernon had always held Parker in high regard. In an interview for CBS television shortly before Elvis's death, Vernon said, "Colonel Parker is an honest guy. Once you find out, you don't have to worry about a guy being your manager and what he will do for you. He handles it, you do the show, and everything works out fine."

On August 23, 1977, Vernon Presley wrote a thank-you letter to the Colonel. In it, he effectively gave the Colonel power of attorney. Vernon asked him to continue the January 22, 1976, agreement under which the Colonel had the power to sign Elvis's name to contracts for personal appearances, merchandising, motion picture, and a variety of other agreements.

Vernon sent the Colonel the following letter confirming the agreement:

Dear Colonel:

I know that you have many details to straighten out pertaining to the commitments that you had for Elvis. I am deeply grateful that you have offered to carry on in the same old way, assisting me in any way possible with the many problems facing us.

As Executor of Elvis's estate, I hereby would appreciate it if you would carry on according to the same terms and conditions as stated in the contractual agreement you had with Elvis dated January 22, 1976. I hereby authorize you to speak and sign for me in all of these matters pertaining to this agreement.

I will rely on your good judgments to keep the image of Elvis alive for his many fans and friends. I will call on you from time to time to help me with many other phases and future problems.

Sincerely and Many Thanks,

Vernon Presley

According to those present at Graceland when Elvis's body lay in state, the Colonel never got anywhere near it. In fact, he never went into the same room with the body. The Colonel's friends attributed this to his extreme grief. Esposito quoted the Colonel as saying, "Joe, I want to remember Elvis when he was alive. I want to remember good memories, great times. I don't want to go in there and see him dead."

The Colonel was in the motorcade of limos that accompanied Elvis's body to Forest Hill Cemetery, where Gladys Presley had been buried. He did not dress the part of a mourner. Then sixty-eight years old, the 250-plus-pounds Parker showed up in a Hawaiian shirt and a baseball cap. As the final words were being spoken at Elvis's grave, the bulky beflowered Colonel could be seen sitting on a police motorcycle off in the distance.

Over the following days, RCA was flooded with phone calls. One of the main requests was for data on Elvis's record sales. RCA was unable to furnish this information. It never officially released the total amount of Elvis's record sales. Callers were told that Colonel Parker did not want the information released. One reporter asked whether the Colonel had veto power over what RCA said. The response was, "Let's put it this way, he has influence, and if the

Colonel says he sees no benefit to be derived from talking about Elvis's death and what occurred after it, so be it."

RCA would not even comply with requests for biographical information about Elvis. This was also at the Colonel's direction. He didn't want to be responsible for keeping the company up to date.

RCA had reason to continue appeasing the Colonel. The surge in demand for Elvis's records was largely responsible for RCA enjoying record earnings in 1977 of $247 million, a 39-percent increase over the previous year. RCA helped to pad the Colonel's pocket by giving him $675,000 twice for future services in helping to "package, promote, and merchandise" its Elvis products. The Colonel signed an agreement with the company to release a two-record album of the *Elvis in Concert* soundtrack. He and the Presley estate split a $450,000 advance. RCA paid an additional $50,000 to the Colonel's company, All Star Shows.

Of course, the other information source that the press went after was the Colonel. He refused to make any comments. Reporters were forced to use what little information they had in their files about him. The Colonel never actually turned down a request for an interview. That would be too easy. Instead, he told the *National Enquirer* that the price for a short interview was $25,000, and his long interview rate was $100,000.

Once the deal with the Colonel was set, Factors made a truly royal effort to get Elvis products on the market in a hurry. Within six weeks of Elvis's death, Factors had assembled a merchandising effort reminiscent of Colonel Parker's 1956 Elvis Presley Enterprises campaign.

Harry Geissler did his best to portray Factors, Colonel Parker, and Vernon Presley as one big happy family. Factors' efforts on behalf of the Presley estate were presented as entirely benevolent. "We are aggressive in protecting the rights of the Presley organization," Geissler told the *Memphis Commercial Appeal*. "The pirates are literally stealing money from Elvis's family, and remember, it is a family affair from the grandmother all of the way down to little Lisa Marie." In private, Geissler was much more candid about his feelings. "I don't even like Elvis's music, but I always was a fan of Colonel Parker's."

Colonel Parker and Harry Geissler, seeking to justify themselves, at times seemed to be in competition for the tackiest public remark about Elvis. Probably Parker's best was when he said, "We are keeping up the good spirits, we are keeping Elvis alive. I talked to him this morning, and he told me to carry on." Geissler was less poetic, but just as tasteless. "We are the only protection against people dancing on Elvis's grave." Harry Geissler often referred to himself as the "King of the Merchandisers," and he loved the idea of representing the "King of Rock and Roll."

A September 21, 1977, story in the *Memphis Press Scimitar* reported on the memorial tribute that the Colonel was planning to Elvis. The Colonel was very sketchy about the details. "I can't tell you exactly what will be happening. But one thing's for sure, it'll be a very big event. The only thing different is that Elvis won't be there in person, just in spirit." That "tribute" did not actually take place until September 1978.

Within days of Elvis's death, the Colonel had come up with a new marketing slogan, "Always Elvis." The empire continued without Elvis. The legend seemed to have a life of its own. If anything, life was easier for the Colonel with Elvis safely in the grave. The Colonel was now in the business of licensing icons and shrines. He was virtually in the religious artifact business, and it suited him fine.

Initially he worried about Baron Hilton's reaction. Hilton stood to take one of the worse losses resulting from Elvis's death. Presumably Hilton also held a stack of Colonel Tom's gambling markers. The Colonel's problem was to persuade him that there was still a future and that he should not call in Parker's debts or evict him from his rent-free fourth-floor suite. Parker saw the Hilton as the hub of the empire. And the idea of being deprived of it filled him with superstitious dread.

Colonel Parker became the main player in the Elvis exploitation game. In fact, he very quickly controlled the entire board and revised the rules for his own benefit. For instance, one year after Elvis died, in September 1978, Parker organized a week-long Elvis convention at the Las Vegas Hilton. He called it, what else?, "Always Elvis." It included a few attractions such as continuous Elvis movies and music, but the only truly noteworthy event was the appearance of Vernon, Priscilla, and Lisa Marie together in public for the first time since Elvis's death. They unveiled a life-sized bronze statue of Elvis outside the Hilton show room. Those in the crowd with cameras surged forward with flashcubes popping. The Colonel raised his hands urging the security forward. "No photographs. Pictures of the statue can be purchased for two dollars."

What most fans got for their fifteen-dollar entrance fee was the opportunity to buy more Elvis products from vendors who each paid twenty-five hundred dollars to secure a booth. In the end, after the Presley estate received 50 percent of the proceeds, everyone but Parker came away empty.

There was a display of Elvis costumes and a souvenir market. Elvis's ties to the hotel were milked to the limit, but people kept on coming. One of the tackiest products for sale was Always Elvis Wine. When it went on the market, the Colonel was asked if he didn't think it strange to be selling Elvis Wine since Elvis didn't drink wine. The Colonel's response was, "Elvis never drank wine, but if he did, this is the wine he would have ordered."

People came to the convention. They paid the admission. They bought the pictures, posters, and souvenirs. And in between, they gambled. This was all Hilton needed to see. The hotel qualified as a place of worship, and the pilgrims would flock to it from all over the world. The Colonel kept his suite, his consulting fees, and his perks.

Robert Hilburn of the *Los Angeles Times* wrote of seeing the Colonel in Las Vegas in 1978 signing autographs at the "Always Elvis" convention. "'We made a hell of a team,' he said after the crowd had cleared and he was sure his remarks would be off the record. 'I'd thought we'd go on forever, but,' he stared off into the distance leaning on the cane he carried in later years and pausing just trying to figure out what more to say. 'Sure,' he said softly, answering a question that hadn't been asked, 'sure I loved him.'"

The stresses of Vernon's new responsibilities took an immediate toll on his health. He had been plagued by heart problems for years. His first heart attack had occurred in 1975. In February 1979, after complaining of an irregular heartbeat, Vernon received a pacemaker. After that his health declined steadily. As the pressure of managing Elvis's estate grew, his heart condition worsened. On June 26, 1979, at 9:20 A.M., Vernon's heart stopped. Priscilla, Lisa Marie, Colonel Parker, and Joe Esposito all attended the funeral.

Elvis's will had allowed Vernon to choose his own successor, and everyone was anxious to see whom he had left in charge. He chose three co-executors for the declining estate, Joseph Hanks, Elvis and Vernon's accountant, the National Bank of Commerce, and Priscilla Presley.

At Vernon Presley's death, the financial condition of the estate was truly bleak. It became up to Priscilla to save her daughter's inheritance. She had said for years that she should have managed Elvis's money. Now she was going to get her chance. It would take the intervention of a probate judge to put her on the right track.

Chapter 16

Estate of Elvis Presley v. Col. Tom Parker

★ ★ ★ ★

Colonel Parker had nothing to fear with the change in control of Elvis's estate. The new co-executors were eager to keep him on board. They wanted to continue the estate's relationship with him because they believed that he was the one man who could make the most of whatever opportunities existed to capitalize on the public's continuing but unpredictable fascination with Elvis Presley. Also, they expected that Parker would present Elvis in the same "high quality" manner he had throughout Elvis's career. On June 29, 1979, they sent him the following letter.

Dear Colonel:

As the persons named under the will of Vernon Presley to be
the successor, co-executors and co-trustees of the estate of
Elvis Presley, we would like to extend to you our appreciation
for the work you have done for the estate and to let you know
that we do want things to continue as they have and as set
forth in the letter of August 23, 1977 from Vernon Presley as
the then Executor of the estate to you.

A copy of that letter is attached hereto as an exhibit and the
terms thereof are incorporated herein.

Sincerely,

Joseph A. Hanks
Priscilla B. Presley
The National Bank of Commerce

However, the decision to retain the Colonel was not completely
up to the executors. After Vernon's death, the principals of the
Presley estate were required to go into probate court for the
appointment of the new executors and approval of various administrative items. Vernon's chosen successors, Joseph Hanks, the
National Bank of Commerce, and Priscilla Presley received quick
approval from Probate Judge Joseph Evans. However, one administrative item caught the judge's eye. The new co-executors
intended to extend Colonel Parker's management contract. The
estate needed Judge Evans's permission to continue with the agreement, but his approval had been considered a mere formality. No
one expected the judge to offer any objections.

When Judge Evans learned the details of the estate's agreement
with Colonel Parker, he was flabbergasted. What surprised and

concerned him most was that the contract gave the Colonel 50 percent of the estate's income. The judge was amazed that anyone would pay such a huge commission for the management of a living entertainer, let alone a dead one. He began to wonder if Lisa Marie's inheritance was really in the hands of people who were looking out for her best interests.

To everyone's surprise, Judge Evans withheld his approval of the contract. He first wanted a full investigation of the Colonel's financial dealings, and to conduct it, he appointed a Memphis attorney. The attorney would be Lisa Marie's financial guardian until the matter was settled. For the first time since they had met nearly twenty-five years before, someone was stepping between Elvis and the Colonel.

The man Judge Evans choose to investigate Parker's relationship with the Presley estate was Blanchard Tual. He would be Lisa Marie's financial guardian ad litem (for the time being) or until the issues with Parker were resolved. Later, the judge extended Tual's financial guardianship to Lisa Marie's eighteenth birthday in 1986.

One of Tual's first tasks in November of 1980 was to oversee the filming of *This Is Elvis*, a movie being produced by Warner Brothers. Colonel Parker had sold Warner the rights for $750,000. Tual was on the set to assure himself that the movie was in the best interest of Lisa Marie. He decided that the film was in good taste, would serve Lisa Marie's interests, and would make a substantial profit for the estate. Colonel Parker seemed to be off to a good start with Tual. Their honeymoon would be short lived.

Tual conducted a crash-course in the background of Colonel Parker. He interviewed the Presley estates' attorneys, Priscilla Presley, the Colonel, various music publishing and entertainment attorneys, and several RCA executives. On the basis of his preliminary report from these interviews, Tual was authorized by Judge Evans on December 10, 1980, to secure any and all tax information from August 16, 1977, on concerning Colonel Tom Parker and

Boxcar Enterprises. Parker agreed to turn over his and Boxcar's tax returns for 1977 through 1979 under the condition that their contents be kept confidential. Tual agreed to these terms to avoid a lengthy court battle.

The details of Elvis Presley's dealings with Parker had always been closely guarded secrets. In fact, before Judge Evans came into the picture, the exact terms of their business relationship were virtually unknown to anyone but Elvis, Vernon, and the Colonel. Tual's investigation would reveal for the first time the specifics of Colonel Parker's dealings with Elvis. The public was to discover just how self-serving the flamboyant, charismatic manager had been.

One of Tual's first conclusions was that Parker's 50 percent commission was indefensible. He called the Colonel's continuing claim on Elvis's posthumous earnings "excessive, imprudent, unfair to the estate, and beyond all reasonable bounds of industry standards." He also discovered that the contract raising Colonel Parker's share to 50 percent dated January 2, 1967, contained no consideration for the increase. That is, the Colonel wasn't going to perform anything extra to warrant the higher commission. Therefore, the agreement could be voided for lack of consideration.

In his report to Judge Evans, Tual explained how he believed Colonel Parker had gained such an unprecedented percentage of Elvis's earnings. "Elvis was shy, naive, and unassertive," Tual wrote. "Parker was aggressive, shrewd, and tough. His personality dominated Elvis, his father, and all others in Elvis's entourage."

The deeper Tual dug, the more skeletons he unearthed. In Tual's opinion, Colonel Parker handled the later part of Elvis's career in an utterly self-serving manner. As evidence, he submitted a report on various side deals that the Colonel had made over the years with people he was supposed to be negotiating with on Elvis's behalf. He cited several clear cases of conflicts of interest.

The Colonel had what almost amounted to an obsession with

receiving extras for himself out of the deals that he made for Elvis. Most of the Colonel's side deals and extras involved considerable amounts of money. But sometimes, the Colonel would ask for worthless tokens only to demonstrate that he was in charge. According to a former Paramount Pictures executive, on one occasion Parker demanded that he be given the ashtray on the conference table before he would sign a contract with the movie studio.

Tual said that Colonel Parker accepted still more favors from the William Morris Agency. In 1956, the agency was headed by Parker's close friend Abe Lastfogel. As Elvis's agent, William Morris was entitled to 10 percent of his earnings. However, there is considerable doubt over whether Elvis ever signed a contract with the agency. Parker probably made a handshake deal with Lastfogel on Elvis's behalf.

The agency occasionally provided advice to Colonel Parker concerning the structure of movie and concert deals and probably introduced him to a few important people in show business. But, the Colonel made the vast majority of decisions about Elvis's career on his own.

The agency provided the Colonel with a rent-free office, purchased a home he wanted in Palm Springs which it then rented to him under very favorable terms, and it even provided employees of the agency who worked for Parker at no charge. In theory, these new hires were being "trained" by the Colonel. In reality, they learned almost nothing except how to prepare the Colonel's lunch.

The thing that most amazed Blanchard Tual about Elvis and the Colonel's relationship was how little money Elvis ended up with despite his unprecedented career success. The probate session for Elvis's will lasted only twenty minutes. The last will and testament of Elvis Presley was read in the Probate Court of Shelby County, Tennessee, on August 24, 1977. The document was thirteen pages long, but its primary message was simple. Lisa Marie would get it all.

When it was over, the total value of the estate was still not known. It would take another sixty days to complete a thorough inventory. After leaving the courtroom, Probate Judge Joseph Evans was asked his opinion of the value of the estate. His reply was that it would probably be the largest estate ever filed in the state of Tennessee. Estimates in the media placed the likely value in excess of $150 million. No one had the faintest idea of the real story.

Elvis's unparalleled commercial success gave the judge every reason to believe that he had a fabulous fortune. During the course of his amazing career, Elvis Presley recorded 114 Top 40 songs including a dozen number one hits. He made more than thirty movies, played hundreds of sold-out concerts, and sold 600 million records during his lifetime. His popularity lasted well beyond the glory days of the 1950s, and even today his recordings continue to sell at an astounding rate. Of the 600 million records sold during his lifetime, 150 million were sold during the last eighteen months of his life. As of this writing, that total has surpassed a billion. If they were laid end to end, all the Elvis LPs and CDs sold to date would circle the earth twice. The biggest selling album of all time is Michael Jackson's *Thriller*. To match Elvis's career total, Mr. Jackson would have to release recordings just as successful every year for three decades.

Then there was the money, a virtual ocean of it with tributaries that continue flowing to this day. Elvis was the only performer in history to generate revenues of more than a billion dollars. Some estimates put his lifetime total (from both music and other promotional sources) at more than four billion dollars.

When the inventory of the Elvis Presley estate was finally completed, the resulting list was seventy-six pages long. It included two jet airplanes—the commercial-sized *Lisa Marie* and a nine-passenger aircraft—a checking account with a balance of $1,055,173, the Graceland mansion and grounds valued and $500,000, eight cars, seven motorcycles, seven golf carts, two trucks, a large gun collection, various awards and trophies, insurance policies worth $96,000, jewelry including a cross inlaid with 236 diamonds, a personal wardrobe filling several closets, miscellaneous property valued at $500,000, and promissory notes on money loaned to various individuals totaling $1.3 million including $270,000 to Dr. Nichopoulos. The total value, $7 million. A far cry from previous estimates. It was certainly not the largest estate ever filed in Tennessee as Judge Evans had predicted it would be.

To put Elvis's estate in perspective, compare it to that of John Lennon. Lennon who sold far fewer records than Elvis, performed in relatively few concerts, and appeared in only four movies, yet he left an estate of $200 million. How could the greatest money-making performer who ever lived, a man who should have been the richest rock and roller on the planet, leave behind such a paltry estate? Where, in other words, did all of the money go?

His death did not end the flood of cash. In fact, it did not even slow it down. At the apex of his career, Elvis was earning, after all of his taxes and bills were paid, around a million dollars annually. From the date of his death, August 16, 1977, to the end of that same year, a period of less than five months, the Presley estate brought in more than twice that amount. Since his death, roughly 500 million more of his recordings have been sold producing additional revenues of around four *billion* dollars.

Vernon Presley had much less money to manage when Elvis died than he might have had. Elvis kept less than twenty cents out of every dollar that he earned during much of his career. The rest went to the Colonel, the William Morris Agency, and the Internal Revenue Service. In 1965, for example, Elvis's income totaled $5,225,000, a staggering sum at the time. This total included $2 million for the three movies that he had starred in that year, $1,525,000 in record and music publishing royalties, and $1.7 for movies he had made in previous years. But after he paid his manager, his agent, and the IRS, Elvis was left only $1 million. A million a yearly was hardly the poorhouse, but it was a far cry from the more than $5 million he started with.

What could have possibly caused Elvis Presley to die a relative pauper? One commonly accepted explanation is that he simply spent it all on high living, a swarm of friends, family, and hangers-on, and on extravagant gift giving. Elvis's generosity was a subject of legend. He routinely gave away expensive jewelry and even homes. He gave incredibly costly gifts to family, employees, long-term acquaintances, and complete strangers.

Elvis never actually knew how much money he was making. According to a friend, Elvis said that he never really wanted to "hoard up a lot of money." He was almost embarrassed by the level of financial success that he had achieved and relied exclusively on his personal manager and his father to handle his financial affairs. As long as there was enough money on hand to buy whatever he wanted, the details of his financial situation were of no concern to him. He instructed Vernon to make sure that there was at least one million dollars in his checking account at all times. This was Elvis's measure of true wealth. He never expressed any concern over the amount of money he had or made as long as his checking account was fully stocked.

Blanchard Tual blamed much of Elvis's financial woes on the Colonel. He felt that a combination of self-dealing and mismanagement had cost Elvis his rightful fortune. In Blanchard Tual's opinion, Colonel Parker's negotiations with the International Hotel exemplified his pattern of collecting tribute in exchange for a chance to work with Elvis. In 1969, the Colonel had negotiated the five-year contract with the hotel and often boasted about it, despite the fact that the price was soon surpassed by performers of far less commercial value with far fewer operating expenses.

Tual was careful to point out that Las Vegas shows are typically money losers designed to attract gamblers to the casinos. But, with the Colonel's deal, the International was taking in twice what it was paying Elvis from ticket and drink sales alone. During Elvis's first four-week engagement, the hotel's gross receipts totaled $1.5 million. Elvis received $500,000. The net profit to the International for Elvis's four weeks of performances was $1 million, not to mention their increased gambling business.

International manager Alex Shoofey claimed the contract Colonel Parker agreed to on behalf of Elvis was the best deal ever made by a casino in Las Vegas. Elvis Presley was the greatest attraction in the history of a town known for its stellar attractions.

What induced Colonel Parker to give the International such a good deal? Tual felt that one likely explanation was his fondness for gambling. Parker had become notorious as one the most reckless gamblers in the history of the International. According to a former manager, "The Colonel was one the best customers we had. He was good for a million dollars a year." The International provided Parker with a line of credit to support his habit and, in recognition of his economical delivery of Elvis, generous repayment terms for his casino debt. The Colonel may even have had some of his gambling debts completely forgiven.

In addition to the line of credit, Parker received special favors from the hotel. His freebies including a year-round suite of offices and hotel rooms, food and beverages for his home in Palm Springs,and free transportation to and from Las Vegas anytime he wanted it. The International also engaged Parker as a consultant.

On April 20, 1972, Baron Hilton wrote the Colonel a letter confirming the payment of fifty thousand dollars per year over a three-year period for "talent and publicity consulting services." On March 8, 1976, Hilton sent Parker another check for twenty-five thousand dollars.

In Blanchard Tual's opinion, these side deals were made in exchange for the Colonel delivering Elvis to the International at a cut rate. In his report, Tual stated that he believed Colonel Parker's gambling habit created a direct conflict of interest. "The impropriety of a

manager losing such sums to the same hotel in which he has to negotiate on behalf of his client goes without saying," Tual wrote.

Blanchard Tual's most disturbing revelation came when he
turned his attention to Colonel Parker's dealings with RCA
Records. One reason it was widely assumed that Elvis had left
behind a far greater estate than he did was the belief the royalties
from his records alone must have been pumping out mountains of
money. After Elvis's death, his records were selling faster than ever.

In fact, people thought, the estate's royalty income was far less
than most people thought thanks to the mysterious dealings of
Colonel Parker. Because of that 1973 seven-year record deal he
negotiated with RCA , Elvis was only earning ten cents on singles,
fifty cents on albums, and one dollar on double albums. The album
royalty constituted only a 5-percent increase from Elvis's original
1955 contract, even though record prices had doubled since then.
Other recording artists of the day were receiving $1.10 per album.
The contract also called for a flat royalty rate, which meant that as
record prices rose, Elvis's percentage would actually decrease.

In his report, Tual pointed out that under this agreement, Elvis's
royalty rate was only half that of artists like the Rolling Stones,
Elton John, and the Beatles. A star of Elvis's magnitude should
have commanded a royalty several percentage points higher. At the
very least, the deal should have included a royalty rate that
increased as sales for a particular album reached certain thresholds.

Stranger still, Parker had actually negotiated six separate agreements with RCA all dated March 1, 1973. Four of them called for
RCA to make questionable payments to Parker. These four agreements are summarized as follows: (Keep in mind that All Star
Shows was owned by Colonel Parker.)

Agreement 1: Dated March 1, 1973, between RCA, All Star
Shows and Elvis Presley, whereby as an inducement to Elvis to sign
the seven-year exclusive recording agreement, RCA agreed to pay

Elvis and All Star Shows the sum of $100,000 upon the expiration of the seven-year agreement. The payment to All Star Shows was in connection with Colonel Parker's merchandising that exploited RCA's interest in Mr. Presley and the records of Mr. Presley. The agreement was signed by Elvis and Colonel Parker.

Agreement 2: A seven-year agreement dated March 1, 1973, between RCA, RCA Record Tours, and All Star Shows. All Star Shows agreed to furnish the services of Colonel Parker to assist RCA Records in planning, promoting, and merchandising the Elvis Presley 1972 tour. RCA agreed to pay All Star Shows a total of $675,000 payable $75,000 the first year and $100,000 per year for the remaining six years. In addition, RCA Record Tours also agreed to pay All Star Shows a total of $675,000 payable $75,000 the first year and $100,000 for the remaining six years. In sum, a total of $1,350,000 would be paid by RCA to Colonel Parker. In addition, RCA agreed to pay All Star Shows 10 percent of the RCA Record Tours net profits. Elvis did not receive any money pursuant to that agreement.

Agreement 3: A five-year agreement dated March 1, 1973, among RCA, All Star Shows, and Colonel Parker. All Star Shows was bound for the services of Colonel Parker for five years to consult with RCA Records and assist RCA Records in the exploitation of Elvis's merchandising rights. RCA agreed to pay All Star Shows $10,000 per year for a total of $50,000 over the five-year period. Elvis did not receive any money pursuant to this agreement.

Agreement 4: A seven-year agreement dated March 1, 1973, between All Star Shows and RCA Record Tours. All Star Shows was bound to furnish the services of Colonel Parker to assist RCA Records in planning, promotion, and merchandising in connection with the operation of the tour agreement. RCA agreed to pay All

Star Shows a total of $350,000, payable $50,000 per year over a seven-year period.

Why was the royalty rate for the new seven-year recording agreement so far below industry standards for an artist of Elvis's stature? Tual believed that Colonel Parker had looked out for his own interest when he negotiated the deal. In Tual's opinion, the more than two-million-dollar payment made directly to the Colonel in those additional four agreements induced him to agree to a relatively low royalty rate in Elvis's new contract.

The side deals between RCA and Colonel Parker even continued after Elvis's death. As a result of the new deals Parker made with RCA after Elvis died, the Colonel received at least $950,000 from September 15, 1977, to February 15, 1980, including $675,000 for services related to promotion, merchandising concepts, and packaging suggestions on RCA record tours, $165,000 in "consulting fees," $175,000 for "extra services in preparing product promotion cost merchandising," and $50,000 more for "promotion, merchandising concepts and packaging suggestions."

The final agreement signed by Colonel Parker on that fateful March day in 1973 may have been the single most financially damaging contract in the history of the music industry. It called for Elvis to sell the rights to all the songs he recorded before that date, 700 of them, to RCA for approximately five million dollars. It was a substantial amount of money, and Elvis was glad to get it at the time, but it was insignificant compared with the amount that Elvis would have received over the years had he kept ownership of his songs. And, remember, the Colonel got half and the IRS got half of Elvis's share.

When all was said and done, only $1.35 million remained from the original payment and most of that went to Priscilla to fulfill the terms of their divorce agreement. Elvis sold the rights to the greatest master catalog in music history and was left with virtually nothing to show for it. Thereafter, his estate received no royalties at all for any songs he had recorded prior to March 1973. Said Blanchard Tual, "The selling price was a fraction of their worth. The agreement was unethical, fraudulently attained, and against all industry standards. The tax implications alone should have prohibited such an agreement or at least prohibited it without further investigation."

Tual said, "It should have been obvious to anyone then or now that this was an abominable transaction especially considering the status of Elvis's career at the time. In 1973, Elvis was reaching another career peak. The 'Aloha From Hawaii' NBC television special had aired on January 14. RCA later released a two record album of the 'Aloha From Hawaii' concert which sold over two million copies. That year Elvis was only thirty-seven years old, riding high with no reason whatsoever to consider selling off an almost certain lifetime annuity."

On the other hand, Colonel Parker might have found a buyout very appealing. In 1973, Parker was sixty-three years old, overweight, and recovering from a heart attack. As a result of the agreement with RCA, he received $2.5 million. He was assured of recieving another $3.7 million over the next seven years in addition to 10 percent of the net profits from RCA Record Tours. The guaranteed payments to Colonel Parker provided a great deal of income to a man approaching the twilight years of his life.

Also, by 1972, Elvis's health had begun to fail, perhaps motivating the Colonel's action. According to Tual, "It is not a coincidence that most of the side agreements that Colonel Parker made with RCA and the Hilton were entered into after 1972. Colonel Parker had to be aware of Elvis's mental and physical deterioration."

Blanchard Tual suggested that the Colonel's proposed sale of Elvis's contract was another by-product of his greed. He said, "In April of 1977, only months before Elvis died, rumors circulated that Colonel Parker was putting Elvis's management contract up for sale. Parker denied the rumors then and continues to deny them today. Yet, a contract sale would have made sense given what he must have thought about Elvis's future as a performer. He had cashed out with the RCA royalty sale. Selling Elvis's management contract would have provided Parker with a final gigantic score."

At the time, Colonel Parker justified the RCA deals by saying "The old records don't sell no more." Later Parker would say that the sale had been Vernon and Elvis's idea. In his version of the events, RCA approached Elvis for his royalty rights. Elvis and Vernon were excited about the possibility of a quick infusion of cash. Colonel Parker thought it was a terrible idea and recommended against it, and in the end, it was Elvis's decision to sell the songs. Colonel Parker maintained he simply carried out his instructions. It is hard to imagine Parker ever just following instructions unless he would have benefited as a result. He was, however, successful in getting RCA to pay more than double its original two-and-one-half-million-dollar offer.

The RCA executive who signed the buyout agreement, Mel Ilberman, confirmed that three million dollars was RCA's initial offer to purchase Elvis's masters. However, on other occasions, the same individual has stated that it was Colonel Parker who initiated the buyout, and others told Blanchard Tual that it was all the Colonel's idea. However, whoever did the initiating, the beneficiaries are clear.

The travesty of the RCA royalty sale was magnified when Elvis's death drastically increased the demand for his records. The backlog of Presley in the RCA warehouses was eliminated almost overnight. RCA's first posthumous offering, *Elvis in Concert*, sold more than one million copies in the first few days of its release. Orders for Elvis records came in to the RCA pressing plant with such velocity that the computer system overloaded and shut down. Demand was so great that RCA resorted to contracting with outside record-pressing plants. In England, an RCA record-pressing plant was reopened to help meet the demand for Presley products.

This tremendous call for Presley albums affected the entire record industry. New releases by other artists were delayed because so much of the industry's production capacity was being devoted to pressing millions of Elvis's albums.

How much did the Presley estate lose because of the royalty sale? In the four months following Elvis's death, RCA sold 200 million of his records. In January 1978, RCA reported record-setting profits for the first quarter due to what it termed the "extraordinary posthumous demand" for Elvis's records.

In Tual's opinion, "Colonel Parker's side deals with the International Hotel and RCA which Elvis did not approve or acknowledge were instances of paying Colonel Parker not for services rendered from Elvis but for services rendered to RCA and to the International. This is a clear textbook conflict of interest which no reputable manager should have even considered. RCA must also share the responsibility and blame along with Colonel Parker for the 1973 agreement. The executives who worked with Colonel Parker were not naive. They realized that the key to Elvis was Colonel Parker and the control of Elvis meant millions of dollars for RCA."

During this investigation, Tual also became interested in the activities of Boxcar Enterprises. It was through Boxcar that the Colonel had made the merchandising deal with Factors Etc. after Elvis's death.

Tual questioned Parker about the Factors deal. He wondered whether Parker had sought competing offers from other merchandisers. Parker's response was that he did negotiate with several other mass-merchandisers. Parker said that he chose Factors because they guaranteed a minimum payment of $150,000.

Tual found that Factors may have defrauded Boxcar and the Elvis estate. "Sources of income such as foreign merchandising may have been withheld and may show up in an audit which should be conducted immediately," he wrote. Acting on the information that Tual presented, the court banned Factors from any further merchandising of Elvis Presley.

Colonel Parker also used Boxcar to make some interesting arrangements with RCA. The record company partnered with Boxcar in 1974 for the sale of the album *Having Fun on Stage with Elvis*. The album was sold under the Boxcar label, and RCA agreed to distribute the record worldwide and pay Parker an advance of $100,000 against a domestic royalty of one dollar and a foreign royalty of seventy-five cents. While 50 percent of the royalty went to Elvis, there was no contractual obligation for Boxcar to pay Elvis any of the $100,000 advance. It is assumed that Elvis received none of it. If RCA had paid Elvis directly for this project, the royalty rate per album would have doubled. Thus, RCA helped Boxcar and Colonel Parker gain yet another financial edge over Elvis.

Tual saw Elvis's contract with Parker as the single greatest drain on his income. In 1965, Colonel Parker confirmed to the press that Elvis was the highest-paid entertainer in the world. What the Colonel failed to mention was that he was the highest-paid manager in the world. His 1965 commission was $1.3 million.

Tual was amazed that the agreement gave the Colonel half of Elvis's earnings. Parker's share was truly outlandish. A standard contract between a star of Elvis's magnitude and a personal manager would call for a commission of no more than 10 to 15 percent. Apparently no one in Elvis's inner circle knew about his deal with the Colonel. Priscilla did not learn the details of the arrangement until after her former husband's death.

Tual felt that in exchange for Colonel Parker's incredible remuneration, Elvis received less than stellar management. Blanchard Tual also felt that in addition to dealing in his own interests rather than Elvis's, the Colonel had made several costly managerial blunders. Many of the deals that Colonel Parker made for Elvis, especially during the 1970s, cost him millions.

Tual found one of the most glaring examples of this ineptitude in Parker's RCA deal. Amazingly, in addition to everything else, it contained no audit clause. In fact, there is a blank space on the page where the audit clause is normally inserted, indicating that it may have been purposely removed. Auditing a record company's royalty calculation is normal for an artist in the music business. Most artists are advised to audit the record companies whenever they have had high sales. Tual believed that if an audit were ever conducted for the period of March 1, 1973, to January 31, 1978, the recovery in unpaid royalties would be substantial.

Furthermore, it seemed the accounting provision of Elvis's recording contract had been ignored by Parker right up to the time of his death. Since 1973, RCA has regularly mailed accounting statements to Parker, but he never objected to even one accounting nor had he ever requested an audit. In fact, Parker always discouraged anyone from questioning the record company's books. At one point after Elvis's death, the coexecutors discussed auditing RCA, and Colonel Parker advised strongly against it.

Auditing RCA would have simply been good business practice which was incumbent upon Parker as Elvis's manager. Objecting to at least a few record company accounting statements is a matter of course to protect the artist and keep the option of an audit open. It is a common industry practice.

"Colonel Parker's practice," Tual wrote in his report, "of not objecting to accounting and not auditing in light of the agreements and side agreements to Colonel Parker bolster the argument that Colonel Parker was in effect bought off by RCA, either expressly or tacitly and that for the payments he received, he kept Elvis under control."

In his investigations, Tual discovered little things that defied logic, but which made the case for Parker's incompetence stronger. For example, for some reason that has never been explained, Parker failed to register his client with BMI (Broadcast Music, Inc.) so that he could receive his share of writers' royalties for the songs in which he held a half interest. It is unclear how the Colonel could have made such an obvious mistake, especially since he would have shared in any royalties that Elvis received.

Even today, the public commonly agrees that Colonel Parker was a shrewd and resourceful manager who was greatly responsible for Elvis's phenomenal success. He may have been looking out for himself, but he was still a sharp operator making hot deals. There is no question that Colonel Parker made some great deals for Elvis in the early years of their relationship. In 1956, he negotiated a record contract that paid Elvis 45 cents for every album that he sold. That was an exceptional royalty considering the albums retailed for $3.98 at the time. However, Elvis's royalty rate barely advanced from what it had been in 1956.

In 1962, Bobby Darin signed a contract with Capitol Records that made him the highest-paid pop singer in history. He received $750,000 upon signing plus a guarantee of $2 million against future royalties. This was a better record contract than the Colonel ever negotiated for Elvis.

Elvis was completely out of touch with what would have been a reasonable royalty rate for an artist of his stature. He often bragged to his friends that he received a nickel for every one of his records sold. In fact, a star like Elvis could have commanded twice that amount from any other record company. Colonel Parker was unwilling, for a variety of reasons, to press RCA for a higher royalty. There seemed to be no one around to tell Elvis that five cents a record was not such a good deal, and certainly know one at RCA seems to have made him aware of that fact.

Tual found the Colonel had given Elvis questionable financial advice. Colonel Parker agreed that Elvis should let the IRS calculate his annual tax liability. He furthered the family's general paranoia by telling Elvis that he did not want him to end up like heavyweight boxing champion Joe Lewis who had been ruined financially in a celebrated encounter with the IRS.

In a press release, Colonel Parker once said that Elvis Presley was the highest single taxpayer in the United States. The Colonel seemed to think that paying more income taxes than anyone else was something to brag about. In reality, it was further evidence that Elvis was receiving no professional financial advice. The incompetence with which his tax situation was handled probably cost Elvis around $100 million.

Tual also questioned Colonel Parker's decision to turn down several lucrative foreign tour offers. Elvis himself had always been eager to take such tours and constantly discussed such projects, not only with his entourage, but in press conferences as far back as the 1950s. There were many times when he could have used the money that a tour abroad would have brought him.

By the end of July 1981, Blanchard Tual had completed his investigation and filed a report with Judge Joseph Evans. Tual summarized his findings with a laundry list of serious allegations. "Colonel Parker knowingly violated the artist/management trust in 1973 and continued to abuse it until after Elvis's death. There is evidence that both Colonel Parker and RCA were, at the very least, guilty of unethical conduct.

In his conclusion, Tual wrote, "Lisa Marie Presley is only 12 years old and has her whole life before her. She is entitled to the benefits of her father's talents and should not be deprived of them due to the self-dealings of her father's manager and record company."

Tual went on to recommend the following:

1. The court deny the co-executors' petition to approve the compensation paid to Colonel Parker.
2. The court direct the co-executors not to enter into any future agreements with Colonel Parker.

3. The court direct the co-executors and the estate's attorney to file a complaint against Colonel Parker seeking to void Colonel Parker's contracts with Elvis Presley and the estate on the following grounds:
   a. Breach of contract
   b. Breach of fiduciary duties
   c. Negligence for failure to object to RCA's accounting
   d. Collusion and conspiracy with RCA Records to defraud Elvis Presley of royalties pursuant to the 1973 buyout.
4. The court direct the coexecutors to cease paying any commissions to Colonel Parker.
5. The court direct that any income that in the past may have gone through Colonel Parker to the estate be paid directly to the estate.
6. The court direct the coexecutors to file a complaint against RCA in the proper court seeking to void the 1973 master buyout agreement alleging collusion in conspiracy with Colonel Parker in an effort to defraud Elvis of his royalties from such masters.
7. The court direct the coexecutors and the estate's attorneys to continue its audit against RCA, and if RCA raises any defense of the estate's right to audit back to 1973, then the estate should sue for an accounting and audit back to 1973.
8. The court direct the co-executors to further obtain an audit of Factors, or at least in the alternative, a full and complete accounting.

On August 14, 1981, Judge Evans appeared in court to announce his decision concerning the Blanchard Tual report. The judge issued an order demanding the cessation of all payments to Colonel Parker. He further ordered the Presley estate to bring suit against Colonel Parker for improper activities related to his managerial service for both Elvis and his estate. RCA was to be named in the suit as Colonel Parker's accomplice.

The Colonel did not have to wait long for a chance to defend himself following Judge Evans's order. On August 16, 1981, the fourth anniversary of Elvis's death, headlines in newspapers across the country questioned the integrity of Colonel Parker's management. One headline read, "Former Manager of Presley Denies Cheating Entertainer." Another went, "Did Colonel Parker Take The King For A Ride?"

The Colonel lashed back against the criticism from the press. He issued a statement to the *Memphis Commercial Appeal* stating that Elvis and Vernon were always pleased with his services and that both had wanted to continue their relationship with him indefinitely. Parker also claimed that detailed explanations were always given to Elvis before any contract was entered into on his behalf. And, for the first time, Parker publically criticized Elvis. He referred to him as a moody and headstrong client with little motivation. Managing Elvis was not an easy job, Parker said, and he deserved the compensation he had received. The Colonel also declared that he was fully prepared to defend himself against all allegations made against him.

When *People* magazine reported on the Blanchard Tual investigation, Colonel Parker was asked for his side of the story. He had the following to say: "Elvis knew that I provided services to others. He was satisfied with our arrangement and it worked." Parker said that Tual was making "unjust allegations that not only attack my name and reputation, but also are unfair and insulting to the memory of Elvis and his father, Vernon. I highly respected Elvis Presley, and I have made every effort to honor his name and preserve his memory with dignity."

Following Judge Evans's order, the Presley estate filed a complaint against Colonel Parker, alleging many of the things cited by Blanchard Tual.

Colonel Parker filed a countersuit in Nevada alleging that he was entitled to half of Presley's assets. The basis for his suit was the claim that he and Elvis had become partners over the years. But no one seriously believed that Parker and Elvis had ever been partners. Those close to Colonel Parker at the time say that the suit was just part of his overall strategy to push the Presley estate to the edge of bankruptcy. Colonel Parker had the advantage of being able to afford to continue arguing in courtrooms much longer than the estate. He knew that he could keep the process going until his enemies became more reasonable.

Colonel Parker had health problems in the later years of his life. On one occasion, he fell getting into an elevator at the RCA building in Los Angeles. He could not get up and was repeatedly hit by the elevator door until someone rescued him. The Colonel used his poor health as a tactic during the lawsuit.

The following affidavit was presented to a New York court on the Colonel's behalf. "I am 72-years-of-age and suffer from a heart condition which would make is very difficult for me to travel to New York City in connection with this action. I spend much of my time in Southern California in order to be with my wife who is in a virtually comatose condition and is under continuous nursing care and medical supervision in Palm Springs, California. If I am forced to contest any part of this proceeding in New York it will be a major hardship for me and I will probably be unable to attend the proceedings or assist my counsel on my defense."

The court did not buy his health excuse. However, his attorneys were able to come up with other tricks. For months and months, they used every delay tactic imaginable. Their favorite was to obtain changes of venue. Colonel Parker's lawyers successfully had the case moved from Memphis to New York, to California and back again. The Presley estate found itself paying attorneys in three states.

At times, the estate seemed to be closing in, but the Colonel and his attorneys managed to stay one legal jump ahead. In one particularly tight corner, the Colonel was forced to reveal his darkest and most carefully hidden secret. If he was stateless, the U.S. courts would have no jurisdiction over him.

An Associated Press story in 1956 was the first national report telling Colonel Parker's version of his origin. "Parker was born 47 years ago in West Virginia, where his parents happened to be touring with the carnival. His mom and dad died before Tom reached the fifth grade, so he wound up with his uncle's traveling show, the Great Parker Pony Circus. At 17, a young Tom struck out on his own with a pony-and-monkey act. Parker soon traded the pony for a typewriter and became a press agent for a series of carnivals, circuses and showboats. He developed first-name friendships with Tom Mix and Wallace Beery, both carnival men until the movies found them."

In June 1982, Colonel Thomas Parker, American showman, promoter, and entrepreneur extraordinaire announced that he was in reality Andreas Cornelis van Kuijk, a native of Holland who had immigrated to this country illegally in his youth. No soap opera writer in the world could have come up with a more startling or unlikely plot, and it succeeded in throwing all the legal battles into chaos.

In a written statement, the Colonel said, "I was born in the Netherlands on June 26, 1909 of parents who were lawfully married and Dutch subjects. After I left the Netherlands and immigrated to the United States, I enlisted in the United States Army in or about 1929 in which I served until I was discharged in 1933 or 34. In connection with my enlistment, I was required to and did willingly swear allegiance to the government of the United States of America. I did not seek or obtain the permission of the Dutch government to serve in the United States Army either prior to or after my service. I am now informed my failure to seek and receive such permission affected an automatic forfeiture of my Dutch citizenship. I am not a citizen of the United States having never become a naturalized citizen of this country or of any other country."

At last the Colonel's reason for turning down all offers for tours outside of the United States was clear to the public. He had no passport and could not get one without revealing his secret. Colonel Parker had cost Presley tens of millions of dollars in earnings in foreign engagements because he was an illegal alien.

This shouldn't have been such a revelation. A Dutch journalist had discovered the Colonel's secret several years earlier. A pamphlet-sized book written by Hans Longbroceh was the first public suggestion that Colonel Parker's background was not at all as what he had presented. According to Longbroceh, the Colonel was born in Breda, Holland, and his real name was Andre Von Kuyk. The book was only narrowly distributed and did not attract the attention of the U.S. press. Those who did read the book discounted Longbroceh's claims because the book contained several obvious errors, the most glowing of which was the statement that the Colonel had once managed cowboy movie star Tom Mix, and then brought him to London in 1947. Tom Mix died in 1940, and the Colonel never was in London.

Dutch journalist Dirk Vellenga later picked up the story. He wrote articles for the Breda newspaper, *Desten*, claiming that the Colonel was born in Breda. He tracked down the Colonel's brother and two of his sisters. He learned from them that the Colonel's birth name was Andreas van Kuijk, not Andre von Kuyk. The van Kuijk family had their own version of the Colonel's background. They agreed that his birth date was June 26, 1909. However, this is where the similarity between their account and the Colonel's ends.

According to them, the Colonel inherited his two main personality traits, military discipline and carnival conning, from his parents, Adam van Kuijk and Maria Ponsie. His father was a soldier for many years. The cream of the social class in Breda was a military officer. They were viewed by civilians as well as military personnel as near-royalty. As a boy, the Colonel lived close to the military barracks and witnessed first-hand the troops subservient to their masters' barking orders. Vellenga had hit upon the real story.

The Vellenga article came to the attention of Lamar Fike when he was helping Albert Goldman with his Elvis biography. Goldman's book was the first to publicize the Colonel's Dutch origin in the United States. Fike went to Breda, and Vellenga took him to Colonel Parker's sister's home. Fike was shocked by her resemblance to the Colonel. She showed Fike a family album with a picture of the Colonel when he was a boy.

Fike had never suspected that the Colonel was anything but American. He did notice that he had trouble pronouncing his "r"s, which is typical of those with a Germanic language background. However, Fike and everyone else though that the Colonel had a speech impediment. The Colonel would also occasionally rattle off a few words of what people assumed was German. It was, in fact, his native Dutch.

After returning to the U.S., Fike telephoned the Colonel to ask why he had kept his true identity secret. Lamar Fike said, "Gee Colonel, how come you never told us you were a Dutchman?" The Colonel's answer was, "You never asked me." Then he tried to cover his tracks by saying that Elvis knew. His brother Ad had come to Hollywood, and Elvis had met him. Fike told the Colonel that he was lying, and the Colonel hung up on him.

In retrospect, several of the Colonel's former associates recognized that he had given hints of his real origin. When the Colonel got angry, he would occasionally rattle off a sentence in a foreign language. When they assumed that it was German, the Colonel would tell them that they were wrong, that it was Dutch, and then laughed as if it were a joke.

According to Todd Slaughter, the Great Britain Elvis fan club president, the Colonel never tried to hide the fact that he was from Holland. He claimed that the Colonel made trips to Australia and Japan while Elvis was still alive. He also said that when he brought fans from Holland to the U.S. to see Elvis, the Colonel openly spoke Dutch to them.

Scotty Moore heard from Hank Snow's band that the Colonel was in the country illegally. "It was never any deep secret," Scotty said.

Lamar Fike and several other members of the Memphis Mafia say that there is no way that Elvis knew about the Colonel's past. However, a letter written by Elvis to the Colonel in January 1960 suggests that Elvis just might have known more about the Colonel's background than Fike and the others thought.

Dear Colonel,

Happy 1960. I received your package yesterday and I'm still searching for the gift. Damn, I couldn't believe that you were sending me a script. It sounds more like work than joy to me. Sending you a couple of clippings from German magazines so that you can test your knowledge of *Deutsche* language. So far everything is prepared and organized for change homes. You oughta see all of this boxes and suitcases. In fact, I think that they'll need a separate plane for all that kinda stuff. I will give a couple of interviews to some of the teen magazines and newspapers starting next week. Just keep me informed about that TV thing.

Respectfully,

Elvis

The script that Elvis was referring to was *Wild in the Country*. The double-underlining of Deutsche was perhaps Elvis indicating he knew Colonel's native language was Dutch, was not going to write it outright.

The Colonel never took steps to legalize his immigration status. He could have become a U.S. citizen, but didn't. Normally an individual who comes forward after living for several years in the U.S. and who is gainfully employed and has no criminal record is granted amnesty and allowed to remain in the country. In fact, anyone who could prove that they had been in the country since June 30, 1948, would be granted administrative amnesty by the Immigration and Naturalization Service. The Colonel definitely met this criteria.

Why didn't the Colonel become a U.S. citizen? Maybe he wanted to hold the man without a country as a trump card. He always said he tried to put together the perfect contract. Maybe he viewed not being a citizen as the perfect way to break a contract if need be.

Also, the Colonel may have never worried about deportation because of his political connections. He had several powerful friends, including President Lyndon Johnson, who he knew from Johnson's first run for the U.S. Senate in 1948. Johnson's daughter, Lynda Bird, even visited Elvis on the set of *Girl Happy*.

The Colonel never returned to Holland after 1929. It wasn't until 1961 that the van Kuijks finally learned what had happened to Dries. One of the sisters was reading a Dutch magazine when she saw a picture of Elvis Presley and his manager, Colonel Tom Parker. She immediately recognized the Colonel as being her brother. The family contacted Colonel Parker. Parker paid for his brother Ad to come to America. Ad went back to Holland, but discussed the matter with no one outside the family. Speculation is that the brother was either paid money or threatened by the Colonel to keep quiet. The family never contacted or saw the Colonel again. It is still not generally known in Holland that the Colonel was Dutch.

The Colonel's nationality revelation did not succeed in getting the case dismissed. It did, however, further delay the proceedings as he hoped it would. In the summer of 1983, Colonel Parker's delaying strategy was paying off. The Presley estate attorney informed the co-executors that they were in a no-win situation. The estate had already spent more than two million dollars pursuing its lawsuit against Colonel Parker. To cover its legal expenses plus additional fees, it would have to spend to win the suit, the estate would have to demand millions in dollars in damages from Parker who could at that point declare bankruptcy and the estate would get nothing. Even if the Colonel did pay the estate, the IRS would claim the majority of the money in taxes, and the estate would end up with a loss. If the estate pursued the case and lost, it would be bankrupt.

They had a choice. They could either go broke pursuing a principle, or they could settle. In June 1983, they settled. The Colonel would sever all connections with the estate and give up his claim to all future income. In return for giving up his interests, the Colonel would receive from RCA two million dollars paid in installments of forty thousand dollars per month concluding in May 1987 for his "right, title and interest in all Presley related contracts." The Colonel would also be entitled to 50 percent of all record royalties prior to September 1982. After that, everything would go to the estate. After twenty-eight years, Colonel Parker was finally relieved of duty. RCA had agreed to provide the two million dollars in return for exclusive rights to release Elvis Presley recordings.

After the lawsuit was settled, the principals tried to put up a friendly front for the public. On June 16, 1983, the Presley estate, Colonel Parker, and RCA issued a joint announcement saying that they had "amicably resolved the various matters of controversy between them." The Presley estate also paid tribute to the "significant contribution of Colonel Parker and RCA Records in the unparalleled career of Elvis Presley." In reality, there was still considerable resentment and dislike on all sides.

Representatives of Elvis Presley Enterprises have said that a new deal has been reached with RCA in which the estate receives royalties on packaged anthologies of pre-1973 Elvis Presley records. The estate will not comment on the size of the royalty payment except to say that "the particulars are our business." In truth, Elvis Presley Enterprises receives only token goodwill payments on any song Elvis recorded before March 1973.

Privately those inside the Presley organization have varying opinions of Colonel Parker. Publically they are unanimous in their praise of him. In fact, the estate now claims that Colonel Parker's management style and contract with Presley was not unusual compared with other artist/manager relationships of the 1950s and 1960s, and they do have a point. Modern-day norms of management don't just make Colonel Parker look bad, they reflect poorly on managers of that era in general.

After all the revelations and the lawsuit, Priscilla Presley continues to defend Colonel Parker, and is quick to praise him in the media. When a company released a book about Graceland, produced with the cooperation of Elvis Presley Enterprises, that turned out to contain a tirade by the author about Colonel Parker, Priscilla tried unsuccessfully to have the publisher pull all copies of book from stores. She even attended Colonel Parker's eighty-fifth birthday party. The event was held at the Las Vegas Hilton, and was hosted by the Colonel's old friend, Baron Hilton.

During her years with Elvis, Priscilla said she closely followed the way in which Colonel Parker promoted her husband's career. She admired the contribution that she believed the Colonel had made to his success. Despite later revelations of the Colonel's misdealing, she came to view him as something of a role model as she assumed more responsibility for the estate and took on the role of keeper of Elvis's memory.

It is unclear why Priscilla continues to defend Colonel Parker, a man who clearly cost her ex-husband and daughter many millions of dollars. Perhaps the settlement of the lawsuit includes a provision that compels her to do so, or maybe she is trying to preserve the myth that Elvis Presley and Colonel Parker were the greatest artist/manager team in the history of show business. The dark side of Colonel Parker conflicts with the fairy tale that she continues to sell to the public.

With all we know now, it is easy to blame Colonel Parker for everything that went wrong with Elvis Presley's career. But Elvis must carry his share of the blame. He could have put professionals in the positions he reserved for friends and family. He could have toured Europe if he had demanded to do so. He could have appeared in quality films instead of low-budget clunkers. He could have insisted on recording top-notch songs instead of forgettable tunes for which the Colonel could get him a piece of the publishing rights. And if he had wanted to, he could have fired Colonel Parker.

In his final report, Blanchard Tual said that Elvis had contributed to his own financial difficulties. "I'm sure Elvis never read any of the contracts," Tual wrote, "He went along with the Colonel because he was unsophisticated and from a very young age had all the money he could ever want. Elvis did not care whether the Colonel made 5%, 50% or 80%. Elvis received tax advice and assistance from accountants and attorneys such as Joe Hanks, Charlie Lewis and Beecher Smith, III. However, he did not seek their advice on a regular basis, never sought any advice on any agreement with Colonel Parker and generally tended to ignore his lawyers until he got in trouble."

Chapter 17

1983 to 1997

With Elvis snatched away from him, the Colonel found himself suddenly retired. He returned to his new home in Las Vegas with his second wife, the former Loanne Miller.

Marie Parker had been in a coma the last year of her life. The Colonel wanted her at their Palm Springs home rather than in a hospital. He hired the equivalent of an intensive care unit for her at a cost of six thousand dollars per month. Marie Parker died in 1980.

The Colonel and Loanne Miller were subsequently married. Loanne Miller had been Alex Shoofey's secretary at the International Hotel before going to work for the Colonel in 1975. Eventually their relationship became personal.

Soon after Elvis's death, reports began surfacing in the media that the Colonel would take over the management of Rick Nelson.

In 1976, Greg McDonald had become Rick Nelson's manager. McDonald worked for the Colonel as a teenager, and the two remained in contact over the years. After Elvis died, speculation over the Colonel working with Nelson arose because of his relationship with McDonald. It never formally happened, although Nelson did consult with the Colonel on several occasions. In 1977, the Colonel arranged a lucrative engagement at the Las Vegas Hilton for Ozzie and Harriet's younger son.

Greg McDonald lived in Palm Springs. Whenever Rick Nelson went to visit McDonald, he would stop by the Colonel's house. "There weren't many people in the music industry whose opinions Rick respected," said McDonald, "but, he went to the Colonel about all sorts of things, even personal matters and could really talk openly with him."

The rumor that the Colonel would take on a new client extended into the nineties. Because of his connection to Las Vegas, Wayne Newton's name was often mentioned. However, after managing Elvis, the Colonel had no desire to handle anyone else. He had shaped the greatest career in music history. There was nothing left for him to accomplish in the artist management arena.

In 1984, Colonel Parker made his first appearance at an Elvis Presley event since the court settlement. He was the guest of honor at a small celebration held in Tupelo, Mississippi, on the seventh anniversary of the death of that community's most famous son. The Colonel did not make an appearance at another Elvis-related event for another three years.

In 1987, Parker held a Hilton press conference to honor the tenth anniversary of Elvis's death and to promote a tour of Elvis memorabilia. "I think the thing that he liked the most about performing here, and it was the thing that I liked the most, was our check every week," the Colonel said. In response to a question about the goal Elvis never accomplished but would have liked to, the Colonel said,"Stay alive."

The Colonel side-stepped a question about Presley's drug use with "We are here to honor his memory; I didn't hear you very well. Thank you." When a reporter did not get the message, he just ignored the follow-up drug question all together.

The Colonel was asked to comment on the charge that he had controlled Elvis's every move. "Elvis lived his life, and I lived mine," the Colonel said. "We may have had dinner [together] three times a year. I never handled his money. His dad Vernon did that. But, whenever there was a problem, they called the Colonel."

When asked whether he thought that Elvis's grueling work schedule had contributed to his death, the Colonel answered, "No, he never worked too hard. If you add that up, he worked about four months a year."

The Colonel next was heard from publically in the August 14, 1987, edition of the *Chicago Tribune*. The Tribune published a short interview with him that took place in the coffee shop of the Las Vegas Hilton. Before the interviewer had a chance to say more than "hello," the Colonel told him that he had just turned down a fifty-thousand-dollar offer to make a speech. He then pulled out a picture of himself and autographed it for the reporter.

The Colonel volunteered that he always remained in the background and let Elvis have the limelight. The reporter asked the Colonel whether putting his picture alongside Elvis's on the annual Christmas card seemed like someone who "stayed in the background." The Colonel countered that Elvis's name had always been listed first on the cards.

The Colonel said that entertainers continued to ask him to manage them, but he had nothing left to prove. The interviewer concluded by asking the Colonel if he missed Elvis. The Colonel said, "Every day. There's not a day when I don't think about him. A lot of days I cry." A few hours later, the reporter spotted the Colonel sitting by himself at the twenty-five-dollar slot machines. He stuck the tokens in one after another as fast as the wheels would stop turning.

In 1990, the Colonel formally resumed his connection to the Elvis Presley estate. That year, the estate bought Colonel Parker's collection of Elvis memorabilia in a multimillion-dollar transaction.

The Colonel had been a pack rat during his long association with Elvis. He amassed what amounted to the largest and most significant collection of Elvis Presley memorabilia outside of Graceland. In total, the Colonel had more than seventy thousand pounds of Elvis photographs, movie costumes, contracts, novelty items, and the like. For years, he was courted by Elvis collectors and entrepreneurs to sell his collection. Finally a multimillion-dollar offer from a group of Japanese investors in 1989 convinced the Colonel that it was time to sell.

In a rare moment of sentimentality, he decided that his preference would be for the collection to go to Graceland where it would remain intact with the collection of Elvis artifacts there. The Colonel approached Priscilla Presley with the offer from the Japanese group. He gave her the chance to match it. Out of fear that the Japanese group might open an attraction that would compete with Graceland, Priscilla agreed to buy the Colonel's collection.

The transaction was completed in October 1990. A fleet of semis was dispatched to the Colonel's Madison offices where the collection was stored. It took two days for a crew of twenty to pack the contents of the four buildings full of Elvis history onto the trucks. The prized piece of the Colonel's treasure was the gold lamé suit from the 1950s. This suit had not been seen since Elvis's 1961 USS *Arizona* memorial benefit concert. It was assumed to have been lost. In reality, Colonel Parker had it packed away for thirty years.

The Elvis postage stamp brought the Colonel out of hiding in 1993. He took part in the ceremonies in Las Vegas when the stamp was issued. Of course, reporters were more interested in the Colonel than they were in the stamp. When asked for his response to the charge that he exploited Elvis, the Colonel said, "I don't think I exploited Elvis as much as he is being exploited today."

In February 1994, the year he turned eighty-five, a year-long tribute to Colonel Parker was begun at Graceland. A special exhibit devoted to him was put on display at one of the Graceland museums. Special commemorative merchandise was created for the occasion. The Presley estate even published a commemorative magazine devoted to Colonel Parker and Elvis's relationship. The magazine was called "Elvis and the Colonel, The Partnership Behind the Legend." It portrayed their relationship as a kind of fairy tale, as if the lawsuit never happened.

The CEO of Elvis Presley Enterprises, Jack Soden, released a statement explaining why the same organization that had sued Colonel Parker to sever his business relationship with it was now paying him such a tribute. "Elvis and Colonel Parker made history together," the statement read. "They also shared an abiding friendship that is often overlooked and misunderstood by the press and the public. We see his eighty-fifth birthday year as a perfect occasion to recognize his contribution to the Elvis Presley phenomena and to thank him for his friendship."

The Colonel gave an interview to the *Memphis Commercial Appeal* on the occasion of the release of the tribute magazine. In the interview, he told the story of his negotiations for Elvis's first movie, *Love Me Tender*. "I pretended to know a lot about pictures, but I had an intuition when I saw all these important people that I didn't have a chance with these guys. The top man said, 'You know, Colonel Parker, making a picture with Elvis, we're taking a big chance when he heard the fee the Colonel was asking.' The producer went on to say, 'Jack Lemmon don't get that.'" Parker response was "maybe he needs a new manager."

About the tribute magazine, the Colonel said, "The book is the greatest thing that ever happened to the fans. Now they'll know a little bit of what they've always wanted to know about Elvis and me. There will never be two people who argued so hard together, and laughed when it was all over. Some of the best deals I made for Elvis was when we were arguing."

On Wednesday, January 22, 1997, the Colonel, once again, made newspaper headlines across the country, possibly for the last time. The headlines read, "Presley Promoter Dead at 87 After Stroke." On Monday, January 20, Colonel Parker had suffered a stroke. He was rushed to Valley Hospital in Las Vegas. The next day, at 10:00 A.M., he died. His wife Loanne was at his bedside.

Many of the more prominent people in the life of Colonel Parker gave public statements in reaction to his death.

Priscilla and Lisa Marie Presley issued a joint one. "We were saddened to learn of the Colonel's death. Professionally and personally he has been a great and constant friend to both of us. He and Elvis were an amazing team and the work they did together changed the course of pop culture history."

Las Vegas Hilton President Gary Gregg said, "All of us here at the Las Vegas Hilton and in the Hilton Hotels Corporation family are deeply touched and saddened by the death of Colonel Tom Parker. For more than twenty-five years, the Colonel was a key figure behind much of the worldwide entertainment success of the Las Vegas Hilton. There in the Hilton Showroom, Elvis entertained 2.5 million people during 837 unforgettable live performances. Through all of that time, there was the Colonel, the strength behind the King."

"He was the most incredible promoter that I've ever met. There was no way that you could drive, fly, take a train or any other way into Las Vegas without being completely inundated with Elvis Presley in Las Vegas," said the Hilton Hotel's Bruce Banke.

Eddy Arnold said, "Tom Parker was a diamond in the rough. He had a sharp mind. He really was not an educated man formally, but businesswise, he was very educated."

"I think Elvis would have probably lasted no more than four to five years if it had not been for the Colonel. He was the best manager I ever knew," said RCA's Chet Atkins.

Sam Phillips said, "There are probably some things that Tom maybe should have done to have helped Elvis a little bit along the way when he was really having problems, but Parker was only trying to just be a true promoter for Elvis Presley. He was a good manager in many, many ways, but he had the best product that any person in the world, including me, could have ever had, and that was Elvis Presley."

Horace Logan, the announcer for the Louisiana Hayride radio program, said, "Parker takes credit for discovering Elvis. He takes credit for building Elvis's career, he takes credit for molding Elvis. The son of a bitch ought to be hung up by his balls. He practically destroyed one of the greatest talents that ever lived. Those boring movies, my God. A lesser talent would have been destroyed by that crap."

Colonel Parker's ninety-year-old surviving sister was asked to comment on her brother's death. She refused, except to say, "He left us and never gave us anything."

Memorial services for the Colonel were held at the Las Vegas Hilton. Some 160 people attended including Priscilla Presley, Eddy Arnold, Tom Diskin, Joe Esposito, and Henri Lewin. A life-size photo of the Colonel wearing a cowboy hat was placed by the lectern alongside an urn containing the his ashes. Soft music provided by a piano and violin played in the background.

Priscilla Presley said that few people realized the role that Colonel Parker played in bringing Elvis to prominence. "The Colonel is somewhere working up another great promotion. I think most of us assumed that he'd live forever," she said.

Bruce Banke, the former vice president of advertising and publicity at the Las Vegas Hilton, said the Colonel was asked after Elvis's death if he thought the King was still alive. "If he is, would you tell him to get in touch with me because I've got work for him," the Colonel answered.

Wayne Newton said, "He forgot more than most of us will ever know. A great many managers start to believe that they are the artist. That never happened with him."

At the end of the memorial service, the lights were dimmed and a recording of Elvis singing "How Great Thou Art" was played. His boy had performed for the Colonel one last time. The Colonel's ashes were then transported to Palm's Cemetery in Las Vegas for burial.

It was inevitable that books about the Colonel would follow on the heals of his death. Loanne Parker was the first to jump on the Colonel Parker insider bandwagon. On May 12, 1997, in the *Las Vegas Sun*, Loanne Parker announced that she planned to write a biography of the Colonel, detailing "the true story behind the incredible relationship between the Colonel and Elvis." She went on to say that her biography would be the only one authorized by the Colonel's estate. She would make use of her husband's collection of photographs, memorabilia, and records.

The Colonel frequently mentioned that he was going to write his autobiography. He started doing this not long after Elvis exploded on the scene in 1956. He was going to call it *How Much Does It Cost If It Is Free?* He would tell everyone he mentioned the autobiography to that he was going to put their name in the book. At the end of the book, he was going to put all these people's names in alphabetical order. The Colonel knew that he could count on each of them to buy the book, along with a few extra copies to impress friends and relatives.

The Colonel told *Variety* that he constantly received offers to write a book about Elvis, but he turned them all down. He said, "You know what they want. Dirt. I'm not a dirt farmer." Many people had hoped that his death would finally bring this often-rumored book to print. In the end, there was no such book. It had been another one of the Colonel's snow jobs.

When Elvis died, John Lennon issued a statement that sums up the essence of Colonel Tom Parker. "Elvis died the day he went to the army. The difference between Elvis and us is that Elvis died and his manager lived. Our manager died and we lived," Lennon said. He was referring to Brian Epstein, the Beatles manager.

The Colonel will continue to live in our history as the greatest promoter of all time. That's all that Andreas Cornelis van Kuijk ever really wanted.

Appendix 1

Colonel Parker's Promotional Plan For the Movie Spinout

★   ★   ★   ★

S pin out publicity plan.

1966

All star shows/Colonel Tom Parker's promotion and exploitation program for the MGM picture, "Spin Out" staring Elvis Presley.

No attempt is made to give details of various projects. Rather, an outline follows the basic programs and a list of material used. These programs were drawn up by Colonel Parker and involved not only his entire staff but the entire distribution facilities of RCA Victor records and our music firms. In addition, every feasible avenue of publicity was utilized. All of these efforts were carefully timed and coordinated with the release of "Spinout" by Metro Golden [sic] Meyer and close liaison was maintained with Mr. Strickling and the MGM publicity and promotion staff as to integrate all the programs for maximum impact.

Direct Mail Campaign—Several thousand direct mail announce-ments to fan club, publications, clubs and members both domestic and foreign. A series of flyers, heralds and bulletin type letters were used.

Advertising—A series of full paged "Spinout" ads in trade and consumer publications as well as the National Elvis Echo and Elvis Monthly of Great Britain and The Elvis monthly of the European Continent. Each of which have several thousand readers. The trade ads featured special "Spinout" release announcements of both the picture and the record material. Several thousand dollars were bud-geted for this phase of the campaign.

Radio Spots—In several situations a radio spot campaign directly financed and directed by Colonel Parker was carried on and tied in with the release date of the motion picture and sound-track LP album. These campaigns were an extra plus to those car-ried on by the record and film distributors.

Theater Kits—Several thousand theater kits were assembled and distributed. The kits, assembled by Colonel Parker's staff, included a large number of 8X10 give away photos, Elvis wallet sized calendars, Elvis catalog, Heralds, press stories and two dozen large, portrait sized photos of Elvis to be used as contest prizes. Also included were banners and streamers carrying the name of the movie.

Publicity Exploitation—complete coverage of all available news-paper and magazine publicity outlets included the mailing of spe-cial press stories and Elvis photos to the amusement editor of every major newspaper in the country. IN addition, special kits were also sent to leading syndicated and wire service contacts and included a variety of Elvis items. Extensive contact was made with leading show personalities and television and radio personalities with little Elvis souvenirs. These contributed to a number of picture plugs on network and local shows.

Direct Publicity by Elvis—Prior to, during and following the production of "Spinout" Elvis participated in a great number of personal interviews, sit visits and was the recipient of several awards presentations which were tied in with The "Spinout" activity and accordingly resulted in widespread picture and news plugs for "Spinout." At this time a number of polls award announcements in various countries made possible the mention of Elvis's "Spinout" activities.

RCA Victor Tie—in Promotion as Coordinated by Colonel Parker of "Spinout" record material and motion picture.

Direct mail campaign—The vast distribution network of RCA records involves a small army of field salesmen, record managers of the distributors, records salesmen, field promotion men and field supervisors. The release of an Elvis Presley record will get the immediate attention and efforts of several hundred of these men. Thus, a tremendous "in depth" coverage results when the record company releases material used in an Elvis picture and which requires the approval of Elvis and the Colonel. The initial announcement of this distribution network is in the form of flyers and heralds and mats for re-printing announcements to be distributed among the several thousand record dealers. The direct mail program starts just as soon as the decision has been made to release record material from "Spinout" and continues right through the pictures first and second runs and often beyond.

Record Releases—A single record from the "Spinout" soundtrack was first released in September and featured "Spinout"—All That I Am. In early October, The complete "Spinout" soundtrack was made available on an LP album together with three bonus songs. This program was carried on in both domestic and foreign markets.

Advertising—Several thousand dollars worth of full page ads were placed by RCA to tie in with the release of both the "Spinout" single and the soundtrack album. Those ads appeared in all the trade publications and the principle consumer publications. This program was on the national level and further backed up by ad campaigns from each individual RCA distributor in local papers, magazines, school papers and a series of "Spinout" flyers to be available to record dealers. In addition, allocations were made for several window displays. Tie-in advertising of the "Spinout" records as leader merchandise by the large department discount stores and receiving prominent newspaper space and special release announcements.

Radio Spot Announcements—Through the network of distributors very heavy radio activity included announcements on Elvis's "Spinout" material, contests by disc jockeys and television personalities, specialized promotion activities by RCA record promotion men and an all out push through every step of the release to get all the radio and television promotion action possible. Any plug for the "Spinout" record material also meant applause for the picture and release. Here too, these campaigns were initiated with the announcement that the "Spinout" material would be made available and continued at an accelerated pace right through the picture's release and subsequent run.

Special Promotion Devices—Fifteen thousand streamers were distributed to record dealers throughout the country for window and store display on the single "Spinout." Fifteen thousand streamers were also similarly distributed on the release of "Spinout" soundtrack LP album.

250,000 12" × 12" color portraits of Elvis were distributed free of charge in the first release of the LP album. An extensive announcement campaign was carried out to make this free offer known to fans.

One million 1967, Elvis Presley wallet sized calendars were placed to thousands of record dealers throughout the country to be given free to record buyers. This project was also tied in for greater impact with discount merchandise.

One million Elvis record catalogs were distributed through record dealers made available to fans free of charge and carrying prominent promotion for "Spinout."

Five hundred thousand Elvis stereo eight catalogs were distributed through record dealers all over the country and made available to fans free of charge. This giveaway was also timed so as to stimulate greater interest in the Elvis "Spinout" activity.

Several thousand window displays on "Spinout" appeared in record shops across the country. These window and the in-store displays were set up and supervised by the distributor's personnel.

Field force Entries—The entire RCA record division field force and field promotion men closely integrated the foregoing activities that MGM film distributor's promotional personnel to work for maximum impact and coverage of all "Spinout" projects. Through meetings and advanced planning it was possible to bring about the most effective campaign with mutually beneficial results. This spirit of cooperation well established through our long association with both RCA Victor records and MGM studios has developed a fine teamwork that is not confined to an immediate project but that carries on from day-to-day in cooperation on motion picture and record releases, new or old, and in which there is a mutual interest.

Elvis Presley Music and Gladys Music Projects Is Devised by Colonel Parker for Promotion of the Elvis Presley Picture "Spinout"

Special promotion Devices—Both music firms printed up thousands of copies of each song in the soundtrack on sheet music to be distributed to music stores and on music racks in thousands of outlets throughout the country.

Full facilities of the firm's promotion arms were made available to the "Spinout" projects and to employ every effort in promoting the picture release and the record release. Avenues of exploitation normally used in the music business were followed and amplified for an all out effort. IN addition to the music distribution outlets, radio stations, television stations, recording artists and publicity representatives all were contacted to give wider and more complete coverage to the activities of the record company and the film distributors.

Several trade ads and stories were also placed. Flyers went out to the hundreds of music outlets. All of these activities amounted to an "extra plus" for the campaign already in operation.

A partial list of the merchandise used in the foregoing campaign:

1 million—Elvis wallet sized 1967 calendars

1 million—Elvis RCA record catalogs

500,000—Elvis RCA Stereo Eight catalogs

500,000—Elvis photos, post card sized

50,000—Elvis photos, 8X10

50,000—Elvis portraits 12X12 kits

250,000—Elvis portraits, 12X12 with album

50,000—Elvis "Spinout" flyers

5,000—Elvis "Spinout" kits

5,000—Elvis "Spinout" stories

15,000—Elvis "Spinout" streamers on LP album

15,000—Elvis "Spinout" streamers on single

Full paged ads in trade and consumer publications, newspaper cooperative ads and special mailings all involving thousands of dollars.

Extensive radio and television spot programs.

$\mathcal{A}ppendix$ 2

$\mathcal{T}he$ $\mathcal{C}olonel's$ $\mathcal{W}ill$

$\mathcal{L}$AST WILL AND TESTAMENT OF THOMAS A. PARKER

I, Thomas A. Parker, a resident of the city of Las Vegas, Clark County, Nevada, being over the age of eighteen years and of sound mind and disposing memory, and not acting under duress, menace, fraud or undue influence of any person whomsoever, do hereby make, publish and declare this as my last will and testament, hereby revoking all former wills, testaments, codicils and any other instruments of a testamentary character heretofore made by me.

Article One. *Personal, Marital and Family Status*

I declare that at the time of the making of this will I am married to Loanne Miller Parker . I further declare that I have no children. I recognize that I may have living family including brothers, sisters, nephews, nieces and cousins. I declare that I have considered all such persons in making the distributions as hereinafter provided.

November 26, 1990.

Article Three. *Personal Affects, Household Affects and Memorabilia*
I give to my wife, Loanne Miller Parker, if she survives me, all personal affects including china, glassware, jewelry, silverware, clothing, household and kitchen furniture, furnishings and supplies, carpet, books, pictures, musical instruments, all similar articles of domestic use or adornment used or possessed by me and in addition all of my memorabilia, collections and other personal property owned by me.

Article Five. *Specific Bequests*
If the below listed individuals survive me I give and bequeath to each of them the following amounts. 1.) To Sharon Ross Wright, The sum of $30,000 2.) To Thomas Ross the sum of $30,000, 3.) To Jim O'BRIEN, The sum of $25,000, 4.) To Mary Diskin the sum of $25,000, 5.)To Patty Diskin the sum of $25,000, 6.) To Tom Diskin, The sum of $25,000, 7.) To Linda M. Brown the sum of $30,000, 8.) To Jerry Shilling the sum of $2,500, 9.) To Joe Esposito the sum of $2,500, 00.) To Greluen Landon the sum of $2,500.

Unless otherwise provided herein in the event any one or more of the above named individual beneficiaries fail to survive me, such beneficiary bequests will lapse and his or her share will become a part of the residuary estate as hereinafter specified.

Article Six. *Gift of Residue*
I give, devise, bequeath all the rest, residue and remainder of my properties to my wife, Loanne Miller Parker, provided that she survives me. In the event that my wife, Loanne Miller Parker, does not survive me, then I give all the rest, residue and remainder of my properties and all my personal effects, household effects and memorabilia as described in Article III herein above, to the Trustee of the Charitable Trust created herein.

Article Seven. *Charitable Trust*

A. Name. This trust shall be known as the "Colonel Thomas A. Parker Trust" [Hereafter, The "Trust.].. In making the bequests hereunder, I direct that my Trustee shall distribute the annual distributions of the trust to or for the benefit of one or more charitable organizations provided such organization or charitable organizations as defined herein which will generally or particularly: 1) promote the various fields of entertainment, 2) Promote a particular field of entertainment, including, for example, The Country and Western and Rock and Roll fields or the Development of Artist or Artists in said field or fields. 3) Provide for the study of entertainment and its effect on the culture of the United States or any segment thereof. 4) Provide support through scholarships, grants and/or honoraria to students enrolled in accredited institutions of higher education or pursuing studies in music or the history of music or entertainment or, related fields that are designed to directly or indirectly enhance entertainment generally.

Article Eight. *Appointment of Fiduciaries*

I nominate and appoint my wife Loanne Miller Parker as executrix of This, my last will and testament, and I direct that no bond be required for the faithful performance of the duties of said executrix. If my wife, Loanne Miller Parker, fails to survive me, or is otherwise unwilling or unable to serve for any reason, or upon her later death, I direct John F. O'Reilly shall serve as executor.

Article Thirteen. *Contestability*

Each request made to or for the benefit of an individual herein is made on the express condition that such beneficiary must not directly or indirectly oppose the probate of this will or contest all or any part hereof. And if any such beneficiary does directly or indirectly oppose the probate of this will or contest all or any part thereof, then in such event, I revoke and annul any bequest, legacy or devise herein made to such person and I direct that such bequest, legacy or devise become a part of the residue.

First Codicil of Thomas A. Parker.

I, Thomas A. Parker, of Clark County, State of Nevada, do make, publish and declare this to be my first codicil to my last will and testament dated November 26, 1990, heretofore made by me. First, I do hereby delete article five specific request of my last will and testament dated November 26, 1990, in its entirety and replace it with the following:

Article Five. *Specific Bequests*
If the below listed individuals survive me I give and bequeath to each of them the following amounts to each of them.

1) To Sharon Ross Brennan the sum of $15,000.

2) To Thomas Ross the sum of $15,000

3) To Jim O'Brien the sum of $15,000

4) To Mary Diskin the sum of $15,000

5) To Patty Diskin the sum of $15,000

6) To Tom Diskin the sum of $15,000

7) To Linda Brown the sum of $15,000

This is dated September 1, 1992.

Second Codicil of Thomas A. Parker

I, Thomas A. Parker of the County of Clark, State of Nevada, do hereby make, publish and declare this to be my second codicil to my last will and testament dated November 26, 1990, and the first codicil dated September 1, 1992, heretofore made by me.

First I hereby delete Article Five, *Specific Bequests* of my last will and testament dated November 26, 1990 in its entirety and I hereby delete Article Five, *Specific Bequests* of the first codicil dated September 1, 1992, in its entirety and replace it with the following.

Article Five, *Specific Bequests*

If the below list of individuals survive me I give and bequeath to each of them the following amounts.

1) To Sharon Ross Brennan the sum of $10,000

2) To Thomas Ross the sum of $10,000

3) To Jim O'BRIEN the sum of $5,000

4) To Mary Diskin the sum of $5,000

5) To Patty Diskin the sum of $5,000

6) To Tom Diskin the sum of $10,000

7) To Linda M. Brown the sum of $10,000

This is dated April 2, 1996.

Appendix 3

Elvis's Concert Schedule for the 1970s

★ ★ ★ ★

1970: Two four week bookings in Las Vegas and a 17 city tour.

1971: Eight weeks in Las Vegas, two weeks in Lake Tahoe, 12 concert appearances in large arenas.

1972: Eight weeks in Las Vegas, 37 city tour mixing both large and medium sized arenas.

1973: Two engagements in Las Vegas, one engagement in Lake Tahoe, 24 city tour.

1974: Two engagements in Las Vegas, two in Lake Tahoe, and a 45 city tour.

1975: Elvis made one engagement in Las Vegas and had performed in 43 cities by July. His August Las Vegas appearance was shortened due to illness. He made no more appearances the rest of the year.

1976: Elvis was back on tour in March. He was booked for 88 appearances and two performances in Las Vegas.

1977: When Elvis died, he had already made 55 appearances. He was scheduled to go on a 10 day tour the day that he died.

Appendix 4

Concert Contract Used by Colonel Parker in 1956

★ ★ ★ ★

*T*he Colonel prided himself as never making the same mistake twice. He once explained how he formulated the standard performance contract that he used for Elvis. He said that the first few contracts he signed as a promoter all contained clauses that later came back to haunt him. He made a file of all of these clauses for use in the future. Soon he had assembled his own contract made up almost entirely of the "smart ass clauses."

Personal Appearance Agreement

Elvis Presley with his variety show, vaudeville acts, Waco Coliseum, one performance, 8:15, Friday, October 12, 1956, for the following terms:
Five thousand dollars guaranteed in percentage coverage, if any, at closing of box office"

No other talent is to appear on this show other than listed above. The above listed talent and show is contracted from Colonel Tom Parker by party known in this contract as the sponsor.

Sponsor's name, Heart O Texas Fair, Othel Neely, General Manager.

Sponsor agrees to pay for all advertising costs, radio, newspaper, a suitable auditorium, sound system, stage hands, ticket takers and pay for same. Pay all amusement taxes, city, state, federal, county and licenses if needed.

It is understood that the sponsor is in good standing with the Federation of American Musicians.

It is mutually agreed by both parties that if either party in this agreement should be unable to carry out the terms of this agreement by reason of sickness, accident or death, strikes or any other act of providence, then in that event, neither party shall be held liable upon this agreement.

Colonel Parker reserves that right to substitute other talent if necessary or desirable. This however, does not apply to the star of the show, Elvis Presley.

Admission prices for this attraction must be approved by both parties. All seats, one dollar and fifty cents in advance, two dollars at the door. Sit where you like, including federal taxes.

It is understood that The Elvis Presley show will have The free and expressed privilege to sell its souvenirs, novelties, song books, phonograph records and photos at all shows. And any Elvis Presley merchandising they decide at this performance on an exclusive basis only at no cost to show.

Special added terms: Sponsor to furnish at least a minimum of ten police officers to supervise the stage presentation on the inside of the coliseum and suitable police protection at the front and back stage.

Dressing rooms, a minimum of two microphones, piano, spotlight at least radio spots to advertise the show, and not less than sixty inches of newspaper advertising in promote the appearance of the show to the fullest of all mediums possible. Advance sale of tickets must be at least ten days before show date. Police escort is to be furnished to Mr. Presley from coliseum to hotel and back.

No Elvis Presley merchandise of any type can be sold in the coliseum except through the Elvis Presley concession department. This also includes in front of the coliseum on the outside. The show will expect 100% protection from this agreement.

A deposit check to be made out to Elvis Presley Enterprises.

Guarantee is per contract.

Show to be presented in its regular presentation as per lease established on other appearances.

The stage show is to run approximately one and a half hours. The show management reserves the right to inject an intermission at its discretion. No advertising of any nature can be sold in conjunction with Elvis Presley's appearance. The name Elvis Presley on its singularity cannot be used for any advertisement on any merchandise other than under our contracts. Our advance agent, Mr. Oscar Davis, will be in Waco to set up advertising campaign with Mr. Neely and his representative prior to the opening of the show.

Television: No television appearance of any nature before or during the show can be permitted due to exclusive contracts in effect.

Radio: No radio appearances before or during the show can be permitted.

Motion Picture: The show reserves the right to cancel the contract due to motion picture commitments.

Signed for the Elvis Presley show _____
Colonel Tom Parker management,
approved by sponsor _____

Exclusive manager—Colonel Tom Parker—P.O. Box 417, Madison, Tennessee.

Acknowledgments

The author would like to thank the following individuals and organizations who helped make this book possible.

Stan Allison, Davis Bassman, Eleanor Biggs, Walter Bishop, Sue Carlson, Lauren Chesterfield, Clark County Court, Richard Dewitt, Alberta Dink, Federal Bureau of Investigation- Freedom of Information Section, Al Gabelli, Phillip George, Kathy Gray, Hillsborough County Historical Society, Tracy Isher, Nancy Jarvis, Larry Jenkins, Joe Lawson, Constant Lenson, Mark Meijer, Memphis Public Library, Stewart Mooreland, Nancy Miller, Mary Mott, Fred Neal, T.W. Nice, Christine Orange, Lester Phillips, Probate Court of Shelby County Tennessee, Rich Roetemeyer, Sarasota Historical Society, Rick Senn, W.C. Shipley, William Smith, Steve Stepp, George Tan, Edith Twilley, United States Army, Ray Walters, Andrew White, Kerri White, and Paul Williams.

Bibliography

★ ★ ★ ★

Arnold, Eddy. *It's a Long Way From Chester County*. Old Tappan, New Jersey: Hewitt House, 1969.

Bashe, Philip. *Teenage Idol, Travelin' Man*. New York: Hyperion, 1992.

Burk, Bill. *Elvis Memories*. Memphis: Propwash, 1993.

Clayson, Alan. *Aspects of Elvis*. Convent: Sidgewick and Jackson, 1994.

Cusic, Don. *I'll Hold You in My Heart*. Nashville: Rutledge Hill Press, 1997.

Dannen, Fedric. *Hit Man*. New York: Vintage Books, 1991.

Doll, Susan. *Best of Elvis*. Lincolnwood, Illinois: Publications International, Ltd., 1996.

Eliot, Marc. *Rockonomics: The Money Behind the Music*. Seacaucus, New Jersey: Citadel Press, 1993.

Escott, Colin. *Good Rockin' Tonight*. New York: St. Martin's Press, 1991.

Esposito, Joe. *Good Rockin' Tonight*. New York: Avon Books, 1994.

Geller, Larry. *If I Can Dream*. New York: Avon Books, 1989.

Gordon, Robert. *The King on the Road*. New York: St. Martin's Press, 1996.

Gray, Michael. *The Elvis Atlas*. New York: Henry Holt, 1996.

Gregory, Neal. *When Elvis Died*. New York: Pharos Books, 1980.

Lacker, Marty. *Elvis, Portrait of a Friend*. New York: Bantam Books, 1979.

Lewis, Myra. *Great Balls of Fire*. New York: St. Martin's Press, 1982.

Mann, May. *The Private Elvis*. New York: Pocket Books, 1977.

Presley, Priscilla. *Elvis and Me*. New York: G. P. Putnam and Sons, 1985.

Snow, Hank. *The Hank Snow Story*. Chicago: University of Illinois Press, 1994.

Whimer, Peter. *The Inner Elvis*. New York: Hyperion, 1996.

Yanzey, Becky. *My Life with Elvis*. New York: St. Martin's Press, 1977.

Index